SCALES
ON
WAR

SCALES ON WAR

THE FUTURE OF AMERICA'S MILITARY AT RISK

MAJ. GEN. BOB SCALES, USA (RET.)

NAVAL INSTITUTE PRESS
Annapolis, Maryland

Naval Institute Press
291 Wood Road
Annapolis, MD 21402

Library of Congress Cataloging-in-Publication Data
Names: Scales, Robert H., date, author.
Title: Scales on war : the future of America's military at risk / Maj. Gen. Bob Scales, USA (Ret.).
Description: Annapolis, Maryland : Naval Institute Press, [2016] | Includes bibliographical
    references and index.
Identifiers: LCCN 2016022664 (print) | LCCN 2016032121 (ebook) |
    ISBN 9781682471029 (hardcover : alk. paper) | ISBN 9781682471036 (ePDF) |
    ISBN 9781682471036 (ePub) | ISBN 9781682471036 (mobi)
Subjects: LCSH: United States—Military policy—21st century. | United States—Armed
    Forces—Operational readiness. | Military art and science—United States.
Classification: LCC UA23 .S29498 2016 (print) | LCC UA23 (ebook) |
    DDC 355/.033573—dc23
LC record available at https://lccn.loc.gov/2016022664

24 23 22 21 20 19 18 17 16   9 8 7 6 5 4 3 2 1
First printing

CONTENTS

PREFACE

I first "met" Jim Mattis virtually (though not yet in person) when my coauthor, Professor Williamson Murray, and I wrote our book *The Iraq War: A Military History*. The publisher, Harvard University Press, wanted to be first with a book about the March on Baghdad in 2003, so they gave us only a few months to produce it. We worked like dogs, and by the next fall it was on the shelves.

Two characters stood out in the book: Maj. Gen. David Petraeus, commanding the Army's 101st Airborne Division, and Maj. Gen. James Mattis, his Marine counterpart, commanding the 1st Marine Division. By the end of the campaign both had achieved near-legendary status—Petraeus for understanding the need for a shift to counterinsurgency and Mattis for his remarkable skill as a fighting and intellectually gifted infantryman.

Two years later, Mattis was commanding all Marine forces in Central Command, leading the headquarters responsible for the fighting in Iraq and Afghanistan. As he watched the battle from his perch in Tampa, Florida, he became concerned with the tough battle being fought to retake the Iraqi city of Fallujah. When it was over the city was ours but at a cost of more than ninety Marine lives. Early on a November evening just after Thanksgiving, Mattis called me at home.

"General, it's me, Mattis. I just read your book." Of course I thought he was referring to *The Iraq War*. "No, I mean *Yellow Smoke*." I had published *Yellow Smoke* before the invasion of Iraq. I had written it to offer a future vision of ground warfare. "I keep your book by my bedside," Mattis said. "You say some things in it about tactics and the human dimension in small units. Many of those things I saw play out in Fallujah. We need to talk." Here was a fighter, the archetype American warrior, wanting me to talk to him about tactical warfare. Of course I agreed.

The phone call started a relationship between us that continues to this day. His next assignment after returning from the second battle of Fallujah was as commander of the Marine Corps Combat Development Command (MCCDC), and it came with promotion to three stars. MCCDC is essentially the Marine Corps' in-house think tank. It develops fighting doctrine and runs schooling, training, and the requirements for new weapons. It was here that I became reacquainted with "Rip" van Riper, a retired Marine lieutenant general, who like me was a military writer and intellectual. We became something of a brain trust for Mattis.

Mattis knew something was not right about how the Marine Corps fought at the tactical level of war. He thought at the time that some of my ideas might prove useful in making changes after Fallujah. In January he put me in front of all Marine brigadier generals in the auditorium at Henderson Hall, the Marine Corps Headquarters in Arlington, Virginia. The next month I gave the same briefing to the Marine Corps' "Executive Offsite." Present were all the senior Marine generals and the Commandant of the Marine Corps, Mike Hagee. It was a tense moment for me: a retired Army artilleryman lecturing to a body of men who considered themselves to be leaders of the most competent tactical body on Earth. Of course it was a risk for Mattis to invite me, as well.

I talked for an hour and a half and then answered questions. I kept the notes of that talk, and those notes generally form the outline for this book. General Hagee was extremely kind to me, and he told Mattis to get on with some of our suggested reforms. They seem so simple today: to construct a system of "combat profiling" that would allow Marines to observe an enemy's body language to determine his intent; to create a virtual "shoot house" to teach Marines how to react to various unpredictable circumstances when fighting in towns and cities; to reinvigorate the long-range shooting course, by which (to use my words) every infantryman would be a sniper. The list went on.

The Marine Corps' greatest asset is its relatively small size. As Mattis used to say, "When the captain says hard to starboard, small ships turn faster than big ones." So, very quickly, our ideas began to shape Marine training and tactics. After his stint in MCCDC Mattis took command of the First Marine Expeditionary Force in Iraq and had the opportunity there to put theory into practice. The results were extraordinary. He saved many lives.

Upon return to the States Mattis again was promoted, this time to head a newly created four-star headquarters, the Joint Forces Command (JFCOM). Mattis' energy and "take no prisoners" attitude shook up colonels and generals. Things started to get done. One of his efforts was to elevate the study of the tactical fight, just as he had done at MCCDC. Unfortunately, most generals and admirals considered tactics beneath them. It was sergeants', not generals', business. At JFCOM I worked for Mattis as a contractor, with the vision to create a National Center for the Study of Small Unit Excellence. During this time I wrote a think piece on tactical warfare, a piece that came out of a private conversation with Mattis.

He loved the book *The Defence of Duffer's Drift,* published in 1904 by Ernest Dunlop Swinton and reissued in recent years, because that fictional account of the Boer War captured all of the timeless tenets we hoped to impart to the ground services. He asked me to update *Duffer's Drift* to a modern setting. Instead, I convinced him the book we needed to mimic was *Ender's Game,* a very popular science fiction work by Orson Scott Card. Written in the 1980s and later made into a popular movie, *Ender's Game* told the story of a young teenager who is selected among many millions for his exceptional decision-making skill. Ender spends years undergoing a series of ever more demanding simulations to make him the absolute master of tactical warfare. My version, *Jerry Smith's War,* incorporated most of our ideas about the theoretical future of small units and has become something of a cult piece on the Internet.

The climactic event of our effort was our Small Unit Excellence Conference, held at the Monaco Hotel, in the Old Town district of Alexandria, Virginia, in April 2009. Mattis' JFCOM was the sponsor. I was a director of the event, along with Army general Jason Kamaya. It was without doubt the culminating point in our effort to make the Department of Defense and the other ground services start to pay attention to small tactical units, those who were doing virtually all the fighting and dying in 2009. We invited representatives of all the ground services, from generals to sergeants. We included police SWAT teams, CIA direct-action teams, and Special Forces and Tier I U.S.

Special Operations Command (SOCOM) leaders, to include Delta person-nel, Rangers, and SEALs. We included civilian industry partners and academ-ics, such as Dr. Martin Seligman from the Center of Positive Psychology at the University of Pennsylvania, and also Coach Peter Carroll, then at the University of Southern California. We were on a roll. We had plans to open a national center for small-unit excellence. We had begun to design a huge, virtual "shoot house" at Camp Pendleton, California, that would represent the highest achieve-ment in the simulation of warfare at the small-unit level.

Sadly, the next year it all died. Some liberal national newspapers did a series of articles harshly criticizing JFCOM's association with defense contractors. In a needless overreaction, Secretary of Defense Robert Gates implemented draconian requirements for contractual advisers that literally forced me to leave JFCOM. The next year JFCOM itself was dead, and our once-hopeful effort to reform the military at the tactical level died as well. As a result, the ideal of small-unit reform, an effort that had held so much promise for so many years, died too, and with it died many Soldiers and Marines. They are dying still.

I blame myself for much of this. The idea that the nation doesn't really care about those who do the dirty day-to-day business of killing the enemy haunts me to this very day. This will be my last book. I had to write it to atone for my sins and to try to awaken our national leaders to the need to keep those who perform the act of intimate killing alive in combat.

I'm not optimistic. Jim Mattis has retired. The nation is tired of watching war on television. What the Defense Department really wants is to buy big, expensive stuff that floats and flies, and ISIS is on the march, undoing the brave work done by hundreds of thousands of Soldiers and Marines in Iraq.

But here goes anyway.

And by the way, Jim, thanks for trying . . .

ACKNOWLEDGMENTS

Portions of this book have been repurposed from various articles and op-eds that I have written over the years. Parts were originally published as articles in *Armed Forces Journal International* (AFJI) between 2006 and 2010. Much of chapter 7 was taken from two AFJI articles: "American Infantry and National Priorities" published in June 2007, and "Small Unit Dominance," published in March 2010. The first third of chapter 10 is taken from "Clausewitz and World War IV," published in July 2006. The portion subtitled "Meeting the Mother Ship" in chapter 15 is taken from "A Vehicle for Modern Times," published in 2009.

All of chapter 20, "The Draft," is taken from *Ripon Forum* (May 2008). All of chapter 13, "Ripley's Ghost," is taken from *Atlantic Magazine's* article "Gun Trouble," January 2014. The first two-thirds of chapter 9, "Feeding the Narrative," is taken from a monograph I first published through the Center for New American Security in 2010. *Joint Force Quarterly* first published chapter 4, "Adaptive Enemies," while I was still on active duty in 1999. Various portions from chapter 16, "Firepower," were taken from my 1989 book *Firepower in Limited War,* published by the Presidio Press.

I adapted several chapter segments from op-eds I wrote over the years. Most of chapter 21, "Earning the Right," was taken from two *Washington Post* op-eds written in 2013. I selectively lifted much of chapter 8, "War in Two Epochs," from a *Washington Post* op-ed "The Only Way to Defeat the Islamic State" published September 6, 2014.

[1]

TWO UNNECESSARY HEROES

Now, I'm going to go off-script here for a second and just say I really like
this guy. . . . [W]hen you meet Sal and you meet his family, you are just
absolutely convinced that this is what America is all about.
—President Barack Obama

I was brought to tears when I watched with enormous pride and humil-
ity a November 2010 White House ceremony in which SSgt. Salvatore
"Sal" Giunta became the first living Soldier awarded the Medal of Honor since
Vietnam. For many of us who served in that long-ago war, the circumstances
under which Giunta was awarded his medal felt frighteningly familiar: an
inhospitable and forbidding mountainous battlefield that looks very much like
Vietnam's Central Highlands; a diabolical, fanatic enemy skilled in the tactical
art of war; a lone squad patrol, armed with the same class of weapons we used
more than four decades ago, engaged in a desperate firefight against an enemy
who remained undetected until the patrol entered the kill zone. The results
were both heroic and tragic: two of Giunta's buddies died in what appeared to
have been, sadly, too fair a fight.

Similarly, almost exactly two years later I watched with the same emotion
during the Medal of Honor ceremony celebrating the heroism of Capt. William

Swenson and his team in Afghanistan. Swenson's men had walked into a three-sided ambush. All five members of Swenson's lead element, four Marines and a medical corpsman, had been killed in the opening exchange of fire.

This book is about these two men and hundreds of thousands of other close-combat fighters like them who have done most of the killing and dying in wars fought since the beginning of recorded time. Policy makers, politicians, academics, and big weapon makers still assert that the day of close-in killing by men like these is gone. The techno-warriors continue to promise that technology and the material fruits of Western civilization will lessen the role that the Giuntas and Swensons play in winning future wars. From this expectation come legions of commentators, writers, think-tank gurus, and learned men and women who chase the idea that war has changed. Tomorrow we will fight distant wars from space, fighting machine against machine. Future battles will pit cyber electrons versus cyber electrons; virtual pilots will fight drone against drone.

Washington's defense intellectuals tell America to expect tomorrow's wars to be short, sharp, distant, bloodless, and glorious. Expect our enemies to be "shocked and awed" by our matériel greatness. Expect them to fight the way we fight—and remember that they are stupid, illiterate, and cowardly. President Obama almost started a war against Syria in 2013 based on this premise: a few hundred missiles fired from submarines and destroyers and it is over. This book tells a different story, one from the ground, standing on the firing step of a foxhole or inside the turret of a tank, from where Giunta and Swenson have seen war. The world looks quite different from there. I believe that the past is prologue, that a close look at the circumstances that overwhelmed and almost killed Giunta and Swenson hold the keys to future victories.

The stories of Giunta and Swenson are remarkably similar, in that neither of these incredibly brave men should have been in a position to receive their medals. Had Soldiers in these engagements been adequately provided with a few cheap technologies, they might have avoided the bloody traps that precipitated their heroic actions. The tactical fights of these two heroes raise a question, particularly for those who have served before: Why, after fourteen continuous years of combat in Iraq and Afghanistan, are our Soldiers still involved in these fair fights against primitive, ill-equipped, and poorly trained enemies?

In his debrief, Captain Swenson railed justifiably about the failure of staff duty officers hidden away in a distant command-and-control center to approve the delivery of artillery and airpower in support of his desperate action. Imagine for a moment that Swenson had a simple GoPro-like camera on his helmet capable of displaying the ground situation and linked to screens in the control center. Had officers in the center seen the action in real time though Swenson's eyes, these graphic images might have convinced them immediately to approve supporting fires from a mortar unit located only a few kilometers away. You can buy the GoPro-like camera at Walmart.

According to unclassified reports of the battle, an aerial drone had shown up over Swenson's unit five hours after the Taliban sprang the ambush. What if our military had been able to deploy enough drones to put a set of aerial eyes over every ground patrol marching into a dangerous and uncertain situation? Surely had a drone been overhead the Taliban would never have dared to open fire. You can buy small drones with a camera attached during your shopping trip to Walmart.

What if one of the lead Soldiers in Swenson's patrol had carried a sensor that detected movement or the metabolic presence of humans nearby? Such devices are easy to develop; the technology has been in use by civilian security companies for years. Again, had Swenson's team been warned, there would have been no ambush and no medal. You can buy a home security system that detects human movement at Walmart. Add another item to your cart. . . .

The Taliban engaged Swenson's team from behind the protection of large boulders and stone walls. Swenson was able to keep his attackers at bay only by throwing a hand grenade at them, just as his grandfather did in World War II. Had Swenson had a means actually to engage enemies behind the wall, maybe he would not have enjoyed his visit to the White House. The Germans developed such a weapon system—the M-25 "Smart" grenade launcher—before 9/11. The U.S. Army did not buy the system until 2014 and has yet to get it to troops in combat.

After fourteen years of war the ground services, the Army and Marine Corps, remain starved of new, cutting-edge, lifesaving matériel, while the Department of Defense and its big defense company allies continue to spend generously on profitable big-ticket programs like planes, ships, missiles, and computers.

Soldiers' "stuff" today is more *Popular Mechanics* than *Star Wars*. However, Captain Swenson and his six colleagues might have had a better day in Afghanistan had the nation spent a bit more to give them an overwhelming, in fact dominant, technological edge over the enemy.

After suffering almost nine thousand dead Soldiers and Marines, the nation still cannot offer an advantage to those who do most of the dying. Our Soldiers and Marines should have gone into Iraq and Afghanistan ready for an *unfair* fight—that is, unfair in their own favor—at the squad level. Giunta's life was saved by state-of-the-art body armor. More Soldiers and Marines might have been saved had this body armor been provided before they started on the march to Baghdad in 2003. Too many Soldiers and Marines died from primitive roadside bombs, "improvised explosive devices," or IEDs, during the early days in Iraq and Afghanistan. The Pentagon weapons-buying bureaucracy was too slow in supplying the troops with explosive-resistant vehicles to protect against IEDs. We must also ask why the Taliban were able to see Giunta's squad first, simply by observing his Soldiers from the surrounding high ground. After fourteen years of war, no small unit in such peril should ever have to move exposed to unimpeded observation.

Army and Marine Corps infantry squads were outgunned in Vietnam by the North Vietnamese army's superior AK-47 assault rifles. One would think that maybe, fifty years later, infantry Soldiers would be able to fire a bullet costing about thirty cents that did not disintegrate in the air. A two-hundred-dollar aiming device developed for hunters would provide the precision needed to hit a distant enemy target with the same relative precision as that of the rifles used by the Taliban. The Army has yet to buy it.

For more than two-thirds of a century, this country has preferred to crush its enemies by exploiting its superiority in the air and on the seas. Unfortunately, these efforts to win with firepower over manpower have failed to consider the fact that the enemy has a vote. From Mao Zedong to Ho Chi Minh to Osama bin Laden, all our enemies have recognized that our vulnerable strategic center of gravity is dead Americans. It is no surprise that the tactic common to them all has been to kill Americans, not as a means to an end but as an end in itself. Every enemy has ceded us those domains where we are dominant—the air and the sea. They challenge us instead where we are weak: small units, on ground unfamiliar to us but familiar to them.

Memories fade fast. Already the process of denial has begun again, even as smoke still obscures battlefields in the Middle East and South Asia. Politicians on both ends of the political spectrum have called for cutting the ground-force budget as a means of paying down the national debt. The experiences of Captain Swenson and Staff Sergeant Giunta and their gallant men should remind lawmakers of their unpaid debt to those who do the dirty business of intimate killing. We hope policy makers watched both White House Medal of Honor ceremonies and paused to reflect on their stories. Our leaders should be asking why the richest nation on Earth could not have done more to help these small infantry units prevail on the tactical battlefield. For the sake of both these great men, please: no more fair fights.

Who are these (mostly) men? A popular rallying cry for those who want to redistribute the nation's wealth is, "The wealthy 1 percent versus the rest of us!" In American wars there is the other 99 percent, those who do not have to go to war thanks to the 1 percent who serve. A cynic might say that all the good citizens who shake hands with servicemen and say "Thanks for your service" are really saying, "Thanks for doing this so my son can go to graduate school."

Yet the Swensons and Giuntas—the ones who do the real fighting and dying—constitute an even smaller slice of American society than the honored "1 percent." In fact, the United States' "intimate killers" account for only about 0.02 percent of the population. For the most part, America is clueless about the uniqueness of guys like these. I witness this sad perceptual divide every time I pass through the Baltimore-Washington Airport on my way overseas. Take a moment sometime and walk over to the BWI Military Airlift Command Gate as young servicemen and women drag themselves through the dark corners of the customs gate to debouch into sunlight and the arms of loved ones and the hugs of grateful citizens. It is an interesting study. A natural line forms. Single file, these desert sand–clad youngsters shake hands as if they were walking off the court after an NCAA basketball game. The greeting crowd is always drawn to the American beauties. The first to be deluged is always a tall, blond airman (actually an "airwoman") with tightly braided hair, smelling fresh even after twenty hours stuffed into a crowded aluminum tube. I look at her rank and badges and know from them that this is her first tour and that she has spent the past four months in an air-conditioned "hooch" with shiny toilets, running water, and an Anthony's Pizza or a Starbucks just around the corner.

Walking some distance behind, bending under a heavy rucksack, is a kid who looks much older. He is not smiling. Most likely, he is trying to get around the pack and into a taxi that can take him to the nearest bar. His boots give him away. They are worn and discolored. He has pushed his trousers cuffs down over his boot tops to make his short stride more comfortable. If he is white, he is darkly tanned. Most of them sport unhealed blisters and deep scratches. Some show signs of having been recently wounded. And they all wear the same black badge. It is a long, thin rectangle about four inches long surrounded by a wreath. If you look closely you will see the faint outline of a Revolutionary War–era musket embedded in the rectangle. It is the Combat Infantry Badge (CIB), the most coveted and respected piece of apparel in the military services— because (to those few who know) it is worn by a tiny percentage of the 1 percent who do virtually all of the killing and dying in America's wars today.

Only infantrymen can wear the CIB. Only recently has it come to symbolize those most likely to die in war. During World War II, the greatest chance of dying at the hands of the enemy was faced by submariners; the odds of a submariner dying at the hands of a Japanese destroyer or aircraft was about one in five. Next in this frightful roll came bomber pilots flying over the skies of Germany. Like the submariners of that war, airmen who flew in the Eighth Air Force have no battlefield memorials. They left no trace of the horror of their demise other than the odd monument or the headstones lined carefully, row on row, in our overseas military cemeteries. Third in proportion were infantrymen. Because of their huge numbers in World War II, "grunts" constituted more than 70 percent of all servicemen who died at the hands of the enemy, dying in the hundreds of thousands. If you are related to a member of the "Greatest Generation" who died in that war, chances are he was an infantryman.

Since the end of World War II, the dynamics of the dead have changed. Submarines are still dangerous vessels. But the enemy has sunk no U.S. submarine since 1945. The enemy killed a few bomber crewmen over the skies of Korea and Vietnam, but none have died since the Christmas bombing offensive against Hanoi in 1972. The infantry has not been so lucky. In a strange, ironic twist, the proportion of infantry killed at the hands of the enemy now is actually higher, 81 percent. In Afghanistan the proportion of infantry deaths at the hands of the enemy is even greater, 89 percent. Of those, more than 90 percent occurred within four hundred meters of a road. Today, some elite small units, like Delta Force and the SEALs, have suffered losses in Iraq and Afghanistan that proportionally approach those of submariners in World War II.

The number of Soldiers in this fraternity—it is predominately male, a "band of brothers"—is small. The total number of infantry serving today, Army, Marine, and Special Forces, would not fill FedEx Field, home of the Washington Redskins. Put in its starkest terms: 4 out of 5 of all Americans killed at the hands of the enemy have come from a force that makes up less than 4 percent of men and women in uniform. Not many of our citizens know that.

These men are our warriors. Others serving in uniform are not. In fact, the vast majority of men and women in uniform are employed in professions similar to those of their civilian counterparts: they fix or drive trucks, cook food, staff hospitals, and operate radios and telephones. Over the past fourteen years most of them have served honorably in Afghanistan and Iraq. On rare occasions these "incidental warriors" come under fire, in ambushes or by exposure to IEDs. Some in uniform are "almost warriors," in that they are well trained to fight using small arms and might meet the enemy. These men and women get close to the infantry fight when they fire artillery, fly aircraft, remove explosive ordnance, guard roads, or defend firebases against enemy attacks. I am one of these. I spent my career as an artilleryman.

Only guys like Sergeant Giunta and Captain Swenson had the job that required them to go out every day with the intention of killing, and avoiding being killed by, the enemy. One would expect that those Americans most likely to die would gain the support of those pledged to protect them. Sadly, for too long this has not been the case. This book is mostly about them, the ones most likely to die. It will be the last of seven books I have written over the years about warfare. It is an unusual work, for two reasons in particular: first, it appears after the United States' interventions in Iraq and Afghanistan are substantively over. History has shown that armies reform successfully after wars end, especially after wars that do not end well. During wartime, armies, in particular, are too busy fighting to worry much about the next war. Wait too long after a war, however, and an army ossifies. It fights for money in peacetime rather than thinking of things anew. Second, as the stories of the two heroes testify, the United States has exhibited an unhealthy habit of trying to fight its wars with machines instead of Soldiers. Sadly, as you will read in the pages to come, our enemies continue to succeed against us because they are willing to sacrifice their fighters copiously to offset our matériel superiority.

My hope is that the logic of the argument to follow will convince policy makers in our defense establishment not to make these mistakes again. But I am afraid they will. My fear is that my grandchildren will have to pay in blood for our mindless return to high tech, matériel warfare. So this is my last shot to tell the sad story of neglect, ahistoricism, intellectual hubris, corruption, and ignorance about the nature and character of war that has left too many of our (mostly) Soldier sons needlessly dead on our battlefields.

[2]

THE CINDERELLA SERVICE

In fact, Washington "makes" very little. Yet there is one industry
that Washington can claim as its own: the ideas industry.
—Peter W. Singer, Brookings Institution

America loves its Army, and Washington hates it. Some Americans in the heartland (west of the Blue Ridge and east of the Rockies) think of Washington as a scourge for blue-collar America, a place that receives from and never seems to give back to America's working stiffs. That is the main reason why many in Washington hate the Army and so much of the heartland loves it: because the Army is America's service, a blue-collar haven for the likes of Willie and Joe, the venerable Bill Mauldin cartoon characters who always seem to sit in water-filled foxholes waiting to be screwed by clueless bureaucrats, self-serving officers, and, on rare occasion, the enemy. In our modern wars, media images depict sailors, airmen, and Marines as eager volunteers who seek to join war-fighting elites. Soldiers, in contrast, have traditionally been depicted as the drafted poor who found themselves in foxholes due to bad draft numbers, a judge's order, bad luck, or bad grades in high school. So it comes as no surprise that the hardworking heartland loves Willie and Joe. Virtually every poll taken since the end of the draft highlights the common man's regard for our Soldiers.

Of course, anything popular to the heartland gets attention from politicians. I am continually amazed at the fecklessness of our congressional leaders in this regard. Too often in the green room at Fox News, I listen to the rants of senior solons who complain that generals are stupid, that they do not understand the inner workings of the "system," that they too often give false or misleading testimony. Politicians say they are fed up with listening to visiting generals obsessed with PowerPoint slides. They are too often offended when bemedaled colonels and generals fail to worship the wisdom of slick congressional staffers, usually twenty-something "trust fund babies," who lecture these combat veterans about the world of war as seen through the eyes of their own Georgetown University professors.

Another aspect of Army hatred is that it seems to emanate only from Capitol Hill. An amazing transformation occurs when a politician or administration official (and even some in the media) visits Soldiers in a combat zone. Around reelection time, all politicians will tell anyone who is interested how many trips they have made to the war zone. "What did you think of the troops you saw there?" is my usual question. "They're incredible!" is the inevitable answer. "What discipline! What patriotism, what a great bunch of guys!" Occasionally I will remind them of their forgotten green-room rants: "Please square with me how such great guys, many with half a dozen years or more in the combat zone, suddenly get so stupid when they come to Washington?" No answer. Yet for some reason, as soon as these great Soldiers go from combat to Washington they become the Jed Clampetts of the Beltway cocktail circuit.

Why? It is complicated. But let's start with popular perceptions of armies, perceptions that have sprung from historical events that begin with the very foundation of our country. Englishmen came to our shores in the seventeenth century to escape the depredations of Oliver Cromwell and his professional army, raging across England during its protracted civil war. Remember, preindustrial armies were simply masses of dirty off-scourings of society, scum who Soldiered in predatory machines that needed to move to sustain themselves. While on the march armies took horses and crops and dragooned favorite sons into the ranks. It is this sixteenth-century precedent of a feckless, regicidal band of ravaging Soldiers and officers that today leaves the United Kingdom with a Royal Navy, Royal Marines, and a Royal Air Force but no Royal Army.

The English Civil War experience and the "Glorious Revolution" that followed gave our colonial ancestors an abiding distrust of standing, professional armies. Unfortunately, the colonies were dangerous places, threatened by as yet unbroken Indian tribes and the occasional face-off with the hated French, who occupied an empire beyond the northern and western colonial wildernesses. So our earliest citizens chose to defend their homes by assembling local militias from the citizenry. These pickup crews, like all militia, were terrible Soldiers, but they were usually better Soldiers than the Indians.

Perhaps we would never have become an independent nation had it not been for a badly behaving British Army that forcibly quartered its Soldiers in the homes of Boston's prickly citizens. Hatred for a professional army increased yearly as the patriots' propaganda amplified or made up stories about the horrors of lynching of citizens, burning of farms, and looting that accompanied the British Army from 1775 until the war ended at Yorktown in 1781.

The traditional distrust of a professional army extended itself to the colonial side during the Revolution. Washington's Continentals (read "professionals") won the war but suffered deadly neglect during the winters of 1777 and 1778, in places like Valley Forge and Morristown. Professionals saved the day and won the war at Yorktown (with massive help from French professionals). But over the centuries, history was rewritten by civilians who kept alive the myth of the minuteman who (like Cincinnatus) left his plowshare to take up his musket upon the approach of the British regulars. Minutemen were useful. Local armed citizens fought as bushwhackers and skirmishers, harassing the British lines of communications, and they occasionally reinforced Washington's Continental regulars. The mythology of the militiaman, or the "citizen Soldier," was larger than his contribution, and it would grow after the American Revolution.

The lingering animosity toward professional Soldiers, U.S. or British, was even written into the Constitution by our founding fathers, virtually all of whom served during the Revolution. Article 1, Section 8 of the document states that "the Congress shall have power to . . . raise and support Armies, but no appropriation of money to that use shall be for a longer term than two years." The Navy is treated quite differently: Article 1, Section 8, clause 13 states simply that "the Congress shall have power to . . . provide and maintain a Navy." The implications are clear. The founding fathers considered land forces temporary, to be raised principally in times of crisis with appropriations subject to termination every two years. Early congressmen, in contrast, considered the Navy to be the service that was to be "maintained."

The myth of the minuteman grew during the American Civil War, a war fought by amateurs on both sides. The Confederate armies were formed from local community volunteers. Lincoln raised the Union army principally through a system of "volunteer" recruitment, in which leading civilian citizens, usually rich merchants, lawyers, or judges, would raise personal regiments and, after being elected to command by their Soldiers, lead them in battle. Within a few months, many of these untrained and undisciplined rabbles were dead—not of bullets but of disease caused mainly by amateur leaders who did not have a clue about sanitation or camp discipline. To be sure, most of the fighting generals on both sides were West Pointers. But the troops and junior officers they led suffered and died because they entered combat as raw civilians and were forced to learn to fight by fighting, the costliest way to professionalize an army. The price of amateurism was manifested mostly by wastage, something Lincoln called "the deadly arithmetic." Poor tactical leadership and poor discipline in formations left most of those who remained with the colors dead on battlefields like Shiloh, Antietam, Gettysburg, and the Wilderness.

By the end of the war, both armies had become professional through the deadly Darwinian process of wartime self-selection and luck. Amateurism, not the enemy, killed almost three-quarters of a million men, about one in five of those recruited—more dead than in all subsequent American wars combined. Sadly, in U.S. military history, folklore too often trumps truth. Amateurism has cost many more American lives than virtually any other phenomenon. A uniquely American form of amateurism continued to prevail after the Civil War, from the Spanish American War to Vietnam.

The world wars, Korea, and Vietnam were fought with ground forces remarkably similar in composition and competence. While the technical services (the Navy, Air Force, and noncombat ground Soldiers) were manned by skilled volunteers, the infantry—the branch tasked with fighting the enemy up close—came from the dregs of society. As a rule, infantrymen were smaller and less fit than Soldiers in other branches and services. They were drawn from the lowest mental categories, as determined by newly developed military versions of IQ tests.

Thanks to Hollywood, we have a positive view of the "Greatest Generation," that of the World War II years. Unfortunately, during the opening campaigns amateurism continued to kill U.S. infantry needlessly. The battles of Kasserine

Pass in North Africa and Buna in the Pacific were bloody disasters. Later, on the beaches of Normandy, the 90th Division suffered more than 100 percent casualties among enlisted Soldiers and 150 percent among officers in six weeks of combat. Gen. William DePuy, who served as a regimental commander in the 90th, later recalled that his division was the greatest killer on the battlefield. Tragically, it was the Germans who did the killing.

The crushing ineptitude of American close-combat units was eventually overcome by two factors. First, small batches of "elite" infantry stiffened the line. From the moment Airborne and Ranger Soldiers touched enemy soil they became killing machines. The Germans referred to our Airborne infantry as "Devils in Baggy Pants." Fronts occupied by Airborne regiments were routinely four or five times larger than those held by conventional infantry regiments. The Rangers' incredible, hand-over-hand climbing assault up the cliffs of Pont du Hoc on the Normandy beachhead is legend. Every tourist who stands at the top of this cliff asks out loud, "How did they do it?" The answer is that Ranger and Airborne units were carefully selected from out of the usual rabble. Officers and Soldiers alike were all volunteers. These units were robust. Unlike in traditional close-combat units, the Army assigned extra Soldiers to each Airborne small unit. As Soldiers died or were evacuated, their buddies—well trained and deeply bonded with their comrades in a way well known to all "band of brothers" units—joined their brothers in the fight without the need for additional training or familiarization.

The second factor that made the Greatest Generation great was lengthy immersion in the harsh crucible of war. As in the Civil War, most Soldiers who joined infantry small units failed to stay on the line very long. In World War II, thanks to the germ theory of disease and vehicular evacuation, more diseased and wounded Soldiers made it to field hospitals and survived. But Lincoln's arithmetic persisted. Soldiers rotated though foxholes continually until a few survived to become superb close-combat killers. By the end of the war, our infantry had learned to fight, by fighting. Those units that faced surrendering Germans and Japanese in 1945 were superb. However, returning Soldiers made it clear to the American people that their experiences had been horrific, that many of their leaders had been unprepared to lead, that many of their weapons had been inferior, and that battles such as Iwo Jima, Okinawa, and the Huertgen Forest had been shameful slaughter pens.

Congress and the American people concluded from the stories of returning loved ones that their military had to find a less lethal way to fight its wars. Immediately after World War II, conventional wisdom inside the Pentagon was that nuclear weapons would make conventional ground warfare obsolete. As the Army and Marine Corps began their terrible slide toward combat ineffectiveness, the technical services began an aircraft-building program that would eventually consume almost 10 percent of the federal budget. Bombers were the answer for defending the American heartland. Even the expansion of the Red Army into Central Europe during the Cold War failed to convince true believers that nuclear deterrence alone was not enough, that the nation needed land forces to add depth and offer conventional strategic choices to our leaders.

Then the Army collapsed, for the first, but not the last, time after World War II. To be sure, all services, except for the strategic arm of the Air Force, suffered draconian reductions after this (like every) war. The Navy lost in its effort to build the first supercarrier. The Marines fought back efforts by senior Army leaders to fold Marine divisions into the Army and its air wings into the naval air arm. Yet, and in keeping with the Anglo-American tradition of neglecting regular Soldiers, Congress and the Truman administration effectively made its once proud and enormously competent Army into a constabulary force for occupying Germany and Japan.

As in virtually all wars in the American era, the Korean War started through miscalculation and misunderstanding, as well as the blatant aggression of the North Korean People's Army. Our broken Army performed shamefully. Soldiers were out of shape and poorly trained. Equipment was worn or broken. U.S. anti-tank rockets would bounce off enemy armor. Not until the Korean armistice in 1953 did the Army return to being a competent fighting force. Then President Eisenhower's postwar "New Look" strategy broke the Army again.

This shameful cycle of institutional death in peacetime and rebirth in combat repeated again after Vietnam. I lived through this era, and it was horrible. The post-Vietnam Army fought to maintain its existence in the midst of growing apathy, decay, and intolerance. Forty percent of Army personnel in Europe in the seventies confessed to drug use. A significant minority was hooked on heroin. Crime and desertion were rife; 12 percent of U.S. Soldiers in Europe were charged with serious offenses. Near-mutiny reigned in the barracks as gangs extorted and brutalized Soldiers. Barracks became battlegrounds between blacks and whites, and officers were frequently "fragged" by Soldiers seeking to kill their leaders. I recall vividly one night entering the barracks with a drawn pistol, expecting to be ambushed and assaulted by my own men.

A few who stayed in the ranks sought to overcome the shame of Vietnam by rebuilding the Army virtually from scratch. We vowed that "never again" would we be part of a broken Army. Sadly, the United States still failed to learn. In the late seventies we suffered through the "hollow Army" era, when President Jimmy Carter's defense budget cuts left the Army with inadequately manned and trained combat units. This "hollow force" was humiliated in its failed attempt to rescue Americans held hostage by the Iranians in 1980.

President Reagan committed himself to rebuilding, reinforcing, and modernizing a broken and dispirited service. The Reagan years were the golden era for U.S. ground forces. The "Big Five" fighting systems gave the Army a truly dominant capability for the first time in its history. "AirLand Battle," the Army's new fighting doctrine, fully exploited the service's newly modernized divisions. The Army constructed the National Training Center at Fort Irwin, California, as the first truly objective, force-on-force facility for sharpening the fighting abilities of battalions and brigades.

I remember the spirit and confidence of the Army of the late eighties. My Vietnam-era colleagues were enormously proud of what we had accomplished with the wealth donated to us by the U.S. taxpayer. The nation got its money's worth in the burning sands of Kuwait and Iraq, as Norman Schwarzkopf's legions utterly destroyed Saddam Hussein's army in less than four days of unrelenting ground combat in Desert Storm.

Then the Army broke again. Gurus in the technical services read from our Desert Storm victory that future wars would be won by technology alone, principally from the air. The popular theorists at the time concluded that air forces would be able to "give the gift of time," holding off a future foe long enough for a mobilized National Guard and Army Reserve to destroy them. Future enemies would be "shocked and awed" into surrender by aerial systems that would "lift the fog of war" and win solely from the air. By 1999, both presidential candidates had concluded that the Desert Storm Army of sixteen divisions could be reduced exactly in half.

Then came 9/11. The United States had two totally unexpected land wars on its hands and too few Soldiers and Marines to fight them. To this day I will never understand how the Army and Marine Corps fought two wars in the most inhospitable and inhumane circumstances without breaking again. That they did not is a testimony to the fortitude of a generation of ground Soldiers, some of whom served as many as ten back-to-back deployments to Iraq and Afghanistan. And yet it was not until America was four years into these wars that Secretary of Defense Donald Rumsfeld finally acquiesced to public pressure and allowed the recruitment of a hundred thousand more Soldiers to fight his wars. But by then, too many wars fought for too long by too few Soldiers had left a deep, hidden scar in the soul of the Cinderella service. We may never know the full consequences of this tragic neglect. I have seen and spoken to too many of our young men and women, a force that constitutes less than 1 percent of our nation, not to be repelled by the horrible miscalculation and institutional and political ignorance that have led us to such a shameful state.

Now the Army is breaking again, for the fifth time in my life. Secretary of Defense Ashton Carter recently announced that the Army will not have enough money to train above the squad level until 2020. The Army's new Chief of Staff, Gen. Mark Milley, has stated that, regretfully, the Army cannot afford any new systems for at least a decade. In fact, the Army has simply given up on modernizing its antiquated equipment. In the past four years the Army has cancelled 20 major programs, postponed 125, and restructured 124. Put in layman's terms, the Army will not replace its Reagan-era tanks, infantry carriers, artillery, or aircraft for at least a generation. The number of regular Soldiers will decline from 520,000 to 420,000 in the next 4 years.[1]

So, again, the service that sacrificed the most is rewarded the least. Why? Part of the problem is cost. The air and sea services consist of large machines manned by sailors and airmen. The ground forces consist of Soldiers and Marines who man machines. Manpower-intensive services do not appeal to politically connected big-machine makers. It is much quicker and easier for Congress to eliminate Soldiers than it is to cancel big-budget weapons. To many inside the Beltway, the Army represents the seedy side of military reform. After all, until very recently women were banned from joining the infantry. In spite of evidence to the contrary, Washington gurus still regard the Army as the lesser service, made up of losers who cannot get decent jobs in the civilian world. They consider Soldiers to be machine-age survivals in an information age, muscle-powered antiquarians in a techno-centric universe, men (mostly) who are too prone to die and, after fourteen years and two trillion dollars, are still unable to show success in Iraq and Afghanistan.

To be fair, the Army leadership must share in some of the blame for the Army's fifth breakup in my lifetime. Since World War II, Army leaders have been reluctant to engage in the Beltway food fight for resources. They view themselves as representing "America's Army," a force of the people whom the people trust and support. This might have been true in 1945, but it is not now. More than 99 percent of the American people have never served, and many do not know the difference between an F-16 fighter and an M16 rifle. The tradition of avoiding resource fights in Washington too often leaves Soldiers last in priority. Sadly, some of the criticisms of politicians about the Army leadership ring true. For whatever reason, the Army does not do public relations very well. Listen and compare testimonies from the services; the Army seems at times to be intellectually outflanked. Too many congressional briefings are killer exercises in "death by PowerPoint." When on camera, too many senior Soldiers come across as wooden and humorless. Their speech is heavy with acronyms and Soldier jargon. The Air Force takes congressmen and the media on thrilling fighter rides, and the Navy lands them on aircraft carriers; the Army gives them briefings at Fort Hood.

Next time you see a news video of Americans in action on television, listen to the anchor call them "Marines" although, as those of us who know can tell from their uniforms, they are Soldiers. Even my own network, Fox News, occasionally and inadvertently makes this same mistake.

In strategy as in science, nature abhors a vacuum. Someone always comes along to fill it. Vacuums in warfare are usually filled by people who seek to do harm. We are again creating a global vacuum. Our Soldiers are being given pink slips, and many of the best and brightest are voting with their feet. As our Soldiers disappear, really bad actors like ISIS, Al Qaeda, the Iranian Quds force, and many other Islamic extremists are filling the vacuum. Eventually, "ground truth" will force America to rebuild a ground force to take them on. It will take time, of course, to fix the Cinderella service, and, sadly, the handsome prince holding a glass slipper is nowhere in sight. Soldiers will die needlessly, and when that happens, Washington defense insiders will look for someone to else to blame. "I told you so"s will not count any more. After three hundred years of sordid history, we know who the culprits really are.

[3]

THE AMERICAN ERA OF WAR

"The Curse of Colonel Yahara"
How sad to watch the Kiryan Cape
Now carpeted in green
After it was dyed red
With the blood of warriors.
—Hiromichi Yahara, June 23, 1945

The American era of warfare began in a tunnel. Late into the evening of May 3, 1945, three officers huddled around a map-strewn table in the stifling heat of a Japanese command cave buried safely below the ancient Okinawan fortress of Shuri Castle. The two lieutenant generals—Itsura Ushijima, the commander of the Japanese 32nd Army, and Isamu Cho, his chief of staff—argued tactics. It was an argument in the Japanese fashion: monosyllabic, measured, and interrupted occasionally by the guttural outbursts of General Cho. The question before them was limited to one narrow set of options: should the Japanese attack soon, before U.S. forces overwhelmed them, or should they remain burrowed in their caves, bunkers, and tunnels and continue to defend?[1]

The third officer at the table was Colonel Hiromichi Yahara. He was a tall, quiet officer, deeply cerebral and intellectually gifted, a man with a mild, patrician manner. Yahara's service had been spent mainly as a staff officer and instructor at the Imperial War College. He knew his enemy, because he had lived in the United States as an attaché. But his impressions, amplified after the last five weeks of fighting Americans there on Okinawa, were considerably different from those of his boss. General Cho was an arrogant, impetuous, cruel, and stupid man—typical of a generation of generals brought up in the prewar atmosphere of court politics and savage international aggression.

On occasion Yahara would interject a few words to elevate the discussion. While his seniors argued tactics, Yahara thought strategy. He had lectured them frequently on the unique opportunities that their inevitable sacrifice on Okinawa would signify for Japan. He knew that the battle for Okinawa was actually the opening battle for the Japanese homeland. He considered it a bloody prologue of what was inevitably about to happen on the beaches of Japan's main islands of Honshu and Kyushu. He spoke frankly about how Japan should fight on in the face of a succession of tragic defeats. The United States controlled the air and sea absolutely. By invading the Marshall Islands the previous year, Americans had penetrated the final strategic perimeter of the empire and placed the home islands within range of the cruel killing power of U.S. B-29 bombers. He understood that a land assault on the home islands supported by the overwhelming firepower of naval artillery and carrier strike aircraft would follow immediately after the United States captured Okinawa.

The hard part of these discussions was the context. Four years before, Japan's strategy had been to preserve victory. Now it was to manage defeat. The question that Yahara pondered with his staff was how to translate the looming yet necessary sacrifices of a losing land battle into some form of redemptive advantage for Japan. In typical Japanese fashion, Yahara sought to lessen the shame of what was to come by referring to his concept as an "offensive retreat." His intent was straightforward: kill Americans with such efficiency that they would reconsider the wisdom of invading Japan. Perhaps if his Soldiers could kill enough Americans, an armistice similar to the Versailles treaty that had ended World War I might be negotiated with the United States. Perhaps even the emperor's place as the "son of heaven" might be respected and preserved.

Like any competent staff officer, Yahara based his strategy on the strengths and weaknesses of the enemy. He knew Americans well from personal associations during his time in the States. His superior intuition allowed him to filter out the prejudices of his samurai brethren to form a realistic appreciation of the fighting qualities of U.S. forces. Clearly U.S. matériel strength was far beyond anything the Japanese Imperial Staff could have imagined before the attack on Pearl Harbor in 1941.

Once the battle for Okinawa began in earnest, Yahara discovered that the Americans were harder to kill than anyone had supposed. With a good pair of binoculars, he could watch U.S. Soldiers and Marines moving back and forth between the beach to forward foxholes with relative impunity. He concluded that the only efficient place to kill them was in close, at about one thousand yards, with small arms, mortars, and grenades. Yahara and his field commanders also noted that the fighting efficiency of Americans diminished as they moved toward the line of contact. The closer the Japanese infantry could hold the enemy "in its embrace," the greater chance that it could kill Americans. From the beachhead to the infantry battalion rear area, U.S. Soldiers and Marines were very well trained and motivated. But their infantrymen's performance seemed to fall apart as they closed to small-arms range, the last hundred yards—often less than fifty yards.

Yahara knew that the only remaining American vulnerability was public opinion. Prior to assuming their duties on Okinawa, Ushijima and Yahara had served together as senior leaders at the war college at Zama. From their studies they had concluded that the American public was increasingly concerned about the human cost of the Pacific War. The press exposed the horrors of the Pacific campaign, beginning with pictures of dead Americans on the beaches of Buna in 1942 and continuing through the bloody battles of Tarawa, Peleliu, Saipan, Iwo Jima, and the Philippines. American patience had waned even further in the winter of 1945 after the war in Europe appeared to be substantially won. Opportunities to influence American opinion were amplified by a new openness by the Truman administration, which allowed vivid pictures and written imagry of the Pacific battlefields to be revealed to the American people. The public began to protest the cost of a war against a hated but clearly secondary foe. Why, it was asked, were so many men dying so horribly for bits of rock and coral?

YAHARA'S LONG SHADOW: WAR IN THE AMERICAN ERA

Unlike Ushijima and Cho, Yahara did not die on Okinawa. By the third week in June the once-powerful Japanese forces had been reduced to small huddles of cave-bound Soldiers preparing for ritual suicide. On the 23rd, Ushijima gathered his two colleagues in a small command cave perched just above the cliffs that defined the connection between the absolute end of the island and the emerald-green sea to the south. Yahara watched with resignation as Ushijima and Cho changed into white kimonos and exchanged poetic remembrances of their homeland and past campaigns. In this surreal setting, Yahara noted, he was excluded from the ritual. Ushijima bent forward and spoke in hushed tunes as he gave last instructions to his brilliant and faithful staff officer: "Colonel, the Homeland must be defended next. You have shown us both how Japan must prepare to defend the Emperor. Leave us before it's too late and return to Japan."

The next three days would haunt Yahara for the remainder of his life. Even an officer with such great intellectual gifts believed that in such circumstances continuing to live was a cowardly act. His shame increased unbearably when the U.S. Army captured him only three days after his escape from the funereal cave of Ushijima and Cho. His dead seniors had expected him to convey the secrets learned fighting the Americans back to the defenders of the Japanese home islands. Both had been convinced that in spite of their overwhelming firepower, the Americans could be defeated if only enough of them died.

U.S. command knew it as well. Deep in the bowels of the National Archives rests a set of yellowed papers—only recently declassified—that is the operational plan for the invasion of Japan.[2] Operation Downfall was finalized in Washington as the battle for Okinawa reached its bloody zenith. The preliminary invasion, Operation Olympic, was scheduled to begin on October 25, with an invasion of the Japanese southern island of Kyushu. The invasion would include almost 1.5 million men, thousands of aircraft and ships—the greatest armada the world had ever seen. However, confidence in the Olympic plan continued to wane as stories about Japanese fighting effectiveness began to circulate among the Pacific planning staffs. Only after the war would the Americans learn about the enormously complex defense of the home islands the Japanese had planned.

More than fourteen Japanese divisions as well as seven independent and two tank brigades awaited the invasion. This force was composed of the hard core of Japan's army, well equipped and fed and anxious to die for the homeland. Today a visitor can still walk along the beach defenses on Kyushu: thousands of concrete bunkers and artillery positions. U.S. command learned later that the Japanese had been able to collect more than 14,000 aircraft to support the defense. Clearly, Adm. William Leahy's prediction of 250,000 American dead on Kyushu alone was understated. Okinawa and the strategic genius of men like Yahara had put paid to the optimistic plans of U.S. forces. Yahara's ideas would kill many, many more. Fortunately, for millions of GIs (including my father) Yahara's genius would become irrelevant the day the United States dropped the atomic bomb on Hiroshima.

THE AMERICAN ERA OF WAR

Yahara lived until 1972, long enough to see his strategic wisdom played out as the last U.S. fighting units left South Vietnam. By then, he knew that he had charted a conceptual template that subsequent enemies of the United States would apply with deadly consequence. History would make Yahara's revelations in the death cave the enduring template for challenging the global might of the U.S. military in a new epoch that historians term the "American era of warfare."

Japan's bloody defeat on Okinawa, followed three weeks later by the bombing of Hiroshima, ended a three-hundred-year run of European dominance in war. Virtually all historically significant wars fought between the Treaty of Westphalia in 1648 and the Japanese surrender in Tokyo Bay were shaped by the colonial and state-on-state actions of Western European armies. Of course, not all major wars of this period were fought by European militaries, but the shadow of European military skill, technology, and global reach affected most. Prior to Okinawa every military on the planet either fought using European methods or, in the case of anticolonial forces, sought means to defeat European militaries. After Okinawa, European militaries became witnesses, bystanders, aggressive mimickers of or allies to the new dominant actor so powerful that it displaced the European, in the American era of war.

The foundational element in the epochal shift from the European to American era was the U.S. development of and willingness to use nuclear weapons. The global fear engendered by the horrors of Hiroshima and Nagasaki took off the table any prospect of a third world war fought between great powers. Of course all of the traditional elements of military competition—greed, envy, hegemonic ambitions, and ethnic and religious hatred—remained and flourished after World War II. Yet the prospects of mutual destruction triggered by escalation to a nuclear response served to eliminate total, apocalyptic war as a reasonable option for competition among the great powers, principally the United States and the Soviet Union.

Since the invention of expensive bronze artillery, the power of a military system has been dependent on the economic power of the state. U.S. economic dominance emerged when the horribly destructive bombings and invasions in Europe and Asia left the United States the last untouched great power. The disappearance of global prewar competition was the second factor that served to usher in the American era. U.S. nuclear dominance has led to two generations of "limited" conflicts fought for limited strategic ends, often in the most distant and inhospitable corners of the globe. Often these wars have pitted a Western military (that of Israel, Britain, or France) against a non-Western military, often acting as a surrogate for a competing nuclear-armed adversary.

Not all wars in the American era have been fought by Americans. Nevertheless, the long shadow of U.S. technology, doctrine, and tactical methods can be found in all of them, regardless of opponent or level of war, from preinsurgency in places like the Philippines to something approaching general war in the Middle East and East Asia. We know from many years of observed behavior that aggression in the American era is practiced by an assortment of healthy conventional states, rogue states, and transnational entities. It works for enemies at many places along the spectrum of warfare—from, again, preinsurgency in places like the Philippines to full-blown insurgencies in Iraq and Afghanistan, to what amounts nearly to conventional war in Lebanon and Korea.

At the strategic level, wars in the American era generally have started through mutual miscalculation. The enemy, usually a regional potentate with limited hegemonic ambitions, seeks to achieve his aggressive ends while dissuading a Western power from interfering. From Lin Biao to Ho Chi Minh to Osama bin Laden, our enemies' leaders have embraced a consistent operational and tactical pattern of behavior to confront the militaries of first-world states. Their intent has not been to win in battle so much as to avoid losing. They have sought to stretch out warfare and to kill intruders, not as a means to an end but as an end in itself. They are able to match Western firepower with iron will, familiarity with terrain and culture, willingness to die, and selection of battlefields in very far and inhospitable places.

As Colonel Yahara predicted on Okinawa, none of the United States' more recent enemies have succeeded in winning conventional fights. All of these regional hegemonic leaders have telegraphed their intentions, in unambiguously clear language and actions. They also have established a remarkably straightforward pattern of response based on common sense, a keen sense of U.S. military capabilities, and will to persevere. This collection of bad actors has demonstrated a remarkably refined ability to learn from their mistakes and the mistakes of their malevolent fellow travelers.

In a curious twist of conventional wisdom, enemies in the American era have been remarkably open and forthright about their aggressive intent. Kim Il Sung stated his military objective as the reunification of Korea, and the North Koreans have held to this aim for seventy years. Ho Chi Minh never strayed from his dream of reunifying Vietnam under his rule. Saddam and bin Laden never wavered from their aggressive intentions. Unfortunately, a succession of U.S. leaders has shifted strategic objectives based on momentary perceptions of popular support. If the enemy's past behavior has been so open and consistent, we should treat his declarations as truthful, sincere, and consequently worthy of our attention. We should add the enemy's confidence, fidelity, and winning style into our calculation of future challenges.

The wisdom of Colonel Yahara provides all sides with a template for winning wars in the American era. He tells our enemies that winning begins with a willingness to translate sacrifice into a national strategic advantage. He tells them that American vulnerabilities begin with American public opinion and the reluctance of American Soldiers to die. So the first principle is to kill as publicly and as horrifically as possible. Also, avoid the "hard kill" whenever possible: infantry knows how to fight back. Truck drivers and cooks traveling in open trucks are easy kills.

Yahara knew that his greatest ally was time. Americans are impatient and want to win quickly. Yahara knew that Americans would die merely from the natural attrition that attends long wars. He learned on Okinawa that the United States can be beaten only on the ground. Opposition on the sea and in the air is a senseless diversion. Thus a successful opposition strategy begins by "spotting" to the U.S. control of the air and sea (what contemporary gurus call the "global commons").

Yahara taught that the will is superior to weaponry. Thus, like the Japanese, contemporary enemies of the United States tend to follow a strategy of repurposing older weapons and technologies to fight superior U.S. technologies. Watch any newsreel today provided by the likes of ISIS, the Taliban, Al Qaeda, or other successful rogues. They have left behind captured air and ground systems in favor of an assortment of portable, low-tech substitutes carried by ground Soldiers—for example, shoulder-fired and tripod-mounted antiair and antitank missiles. Newer weapons of our enemies are also derivative in nature, from cell phones to off-the-shelf drones for aerial reconnaissance. Just as in Yahara's day, the greatest killers of Americans remain the simple mortar, mine, and small arm.

The tactics employed by Yahara remain the tactics of choice for all contemporary enemies: hide from orbiting aircraft and drones, and dig in, fortify, disperse, and hide in cities among the people, where the Americans will not strike. Fight close and make human shields of the innocent to obviate the killing effects of U.S. tactical weapons. Use social media to showcase every error that causes casualties. The Americans who fought and destroyed Yahara's army fought a "war without mercy." By 1945 revelations of endless Japanese atrocities in the Philippines, human banzai attacks on virtually every defended atoll, and of the thousands of Americans dead from aerial kamikaze suicide attacks had left U.S. Soldiers without empathy for their enemy. The Japanese had become so dehumanized that "any dead Jap was a good Jap." Things are different now. If alive today Yahara would envy our enemies who exploit rules of engagement to extract themselves from losing fights. Of course, our enemies fight without such rules.

If war were a football game, Yahara's asymmetric warfare team would yield a winning record of five-two-two over the seventy years since Okinawa. Enemies such as Saddam in 1991 and any number of other Middle Eastern conventional wannabies would suffer a zero-and-seven season when attempting to mimic Western states in the use of their conventional (and expensive) weapons and doctrine.

WHAT DOES COLONEL YAHARA TEACH US?

The first lesson is counterintuitive. Conventional wisdom tells us that we must never fight the next war like we did the last. Yahara tells us that maybe we should. Perhaps wars in the American era would end better if we considered the past as prologue, if we postulated that the pattern of progression in our wars has been essentially unchanged from Greece in 1948 to Afghanistan today. The fundamental conditions of warfare will last for many generations. While Yahara tells us that the pattern of wars will not change, he certainly would concede that it is a losing proposition to try to predict specific times, enemies, technologies, or war-fighting scenarios. It has never worked before, and it likely never will.

From a practical perspective, Yahara is telling us that war is a test of will, not technology. Of course, we need to exploit new technologies, and we must never seek to fight fair. All too often in the American era Soldiers have died needlessly, killed by enemies like the Japanese who used simple things to achieve extraordinary outcomes. Perhaps we should spend first to buy things that work best against wise and diabolical enemies.

Most importantly, Yahara knew where to strike for maximum effect. If he was right and if our most vulnerable center of gravity is dead Americans, perhaps we should place highest priority on protecting those most likely to die.

[4]

ADAPTIVE ENEMIES

War, however, is not the action of a living force upon a lifeless mass . . . but always the collision of two living forces. The ultimate aim of waging war . . . must be taken as applying to both sides. Once again, there is inter-action. So long as I have not overthrown my opponent I am bound to fear he may overthrow me. Thus, I am not in control: he dictates to me as much as I dictate to him.[1]

—Carl von Clausewitz

Once the dogs of war are unleashed and the shooting starts, conflicts follow unpredictable courses. The nineteenth-century philosopher of military strategy Carl von Clausewitz warned that wars are contests between two active, willing enemies, both of whom expect to win. Once begun, war—with its precise planning and cerebral doctrine—quickly devolves into a series of stratagems and counter-stratagems as each side seeks to retain advantages long enough to achieve a decisive end, by collapsing an enemy's will to resist.[2]

Over the last seventy years, Western militaries—particularly the U.S. armed forces—have been remarkably consistent in how they fight. They have an extra-ordinary ability to translate technological innovation, industrial-base capacity, and national treasure into battlefield advantage. But no sooner had Western powers accepted and copied the American way of war than lesser states from

Asia, Africa, and the Middle East began in earnest to learn from the sinister wisdom of Colonel Yahara. The colonel and his intellectual progeny are still watching, learning, and adapting. We, on the other hand, have been slow to perceive the growing effectiveness of an asymmetric enemy, partly because of the characteristic Western arrogance that presumes that an enemy, to be a threat, must mimic the Western way of war.

Colonel Yahara was freed from U.S. custody in June 1945 and returned to his homeland, just in time to witness Japan's former enemy, China, begin to learn from, adapt to, and eventually defeat an enemy who sought to win in the American fashion. Yahara's old enemy continued to prosecute its way of war in subsequent conflicts and its serial failures suggest a pattern that should disturb us all.

THE CHINESE CIVIL WAR

An effort to redefine and codify an Eastern approach to defeating the Western way of war began in the mountain fastness of Manchuria, immediately after World War II. Mao Zedong and his marshals adapted doctrine from their wartime guerrilla campaigns to fit a conventional war against an enemy superior in technology and matériel. Mao perfected his new way of war against the Nationalists between 1946 and 1949. His simple concepts centered on three tenets, the most important of which was area control. To succeed, Mao's army first needed to survive in the midst of a larger, better-equipped enemy.[3] He divided his troops into small units and scattered them. Maintaining cohesion thus remained his greatest challenge.

Once his own forces were supportable and stable, Mao applied the second tenet—to isolate and compartmentalize the Nationalists. The challenge of this phase was to leverage control of the countryside until the enemy retreated into urban areas and to major lines of communications.[4] The final act of the campaign called for finding the enemy's weakest points and collecting and massing overwhelming force against each sequentially, a process similar to taking apart a strand of pearls one pearl at a time. Mao's new style of conventional war, though effective, demanded extraordinary discipline and patience under extreme hardship. It also sought quick transition from an area-control force to one capable of fighting a war of movement.

STALEMATE IN KOREA

Within a year of the Chinese Civil War, America severely tested Mao's methods in the mountains of Korea. Initially, the People's Liberation Army (PLA) badly misjudged the effects of U.S. artillery and tactical airpower. Pushed quickly into maneuver warfare, the Chinese massed in the open, often in daylight, to expand their control over the northern Korean Peninsula. They extended their narrow lines of communications farther down the mountainous spine of Korea as they advanced. However, they soon found their logistic support exposed to U.S. airpower and paid a horrid price for their haste. The spring 1951 offensive mounted by the Chinese sputtered to a halt as U.S. artillery and aerial firepower slaughtered PLA Soldiers in masses and air interdiction cut their lines of supply and forced a retreat back across the Han River.

Brutal experiences led to the relearning of sober lessons from the civil war. The Chinese quickly adjusted to a new situation. Over the following two years their attacks were limited and controlled. The high command learned to keep most key logistic facilities north of the Yalu River, out of reach of U.S. air strikes. South of the river they dispersed and hid, massing only to launch attacks. Soldiers moved at night and chiseled their front lines of resistance into "granite mountains." U.S. casualties mounted while the Chinese stabilized their own losses at a rate acceptable to Beijing. Many more Americans died during the stability phase than in earlier days of fluid warfare. What was an acceptable human toll to China was unacceptable to the United States. The result was operational and strategic stalemate. To the Chinese, stalemate equaled victory.

THE VIETNAM EXPERIENCE

Over the next two decades, the Vietnamese borrowed from the Chinese experience and found creative ways to lessen the killing effect of firepower, against first France and then the United States. They also proved skilled in adapting to the new challenges posed by their Western enemies. The Viet Minh based its tactical and operational approach on Mao's unconventional methods. Its conduct of the battle was remarkably reminiscent of siege operations conducted by the PLA during the Chinese Civil War. In both cases, the secrets of success were dispersion and preparation of the battlefield. The Viet Minh remained scattered in small units to offer less detectable and lucrative targets and to allow its troops to live off the land. Fewer supply lines and logistic sites offered even fewer opportunities for interdiction fires.

To win, the Chinese—and eventually the Viet Minh—needed to attack. That demanded the ability to mass temporarily. The Viet Minh had to exercise great care in massing under the enemy umbrella of protective firepower. Superior intelligence indicated the right time and place. The ability to collect and move tens of thousands of Soldiers at the right moment allowed attacking forces to collapse French defenses before firepower could regain the advantage. This capacity to "maneuver under fire," perfected against the Nationalists and now the French, reached new levels of refinement during the second Indochina War, against the United States.

The North Vietnamese architect of victory, General Vo Nguyen Giap, quickly accommodated his strategic plans to the new realities of U.S. firepower. The North Vietnamese relearned the importance of dispersion and patience. They redistributed their forces to keep their most vulnerable units outside the range of U.S. artillery while moving their logistic system away from battle areas into sanctuaries relatively safe from aerial detection and strikes. Thus, they dusted off and applied many of the same methods that had proven useful in previous Asian wars against Western-style armies.

THE RUSSIANS IN AFGHANISTAN

Half a decade later and half a continent away, in Afghanistan, the Soviets learned the same harsh firsthand lessons of overconfidence, when a first-world military once again confronted third-world forces that had the will, tenacity, and skill to remain effective despite firepower inferiority. Year after year, the Soviets arrayed themselves for conventional combat and pushed methodically up the Panjir Valley, only to be expelled a few months later by a seemingly endless and psychologically debilitating series of methodical and well-placed ambuscades and skirmishes. Borrowing a page from the American textbook in Vietnam, the Soviets tried to exploit the firepower, speed, and intimidation of armed helicopters. They employed them principally as convoy escorts and to provide fire support. At times, Hind helicopters proved enormously lethal, particularly early on, when the mujahideen were psychologically unprepared. The guerrillas eventually turned back to the Vietnam experience, employing heavy antiaircraft machine guns and then Stinger shoulder-fired missiles to shoot down the gunships, and in increasing numbers. Military frustration and defeat in Afghanistan presaged the collapse of the Soviet Union.

ISRAEL AND LEBANON THE FIRST TIME: 1982

Beginning in 1982, after nearly three decades of failure in open warfare, an alliance of Arab state and nonstate actors pushed Israeli mechanized forces out of Beirut. Back streets, tall buildings, and other urban clutter provided the Arabs just enough respite from intensive firepower to wear away Israeli morale in the field and at home. Unable to bring superior maneuverability and shock effect fully to bear, the Israelis paused just short of their operational objectives. Excessive casualties and the public images of bloody excesses on both sides eventually resulted in Israeli withdrawal. This success provided Israel's enemies with a promising new method to offset its superiority in open, mechanized combat. Today a spectrum of low-tech threats, running the gamut from weapons of mass destruction delivered by crude ballistic missiles to acts of terrorism, to children throwing rocks at Soldiers, confront an increasingly frustrated Israeli military and public. An irony of the recent wars in the Middle East is that Western-style militaries have had great success against non-Western enemies who mimic their own firepower doctrines. The Gulf War is the most recent example of such failed efforts by Arab states, stretching back to 1948. In 1973, Arab armies enjoyed some measure of success applying Western methods, but that was in large part a result of Israeli overconfidence and limited Arab objectives.

THE GULF WAR

Despite extraordinary incompetence on the part of its leadership, the enemy displayed considerable capacity to adapt on the battlefield during Operation Desert Storm. As the U.S. air campaign began to focus on destroying Iraqi ground forces in the Kuwait theater during early February 1991, the Iraqi army quickly adapted. By scattering their tanks across the desert and then constructing berms around them, they ensured that aircraft dropping precision-guided bombs could at best destroy only a single vehicle per pass. Burning tires next to operational vehicles spoofed attackers into missing real targets. Moreover, effective antiaircraft fire kept numerous coalition planes too high to do substantial damage. The best-trained Iraqi units endured weeks of coalition air bombardment with unbroken will and combat capability intact. The most impressive indication of the Iraqi ability to adapt came in the operational movement of a substantial portion of the Republican Guard during the first hours of Desert Storm. Elements of two divisions shifted from a southeastern defensive orientation to defensive positions that faced southwest along Wadi al-Batin. There, the Tawakalna Division and the 50th and 37th Armored Brigades would be destroyed by VII Corps.[5] Nevertheless, these units' sacrifices allowed the rest of the Republican Guard to withdraw. Significantly, the Iraqi Republican Guard ultimately escaped to save Saddam despite overwhelming coalition airpower.

NATO AND KOSOVO

Despite its video-game public image, the NATO campaign against Serbia was no exception to the Clausewitzian construct. Belgrade sought to overcome a tremendous matériel and technological disadvantage by capitalizing on its strengths: the ability to gain operational objectives quickly and then disperse to avoid the inevitable aerial assault. The Serbs thought that patience, tenacity, guile, and ground forces sequestered throughout the countryside would provide an interval long enough to outwait the resolve of NATO. The political will of the alliance proved stronger. But skill and perseverance on the part of the Serbian army in the face of a thousand aircraft with precision-guided weapons is a compelling example of how an adaptive enemy can foil the best-laid plans of a superior force, by capitalizing on its own inherent strengths while minimizing those of the enemy.

Placed in historical context, the Serbian response to the NATO onslaught is simply another data point on a continuum of progressive, predictable adaptations by technologically dispossessed forces willing to challenge Western militaries having superior precision firepower. Like their Asian fellow travelers, the Serbs sought victory by avoiding defeat. In a similar fashion, they conceded the vertical dimension of the battle space to NATO. They were content to shoot down a few aircraft using ground-mounted guns and missiles. This hope was underscored by an expectation that a few dead or captured alliance airmen would gradually degrade NATO resolve. Even if a shoot-down was impossible, the Serbs would seek to keep their antiaircraft assets robust, knowing that ground targets would be difficult to spot from high altitudes.

The surest way to avoid defeat was keeping the army in the field viable—both as a defiant symbol of national resolve and as a legitimate Serbian guarantor of sovereignty over occupied territory. To maintain an effective army in being, the Serbs likewise depended on historical precedents. Units quickly went to ground and dispersed widely. They rapidly computed the pace at which the allies could find, target, and strike uncovered assets and then devised ways to relocate mobile targets inside the alliance's sensor-to-shooter envelope. They replicated camouflage, decoys, and spoofing techniques proven effective by Asian armies. As the allies became proficient at spotting troops, Serbs sought greater dispersal and went deeper into the ground.

Toward the end, the coalition gained a significant airpower advantage with the emergence of a rudimentary ground presence in the form of the Kosovo Liberation Army (KLA). This force was not very effective in open combat against the better-armed Serbs, but the very presence of large-scale KLA units among them forced the Serbs to come out of protective cover and to mass. The results were remarkably consistent with past experiences against China and North Vietnam. Troops moving, massed, and in the open present the most lucrative targets from the air. Yet the Serb forces were never severely damaged, because they were too large and well protected to be erased by aircraft. Since total destruction was not feasible, the contest in Kosovo, like all battles of attrition, soon devolved into a test of time and will. Victory went to the side that could endure the longest without a collapse of will. Once it became evident to President Slobodan Milosevic that NATO resolve would not be broken before a threatened ground assault could materialize, he ceded Kosovo to ensure his own political survival.

THE SECOND IRAQ WAR

Fourteen years of American adventures in the Middle East have provided the surest evidence yet of the vacuity of our fighting doctrine that minimalizes the ability of the enemy to endure our killing power as they adapted to find new and creative ways of killing us. We all remember the euphoria that accompanied the "March to Baghdad" in March 2003. Again, Saddam Hussein was too stupid and fixated on his mechanized forces to realize that two U.S. divisions supported by overwhelming airpower would destroy his military in less than three weeks.

Unfortunately, the victory dance was premature. With Saddam out of the way, the Iraqis, particularly the Iraqi Sunnis, were quick to apply the lessons they had learned in the past when fighting against Western militaries. U.S. leadership failed to heed the signs of a shift from conventional to irregular warfare. By the end of the summer of 2003, as the George W. Bush administration tried to find a means to withdraw from the fight, a combination of mostly Sunni ex-Baathist officers and a newly formed Shia militia army started to fight back by killing Americans and each other. In time, during the "surge" of 2006–7, the U.S. command in Iraq adapted to the enemy's adaptation and transformed the military in Iraq into an effective counterinsurgency force. But none of this happened until the chaos induced by an adaptive enemy had resulted in the deaths of thousands of U.S. Soldiers, principally from a tactical system that relied on roadside bombs and carefully orchestrated small-unit engagements in places like Fallujah and Ramadi.

Tragically, the chaos of Iraq created the strategic vacuum that allowed Osama bin Laden's small terrorist organization to morph into larger and more deadly terrorist surrogates and franchises, to include Al Qaeda in Iraq and later ISIS, as well as many others spawned from the Atlantic coast of Africa to the Hindu Kush.

THE SECOND AFGHAN WAR

The first year of successful combat by special operating forces in concert with the Afghan Northern Alliance showcased what U.S. Soldiers can do if they give up on big-machine warfare and practice the art of war among the people. Speed, shock, and surprise combined to break the back of the Taliban. I recall a particularly poignant moment in the early months when my television showed images of Special Forces Soldiers wrapped in native Talib shawls and leggings, mounted on horseback, calling in precision fires from B-52 bombers making "lazy eights" in the skies high above. It was a moment when those of us who had been calling for exactly such an imaginative melding of unconventional and high-tech warfare felt vindicated.

Sadly, the moment passed. A defeated Taliban retreated into Pakistan to fight another day. The Taliban, like all of our successful enemies in the past, knew that American patience in war was lacking. It was just a momentary failure for Afghan insurgents whose ancestors had been evicting enemies for 2,300 years. In time, patience and cunning replaced active resistance. Within a year of victory, the Bush administration had decided to fight two wars, with priority given to the one in Iraq, creating another strategic vacuum, which would be filled by a resurgent Taliban . . . and yet another war fought against an adaptive enemy, a war that is with us still.

ISRAEL AND LEBANON THE SECOND TIME: 2006

Contemporary history teaches about the firepower addiction of a Western-style military, unused to fighting against adaptive enemies. Lieutenant General Dan

Halutz, the first air force officer to be appointed head of the Israeli Defense Forces, said upon assuming his duties in 2005 that he believed the American experience in Kosovo demonstrated that a carefully planned, orchestrated, and technologically precise air campaign could collapse Hezbollah's ability to threaten Israel.

Halutz fell prey to the same demons that were at that very moment confounding his American friends in Iraq and Afghanistan. Hezbollah's demons appeared most decisively in the small village of Bint Jbiel, just over the Israeli-Lebanon border and nearby in the defile of Wadi Saluki. There Hezbollah fighters ambushed and destroyed a battalion's worth of Israel's blitzkrieg-era heavy tanks. The parallel disasters of Bint Jbiel and Wadi Saluki became laboratories for teaching how a well-trained insurgent force—exhaustively drilled, carefully dug in, camouflaged, and armed with the first-rate, Soviet-era precision antitank weaponry—could utterly devastate a modern, technologically superior Cold War force, even if that force commanded the air absolutely. These battles strongly suggest that older-generation portable antitank and antiaircraft weapons in the hands of diabolically skilled infantry fighting what theorists now term "hybrid warfare" can win against heavy, mechanized forces if they meld just enough technology with an irregular force whose members are willing to fight to the death.

IMPLICATIONS FOR THE FUTURE

Non-Western militaries are increasingly internalizing the lessons of wars against technologically superior enemies. Recent works on the operational and tactical problems of fighting Western-style militaries suggest clear warnings. First, non-Western enemies understand Western military vulnerabilities: aversion to casualties and collateral damage, sensitivity to domestic and world opinion, and lack of commitment to conflicts of durations measured in years rather than months. They also perceive that Americans in particular retain a style of war focused on the single offensive dimension of a firepower battle. Moreover, they are already considering how to target Western vulnerabilities while capitalizing on their intrinsic advantages: time, will, and the inherent power of the defensive. Borrowing from Mao and Giap, future enemies have learned the value of time and patience. From their perspective, swift success is not essential to victory.

Future enemies have also realized the advantage of interfering with an intruder's intention to end a conflict quickly and at minimum cost. Moreover, non-Western armies have learned to limit the effect and duration of air campaigns by dispersing not only their forces but their telecommunications, logistics, and transportation infrastructures. They also understand that sophisticated air defenses—whose effectiveness depends on airfields, surface-to-air missile sites, and vulnerable command-and-control nodes—have become liabilities more than assets and must be dispersed, hidden, or eliminated.

Once the ground conflict begins, enemies must, they understand, use superior mass to offset the lethal firepower and precision technology of Western armies. They will capitalize on the positional advantages of the defensive in or near their own territory. As they gain confidence, they will search for opportunities to mass sufficient force to achieve local successes. As in the Kosovo air campaign, they will seek to frustrate Western ground forces with just enough modern weaponry to extend the campaign indefinitely. A few precision cruise missiles against major logistic bases will add to the casualty rates that Western militaries must explain to their citizens. The object will not be decisive victory but stalemate. A prolonged stalemate will erode Western political support for the conflict.

As non-Western militaries develop concepts for defeating the U.S.'s firepower-centered method of war, the character and composition of their forces are changing. The Cold War impulse to clone Western force structures is disappearing. Foreign militaries are taking on their own identities. The mountains of metal, consisting of expensive yet often second-rate land, sea, and air machines that serve as lucrative targets are rapidly vanishing. In particular, non-Western armies are becoming lighter.

Evidence of this trend can be found on the shopping lists of emerging militaries. Instead of sophisticated aircraft and blue-water navies, most are pursuing cheap weapons of mass destruction and the methods of delivering them. Acquisition of sea and land mines, as well as distributed air-defense weapons, suggest that the intent of these militaries is to keep potential enemies at bay. Most expenditures and attention go to land forces, because in nondemocratic states armies provide political legitimacy. They are also useful instruments for waging regional wars of aggression, and they are sure means for suppressing internal dissent and thwarting troublesome outsiders.

[5]

FORECASTING WAR

So I'm here today to say that climate change constitutes a serious threat to global security, an immediate risk to our national security.
—President Barack Obama

The least successful enterprise in Washington, D.C., is the one that places bets on the nature and character of tomorrow's wars. The industry remains enormously influential and well financed, because everyone in Washington knows that bad bets cost lives and waste trillions. As our wars in Iraq and Afghanistan wind down, the services, defense industries, and their supporting think tanks, along with Congress, academia, and the media, continue the search for a new and imaginative view of wars to come. Virtually without exception, they get it wrong—and only in Washington are bad bets rewarded rather than punished.

The future-gazing industry grew apace with the emerging dominance of the United States military after World War II. Since then, two generations of failed future-gazers have made the term "intelligence failure" a hyphenated word. Perhaps at no time in our history has a single governmental function been so singularly (and rightfully) vilified. From 9/11 to the appearance of the Sunni insurgency in 2003, to the more recent return of the Taliban and the profoundly disturbing and unexpected arrival of ISIS, our intelligence agencies have left a sorrowful trail of missed guesses and informational black holes. In fairness to current political leaders, our poor record in forecasting threats has a long and uninterrupted provenance that has led to tragic strategic surprises. Korea caught Truman completely by surprise and unprepared for war. Kennedy and Johnson would never have gone to war in Vietnam had they suspected that the price would be sixty thousand dead. Saddam's surprise invasion of Kuwait in 1990 was an intelligence meltdown of the first order. In 2003, Saddam never had weapons of mass destruction.

Failure to predict the time, place, cost, duration, intensity, and nature of the threat has cost the nation dearly in lives and treasure. Every aspect of defense policy and management is dependent upon anticipating properly whom we will fight and, equally, whom we should ignore. Poor threat prediction has too often led to the purchase of weapons and development of forces ill suited to the exigencies of future battlefields. Failure cannot be ascribed to want of effort. Without question, the most engaging sport inside the Beltway is "threat analysis" by legions of academics and think-tank gurus. The collective bill for intelligence prediction is somewhere north of fifty billion per year. Satellites, drones, planes, and computers spend millions of hours looking and counting. Tens of thousands of well-credentialed analysts work tirelessly, interpreting the data in an effort to divine the future.

Threat prediction fails, in part, because the process is done today using methodologies inherited from the Cold War and hardwired into a bureaucratic process that virtually guarantees failure at every turn. These methodologies generally divide themselves into five analytical "schools." The culture that spawned each school shapes the nature of the inquiry. The sum of the processes practiced by these schools exerts a subtle influence that inevitably identifies future threats more like the enemies we want to fight than the enemies we have fought consistently since the end of World War II.

The "Scenario Development School" is the fastest-growing cottage industry inside Beltway think tanks. Threat prediction using "scenarios" involves a process as simple as it is deceiving. Pick one of the usual suspects with serious military capabilities who sits athwart a piece of ground of strategic importance to the United States and then encourage the stimulation of excuses for going to war with him. Since the end of the Cold War, the list of usual suspects has been monotonously consistent: China, Iran, and North Korea (with, in the background, Russia as the nostalgic favorite). Again, the problem with the scenario approach has been that, try as the pundits might (and they really try—particularly at budget time), they have not been able to elevate the overt intentions of these actors to a level approaching imminent danger.

The "Emerging Technology School" consists of frightened and well-remunerated techno-warriors who constantly scan the threat horizon anxious to alert the security community to enemies who they sense are harnessing the diabolical genius of homegrown weapon makers. To be sure, we must guard against being surprised by leap-ahead technologies in the hands of an enemy, particularly enemies who pursue nuclear weapons technologies. But too often, the technological fear mongering has led to a "Chicken Little" effect that has proven both illusory and very expensive. Technological fear mongering comes from cultural arrogance that assumes our enemies put the same trust in technology that we do. Battlefield experience in the American era strongly suggests that we have been surprised and bested on the battlefield not by superweapons but by enemies who have employed simple technologies creatively. Our combat deaths have been suffered mostly from mortars, mines, and machine guns in Korea and Vietnam and by many of these same weapons adapted to war in Iraq and Afghanistan.

The "Capabilities-Based Assessment School" seeks to perpetuate the Cold War status quo by accepting the impossibility of predicting the threat. The capabilities approach argues for flexibility as the safest means for dealing with the ambiguity of today's conflict environment. Security comes from creating a huge military toolbox from which weapons and forces can be retrieved and tailored to meet unforeseen threats. Adherence to the capabilities school begs the question: How can we justify spending fifty billion on a predictive process so ineffective that it abrogates the very purpose of its existence?

The "New Concepts Masquerading as Strategy School" is my personal favorite. Futurists inside the Beltway frequently fall victim to a new idea expressed as a "war-fighting concept." Remember "shock and awe"? This concept grew out of our victory in Desert Storm. It was premised on the ridiculous idea that U.S. killing technologies would prevail against any enemy. Fear of precision bombing would strike at the psyche of a cowering foe. He would be awed and shocked enough to give up after an overwhelming demonstration of U.S. precision firepower. Of course, Al Qaeda, the Taliban, and ISIS have long put paid to this idea. But sadly, it continues to seduce and spawn other firepower-centered silliness. Take the concept of net-centric warfare, for instance. In the nineties, senior naval officers predicted that our ability to dominate the network would "lift the fog of war" and allow us to see, strike, and kill any enemy from the air. Again, no one in Washington talked to the Chinese and North Vietnamese about this beforehand. Other silliness followed 9/11. The concept of "effects-based operations" (EBO) was the brainchild of Air Force senior officers. The geniuses behind EBO postulated that winning could be guaranteed by simply selecting the proper bombing targets. Build an air campaign based on the desired "effect," bomb it, and we win. The latest embodiment of ridiculous firepower concepts is another Navy stroke of genius termed "AirSea Battle." The concept is a thinly veiled battle plan for defeating the Chinese from the sea. More on AirSea Battle, and what the Chinese think of it, below.

The "Global Trends School" is the most insidious of these schools, because it has been given legitimacy by the Obama administration. In fact, the president and his defense intellectuals contend that climate change is more of a danger to national security than ISIS. This approach seeks to launder politically and socially popular global concerns into future military threats. The global trends movement started to gain adherents after the fall of the Soviet Union, when the intelligence community went looking for alternative avenues to justify post–Cold War weapons and structures. The most fashionable include diminishing global water supplies, urbanization, and the AIDS/HIV epidemic. But the current favorite inside the Beltway is climate change. In fact, at the 2015 Climate Change Summit in Paris, President Obama carried the war against climate change forward by claiming that rising global temperatures actually cause wars. While scientists agree on the dangers of global warming, I have yet to find any respected social scientist who makes a causal connection between air temperature and war.

So where does the administration get its facts about climate change and war? First, it contends that a warming planet causes drought, which leads to mass migration away from areas of creeping desertification. To be sure, rising temperatures combined with overgrazing in places like central Africa have caused displacement of peoples. Yet the misery of these peoples leads to, well, misery—

not war. Tribes striving to exist have little energy left over to declare war against neighbors. Central Africa is in the grip of often-horrific conflicts, started by Boko Haram in Nigeria and Al Shabaab in Somalia. But these terrorists are motivated by "the usual suspects," like religious hatred, centuries-long tribal animosities, and political greed.

One source for connecting war to temperature comes from the political closeness between environmentalists and the antiwar movement. Their logic goes like this: "Global warming is bad. Wars are bad. Therefore they must be connected." Remember, prior to the 1991 Gulf War, environmentalists warned of a decade of global cooling that would come from burning Kuwaiti oil fields, which did not happen. More recently, environmental radicals argued against bombing ISIS oil trucks, fearing the environmental consequences. Again, this did not happen.

In fact, environmental activism aside, the three-thousand-year historical record of human conflict argues conclusively against any causal relationship between war and temperature. Let me be more specific. Never in the written history of warfare, from Megiddo in 1,500 BC to the Syrian civil war today, is there any evidence that wars are caused by warmer air.

I really do not care about the administration's attempted connection between war and climate change; it is certain that many American people do not care either. My real concern is that the administration might translate this into a deflection of resources away from fighting a war against global terrorists to a contrived war against global warming. That would cause real harm to our Soldiers, who are trying to win a *real* war.

There is nothing wrong with the defense intellectual community cranking out concepts, even the patently ridiculous ones cited above. The problem comes when silly ideas become strategies. It begins with a chorus of ahistorical acolytes who preach so loudly that a concept becomes an office in the Pentagon. Soon, the general or admiral in charge of the concept starts to lobby the administration, Congress, and the media. Shortly thereafter, lines in the defense budget appear, and careers are made. The conceptual gurus retire and get good jobs with Lockheed Martin, Boeing, or General Dynamics. Weapons platforms (ships, planes, and missiles) suddenly become perfect instruments for fulfilling the requirements demanded by net-centric, effects-based, or AirSea Battle concepts, and a trillion dollars of your money goes down the drain. Sadly, the consequences are not just wasted money. Every dollar wasted on trillion-dollar gizmos is a dollar taken away from those who actually fight our wars. I find it discouraging that in our recent history, few concepts have emerged from Beltway gurus that advocate for the Soldiers and Marines who engage daily in the bloody business of close combat. There's just no money in that.

WHOM WILL WE FIGHT?

Instead of betting the future on failed conceptual approaches, consider the value of a new approach that exploits contemporary history and human behavior as components of a way to see into the future. Too often, generals are accused of trying to "fight the next war like the last." I suggest that much of our failure to anticipate the future properly rests on the fact that generals fail to look closely at the past, particularly the history and past behaviors of our enemies. Since the end of World War II, the generals have gotten it more wrong than right by ignoring "last wars." President Eisenhower's New Look sought to replace conventional with strategic forces, and the nation went to war in Vietnam woefully underresourced for a manpower-intensive counterinsurgency campaign. We paid a similar price in 2003, when U.S. command delayed too long in applying the lessons of Vietnam to the insurgencies in Iraq and Afghanistan. Of course, in today's Beltway, culture, history, and behavior are neither studied nor understood adequately. Thus, touting the past as a reliable road map for the future is a tough sell.

The power of an historical-behavioral approach comes from the realization that regardless of region, actor, motive, geopolitical circumstances, intensity, or type of conflict, our enemies have consistently repeated behaviors that they believe offer the greatest chance of success against us in battle. Patterns of behavior wind their way through all of our contemporary wars and are repeated at all levels of war, from strategic to tactical.

Lately, the historical-behavioral approach to future-casting has gained serious intellectual reinforcement within the social sciences. The Nobel Prize–winning research of economists Daniel Kahneman and Amos Tversky reveals how humans behave when they make serious decisions in life. Many of these decisions are made less from logic and data than from the psychology of personal biases and past behaviors and experiences. Phillip Tetlock, a psychologist from the University of Pennsylvania (and a colleague of mine), takes Kahneman a step further in his book *Superforecasting*.[1] Kahneman concludes that even the most powerful and politically savvy fall victim to what he terms "scope insensitivity." Every human being, no matter how connected with the outside world, eventually gets to a point where there is nothing more in his understanding of the political environment. Tetlock uses the term "WYSIATI," or "What you see is all there is," to describe the phenomenon of scope insensitivity. In other words, human behavior derives only from what the person sees. Scope insensitivity explains why leaders choose to go to war in circumstances doomed to failure. To someone outside the inner circle, the leader might be totally nuts, as well as dangerous. But the leader acts only on what he sees, on the basis of his perception of the realities of the world. Thus, behavior driven by experiences in dealing with the outside world might just be the most powerful single indicator for forecasting the future decisions of global leaders and the course of world events.

Everyman's scope insensitivity is different from the insensitivity of those who start wars. Everyman is powerless. But leaders who control militaries and populations have the power to act and be destructively swayed by their social insensitivity. The difference lies in an old war-college equation: "threat equals capability times will." An example: in his heyday, Fidel Castro would have reveled in the military defeat of the United States. His scope insensitivity was formed from a wacky Caribbean version of Marxism that drives him to this day. However, Castro was and is powerless. His "capability" against us is virtually zero. Thus, his threat to us is nil. Of course, Vladimir Putin is a different story. No one can really anticipate what Russia will do in the future without understanding Putin's behavioral history, the history of his state since the end of the Cold War, and the limits of Putin's social insensitivities.

So let us apply Tetlock and Kahneman to the usual suspects. Then let us expose their scope insensitivities to the war-college equation, threat equals capability times will, to see what behavior and history tell us about whom we will fight in the future.

Without question, the Beltway believes (and some in that realm even hope) that our future enemy will be China. The Chinese are perfect enemies. Their capability score is big and growing. They may be the only potential adversary whose matériel capabilities make it worthy of our expensive, high-tech weaponry. The big defense corporations can rely on the modernization of the Chinese military to justify almost a trillion dollars (yes, that's with a *t*) of new aircraft, ships, and missiles. The Chinese threat touches all of the schools: the technologists warn of Chinese missiles capable of killing our aircraft carriers; the scenario makers love to anticipate crushing the new Chinese navy in a great sea battle; and the concept theorists are thrilled with the chance to showcase U.S. weaponry as the best tools for confronting nascent Chinese expansionism.

But if we apply the template of behavioral history and score their social insensitivity, the Chinese simply do not fit the profile of an enemy ready to go to war against us. First, the obvious: great nuclear powers simply do not go to war with great nuclear powers. The proliferation of nuclear weapons among enemies like China, Russia, and soon Iran offers good news and bad news: the good news is that no large power can threaten us; bad news—we can never return the favor. There is no logical, strategic reason for the United States to bomb a major power to achieve any end other than national survival. Thus, the presence of nuclear weapons has virtually eliminated any chance of great powers fighting each other in big wars that demand the mobilization of the nation and the commitment of massed forces. Likewise, the muting effect of the nuclear ceiling on great-power violence eliminates the possibility of massive air or naval campaigns, because the risk-versus-reward curve is simply out of kilter.

Second, the tenets of geostrategy argue against a war with China. Simply put, the United States cannot fight a war on the continent of Asia and expect any strategically useful outcome. There are two countries on the planet that are unconquerable: China and Russia. China in particular cannot be conquered because of its vast spaces and a three-thousand-year-old culture, strictly averse to fighting extraterritorial threats . . . that is more than a billion people, by the way, with an army five times the size of ours.

Another even more subtle argument for focusing on China comes from the current administration's new strategy that calls for a "pivot to Asia," a thinly veiled expression of intent to shift focus away from the Middle East. Truth is, the pivot toward China is really just a cynical, strategic "head fake." The administration knows we will not fight China. Yet the pivot allows it to perpetuate the myth of muscular U.S. military power after leaving the Middle East—all without having to expect a real war.

The AirSea Battle gurus beat the drums for a war against China by citing the growing strength of its navy and air forces. Of course, the Chinese military is growing. Throughout history, all emerging great powers have sought to express their places in the world by spending on their militaries. Theodore Roosevelt gave the British fits at the turn of the last century as the United States began to flex its naval muscles. However, this time, the war-college equation gets in the way; a threat is a multiple of capability times intent. If intent is zero, the threat is zero. There is ample evidence in Chinese history that the Chinese, while nationalistic, are not expansionistic. They already have their empire; they just want to keep it.

Of course, the Chinese view us with suspicion. Any two great powers juxtaposed across the Pacific would act in a similar fashion. But suspicion, envy, and cultural jingoism are not sufficient to justify a war against a nuclear power. It just does not make sense to them, and it should not for us either.

Next in the line of the most popular "usual suspects" is North Korea. During my career I served four years in the Republic of Korea—as a major, colonel, and general. All of my service was with tactical units, preparing to fight the North. I commanded an artillery battalion whose mission was to protect the Demilitarized Zone (DMZ), which separates North and South Korea. So I think I know the region and the threat well enough to call myself an authority. Bottom line up front: we will not fight the North Koreans. To be sure, they maximize the capabilities quotient with a million-man army and nuclear weapons. Any shaky Stalinist regime headed by a thirty-something sociopath has to command our attention. No doubt, Kim Jong Un's "scope insensitivity" tops the charts. But from a purely military perspective, the threat of a spontaneous North Korean attack on the south is highly overrated. The North Korean People's Army (NKPA) seems impressive at first glance. The truth, however, is that this army is a rusting relic of the sixties; NKPA tanks and aircraft are museum pieces. Soldiers spend most of their training time scratching for food. Few of North Korea's aircraft are flyable. Its air force is so strapped for fuel and spare parts that North Korean pilots are essentially untrained.

The only conventional capability in the NKPA is their artillery, with its rockets and long-range guns strung along the DMZ in range of Seoul. The North Korean Special Forces pose a serious unconventional threat. These two forces would cause serious damage to the South. Yet the North Koreans know well they would eventually lose against the more modern and powerful South Korean and U.S. militaries.

What about the North Korean nuclear threat? This is where mythology trumps strategy. Kim Jong Un, like his father and grandfather, is the one character who can order a nuclear strike or an invasion of the South. But the historical-behavioral background of the Kims argues that they have been in the shakedown business—not the war-making business—for more than seven decades. Their scope insensitivity is incredibly narrow; they are leaders with no experiential depth. They carry on a predictable comic-opera rant after each of their underground nuclear tests in order to extort food and fuel from the West. In truth the North Koreans know they have nothing that even comes close to a legitimate strategic nuclear capability. It will be years—if not decades—before they put together a rudimentary nuclear missile force, one capable of threatening anyone. These people act like clowns, and their repetitively bad behavior has become tiresomely antiquated. North Korea is nothing more than an isolated, neo-Stalinist enclave sandwiched between superior fighting neighbors who would crush it if it dared to advance beyond its borders . . . and the North Koreans know it.

Next in line among the usual suspects is the sentimental favorite: Russia. Vladimir Putin is indeed another international sociopath who has been given an extraordinary license to bully his "near abroad" neighbors. No one questions that it is Putin's hand that directs the ethnic Russian "separatists" to defy the legitimately elected Ukrainian government. This administration and members of NATO and the European Union (EU) have failed to halt his aggression. Sanctions may harm the new urban middle and upper classes, but Putin's stranglehold on the Russian media and his promise to restore Russian power and prestige maintain his popularity among the people. He and his country score high on both variables: a huge nuclear arsenal and past personal behavior that is both troubling and unpredictable; further, Putin's social insensitivity equals Hitler's.

Putin has publicly stated that his national security objective is to split the NATO alliance. He believes NATO and its prime benefactor, the United States, are the principal impediments to his grand design to return Russia to imperial greatness, and Russia will do what Putin wants. But on the surface, Putin holds a weak military hand. Putin's Russia is not the Soviet Union. It is a failing state only half the size of the Soviet Union, with an economy less than a tenth of those of the United States and the EU combined. Putin's military is getting better, to be sure, but a closer look reveals an establishment made up mostly of unwilling young men who lost the conscription lottery. The Russians do not have a single fifth-generation stealth aircraft. Their conventional navy would last a day in combat against ours. Virtually all of their armored forces date from the Desert Storm era, and we witnessed how well those performed in the hands of Saddam's military.

In November 2015, I visited our Army in Europe to speak firsthand with the leaders of all NATO armies. In sum, all of the European generals I spoke to considered Putin "containable" if the United States placed a few armored brigades within the eastern NATO states: the Baltics and Poland. The cost of such a move to the United States would be minimal. Moving existing matériel to Europe would not require a single new weapons program or any increase in existing manpower. From what I witnessed, I strongly believe that such a force, properly positioned, would create a deterrent sufficiently intimidating to keep Mr. Putin on his side of the line for a very long time.

To anticipate whom we must fear the most, we must return to Colonel Yahara. Take a moment and look across a map of the expanse of Islamic nations in turmoil. Begin your visual transit with the North African states that touch the Atlantic, shift southward into central Africa and across the troubled and chaotic states that border the Mediterranean. Skip to the Levant, then to the true heartland of the Middle East: Pakistan and Iraq. What you see is utter chaos, perhaps the most destructive array of geopolitical mendacity and horror seen since the Assyrian holocaust in the eighth century BC.

Scholars call this turgid sweep the "Arc of Instability." After the collapse of Syria, Libya, Yemen, Iraq, Somalia, and the expansion of the threat from radical Islamism, perhaps a more relevant term might be the "Arc of Failure." This growing horror is persistent, most likely generational . . . and it affects our homeland. Radical Islamist threats are growing. But also, more troubling, they are becoming more skilled at both terrorism and war.

Look carefully at media images of ground fighting across the Middle East, and you will notice that the bad guys are also fighting differently.[2] In the immediate aftermath of 9/11, the West confronted terrorists acting like, well, terrorists. In Iraq and Afghanistan, Al Qaeda relied on ambushes, roadside bombings, sniper fire, and the occasional "fire and run" mortar or rocket attack to inflict casualties on U.S. forces. When terrorists were stupid enough to come out of the shadows, they fought as individuals in a mob of other individuals. Just the rip of a Kalashnikov or a single launch of a rocket-propelled grenade was enough to show their manhood. If they stood to reload they risked annihilation at the hands of their disciplined, well trained, and heavily armed U.S. opponents.

Today it is different. We now see Islamic fighters becoming skilled Soldiers. The thrust of ISIS down the Euphrates illustrates a style of warfare that melds the old and the new. U.S. Soldiers fighting in Iraq used to say, "Thank God they can't shoot." Well, now they can. They maneuver in reasonably disciplined fighting formations, often mounted on board pickups and captured Iraqi Humvees. They employ mortars and rockets in deadly barrages. To be sure, parts of the old terrorist playbook remain: they butcher and execute in front of the global media to make the Iraqis, Syrians, and Libyans understand, in unambiguous terms, the terrible consequences of continued resistance. Like their forbearers, they still display the terrorist's eager willingness for death and the media savvy of the "propaganda of the deed."

We see these newly formed pseudo-armies emerging across the Levant as well. The Darwinian process of wartime immersion has forced them to either be dead or a lot better. Some observers of their transformation admit that Hezbollah now are among the best-trained and skilled light infantry on the planet . . . and thanks to their Iranian patron, they have stockpiled more than 100,000 rockets ready to be fired against Israeli civilians.

And now there is Hamas. Gone are the fleeting "pickup teams" from Operation Cast Lead in 2008. We see Hamas fighting in small, strictly organized, tightly bound teams under the authority of connected, well informed commanders. In their war against Israeli intrusion in 2014, Hamas units stood and fought from building hideouts and tunnel entrances. Instead of charging the Israelis, Hamas waited for the Israelis to pass before ambushing them from the rear, occasionally dressed in Israeli uniforms. Like Hezbollah, they are getting good with second-generation weapons, such as wire-guided antitank missiles. The Israelis started the Gaza campaign trying to fight house to house. Soon, tank and infantry fire was replaced by hundred-ton barrages of precision two-thousand-pound bombs—and Hamas still did not quit.

These groups are now well-armed, well-trained, well-equipped, well-led, disciplined, and often flush with cash to buy or bribe their way out of difficulties. While the story of the disintegration of the Iraqi army is multicausal, the fact that it was never trained to face such a competent opponent was certainly a factor.

Michael Morrell, former deputy head of the Central Intelligence Agency calls the anti-jihad conflict in the Middle East the "Great War of our Time." This frightening new age that Morrell describes will dominate warfare for a generation or more, because of several factors. First, of course, is the influence and global influx of foreign fighters into ISIS. As witnessed by the assault on the ISIS-held cities of Tikrit and Ramadi, Iranian advisers throughout the Middle East are getting better at their craft. Radicalized fighters from the Chechen and Bosnian conflicts have joined the ISIS team as mentors. The terrorists of the last decade used to generate one-shot suicide bombers of little strategic consequence. Now they have learned to craft fighting units, and they teach weapons and tactics very well. Second, ISIS and Hezbollah have made the bloody Syrian war into a first-rate training ground. They are exploiting that terrible war to select leaders, practice tactics, train to maneuver on the urban battlefield, and build political and military institutions with depth, mass, and resiliency. Perversely, having these two Islamist organizations in conflict makes each better, not weaker.

All of these new armies talk to each other, even occasionally across ethno-sectarian divides. Social media and strategic intercessions in Syria, Lebanon, Gaza, and Iraq have created a body of well-informed and battle-hardened leaders and Soldiers who actually share lessons learned. While these new armies are becoming more professional, they still retain the terrorist's specialty in disciplined killing. Terrorist killing used to be mostly random. But now killings are carefully orchestrated, media-driven executions of surrendering Soldiers, political leaders, and former leaders of the opposition. Strategic killing gives them the psychological high ground often well before the clash of arms begins.

What we have seen in Gaza, Syria, Iran, Pakistan, Libya, and Iraq is not only sobering but a cautionary tale for those Beltway gurus who are already calling for a pivot to Asia and a war against the Chinese. The truth is that America's battle against radicalism is now a world, not just a regional, war. It is unfinished and going poorly. Of course, U.S. Soldiers and Marines are still the global gold standard in tactical competence. But their comparative advantage has diminished considerably over the past fourteen years of war against an adaptive, dedicated enemy willing to learn and to die. Inevitably, terrorists groups will amalgamate and turn into armies. Given time, ISIS will become a sovereign state, pairing their fanatical dedication with newly acquired tactical skills. Sadly, we are giving them time and room to get much better. Eventually, any attempt to renew intervention into the ISIS heartland will generate casualties on a different scale—as the Israelis and the Iraqis have learned painfully.

Then there is the eight-hundred-pound gorilla hiding in the Middle Eastern closet: nuclear weapons. No one with half a brain would deny that the Iranians will build a bomb. The ayatollahs have learned from their Iraqi neighbor and their North Korean ally that the only certain deterrent against intrusion by the United States is a nuke. They have learned from watching India and Pakistan that world approbation against new nuclear powers fades eventually. To a state that fears the United States and has the technology, not joining the nuclear club would be the height of foolishness. When Iran gets the bomb, the paranoia and extreme social insensitivity of its theological elites would certainly tempt them to use it, most likely against Israel.

The social insensitivity of Middle Eastern tyrants is off the charts. Their religiously driven ideologies and brutal worldview removes them from the community of civilized leaders. Their ability to close their world to social sensitivities of others means that only a protracted and bloody confrontation will end the horror and inhumanity of their ambitions. We have met our enemy. We do not like it, because wars in the American era do not join well with a protracted conflict against an enemy driven by superior will and a willingness to die. Colonel Yahara would understand. He would know that only Soldiers with rifles and a will to win in the close fight will defeat them.

[6]

THE NEW AGE OF INFANTRY

I love the infantry because they are the underdogs. They are the mud-rain-frost-and-wind boys. They have no comforts, and they even learn to live without the necessities. And in the end, they are the guys that wars can't be won without.

—Ernie Pyle

The progress of war, like other forms of human endeavor, is defined in terms of epochs, cycles of periodic change that sweep through and shape the course of civilization. Political scientists recount the advance of governance in terms of theocracy, monarchy, autarky, and democracy. The history of science and culture measures the advance of Western civilization in terms of three grand epochs: the agrarian, machine, and information ages. Economists speak of the evolution from barter to mercantile to market to global economies.

The magnitude of Colonel Yahara's epiphany can be appreciated by understanding the rarity of his moment in the long sweep of warfare. The nature and character of war changes slowly and is driven by the pace of societal change. Military historians define the grand epochs of war in terms of formations: tactics and weapons that have dominated battle for millennia. Battles are the signposts that illuminate the paths through and between epochs. Rifts that separate epochs are defined by seismic rents in the fabric of war, caused principally by geopolitical and technological change. Epochal rifts are rare. There have been only five. The periods between shifts continually shorten as the pace of change accelerates. A study of contemporary battles suggests that we are in the midst of another seismic epochal rent only a half-century after the last.

The first epoch in the history of land warfare lasted longer than any other in the history of the planet . . . and it belonged to infantry. For much of recorded history from prehistory to the ancient armies of Sumer, Assyria, Babylon, Persia, imperial China, Egypt, and imperial Rome, the art of war in this "classical era" depended on muscle-powered infantry armies. The Greek phalanx and later the Roman legion fought in linear formations. For more than five hundred years, Roman infantry dominated the battlefield with their discipline and ability to win in any terrain and against any enemy. During this antiquarian age, the clash of arms was literally that, killing the enemy by throwing deadly objects: arrows and javelins and thrusting objects at close range, such as swords, knives, lances, and halberds. Linear, muscle-powered slaughter held sway until the Roman Empire—and many others to follow—fell victim to the mounted warrior.

Historians generally date this first "epochal shift" in warfare to the battle of Adrianople in AD 467. There, mounted Gothic horsemen demonstrated how to defeat the infantry legion by combining shock effect and the superior long-distance mobility of the horse. For the next one thousand years, the desert cavalry of the Saracens, the steppe cavalry of Genghis Khan, and heavily armored European horsemen determined who would conquer and rule. Of course, horses had been essential to ancient armies since the beginning of recorded history, but the horse became a truly dominant weapon when the ancients invented the stirrup. This device, whose provenance is shrouded in the mists of history, allowed a rider to gain muscular leverage, both to steady himself and push his chosen weapon into the bodies of his enemies.

The horse became dominant on the battlefield thanks also to improvements in breeding that manufactured the perfect animal as an instrument of war. Saracens bred an agile horse capable of long-distance maneuver in open deserts. Europeans bred huge load-carrying horses capable of advancing a lance while carrying more than two hundred pounds of armored knight. The Mongol steppe pony could transport his charge for hundreds of miles across the Asian steppe while subsisting on desert grass. The Mongol pony was a light and agile horse that could maneuver between dismounted enemies while remaining steady enough for a horseman to fire arrows accurately from a gallop.

The battle of Pavia in 1525, fought between the mounted blue bloods of France and the common-born infantry of Spain, heralded the second epochal rent in the fabric of war. The awakening of the classical era of the Renaissance allowed the Europeans to rediscover from Roman literature the war-fighting power of infantry when placed in massed, disciplined formations. Technology in the form of the first efficient gunpowder weapons proved too powerful for even the most expensive, heavy, and constrictive plate armor. For five hundred years, from the Reformation to the end of European empires after World War I, the common foot Soldier from Spain, France, Germany, and England proved the ultimate arbiter of success in peer warfare: European versus European and, in asymmetric warfare, European versus American Indian, African, Asian, and Islamic foes.

The third epochal shift came with the first "precision revolution" of the late nineteenth century. The Industrial Revolution gave Western powers dominance in both the invention and production of weapons. By the turn of the twenti-eth century, these technologies had turned armies into killing machines with the introduction of smokeless powder, the small-bore rifle, machine guns, and long-range, quick-firing artillery. The range of rifles and machine guns increased from fifty to more than a thousand yards. Artillery ranges increased from hun-dreds of yards to many miles, and explosive shells increased the killing radius of artillery from a few feet to hundreds of yards. The railroad, internal combustion engine, and telegraph turned wars from seasonal to year-long enterprises.

Precision weapons and mass production of killing machines ended five hun-dred years of infantry dominance. It died in the trenches of the western front, where killing technologies made the battlefield too lethal for infantry to cross. The day of unprotected infantry assault was over. Soldiers then, as now, are a conservative lot, and only the deaths of millions sufficed to make the point. After World War I, the Germans combined the internal combustion engine and the radio to reinvent heavy mounted warfare, introduced the world to tank-on-tank blitzkrieg during the battle for France in May 1940 . . . and turned the epochal wheel again, in less than a century.

This fourth rending in the fabric of warfare came at a cost, however. The race to win on the armored battlefield was predicated on the ability of armies to build larger and more complex fighting machines to best the machines of the opposition. As weapons grew larger, heavier, and more complex, they became less employable outside the narrow battlefields of the industrial world. Today, this frenetic rush toward gigantism and overcapitalization is accelerating the premature demise of the blitzkrieg epoch. In a curious twist of historical irony, the forces responsible for the demise of machine warfare were only a century ago victims in the former colonized world that Western armies defeated so easily during the first precision revolution.

The blitzkrieg era began to wane with the appearance of precision munitions during Vietnam. A half-century later, precision antitank guided missiles in the hands of Hezbollah terrorists were killing Israeli tanks in Lebanon. Shoulder-fired antiaircraft missiles in the hands of terrorists succeeded in keeping Western aircraft at altitudes too high to provide effective air support in places like Lebanon, Iraq, Afghanistan, and elsewhere in the Middle East. The battlefield signposts that point to the end of the blitzkrieg epoch are as numerous and unmistakable as those that appeared a century ago to signal the end of the second age of infantry. The problem is that since the beginning of the American era, our military has been caught in an ambiguous crease between epochs, a predicament that has drawn us in conflicting directions—between blitzkrieg-age wars we fight well and post–blitzkrieg-era wars that we would prefer not to fight.

It is important to emphasize that epochal shifts are not clean and sudden and do not occur overnight. Dismounted formations were still important during mounted epochs and vice versa. Cavalry remained a potent force during the classic age of infantry. The Romans employed cavalry as an ancillary arm for scouting and the occasional charge. Infantry remained vital to warfare during the first age of the mounted warrior in the Middle Ages. In the right circumstances, lowborn foot archers prevailed against armored knights. In battles such as Crecy in August 1346 and Agincourt in October 1415, both fought during the Hundred Years' War, British longbowmen slaughtered horse-bound French nobility. There, skill at firing iron-tipped cloth-yard arrows was reinforced by obstacles and terrain that broke the momentum of charging horses.

The mounted warrior continued to be useful well into the second age of infantry, after the battle of Pavia. In the right circumstances, Napoleon's heavy cavalry under masters such as Marshal Joachim Murat could still break infantry formations—often at great cost. Rarely, however, was cavalry able to attack artillery formations, as the British learned during the Crimean War in their abortive attack against Russian guns in the "valley of the six hundred." Some horse-mounted warriors remained useful after the first precision revolution by adapting to become "mounted infantry"—essentially cavalry Soldiers who rode to the tactical fight and dismounted to fight on foot with modern rifles. One can still marvel at the bloody romanticism that old warriors still felt for the cavalry by watching grainy films of German Uhlan cavalry marching off to war in 1914, sporting long lances and steel breastplates. Only a few days into the opening battles of the frontiers, these magnificent-looking totems would lie dead alongside their mounts.

To be fair, I am not the first to put forward the thesis that the fundamental nature of warfare has undergone periodic seismic changes. Several modern prophets have also foreseen the coming of a new age. In the late seventies, the iconic military writer and correspondent William Lind wrote about "fourth generation warfare," a new generational conflict wherein irregular state and nonstate infantry-style forces would challenge and defeat conventional, high-tech "nation-based militaries" like ours. Lind's influence was greatest within the Marine officer corps. Lind's theories caused the senior Marine leadership to question the tenets of the Army's euro-centric AirLand Battle. The Marines' competing concept postulated a "three block" war that melded close combat, peacekeeping, and humanitarian aid. Gen. Charles Krulak, commandant of the Marine Corps just before 9/11, envisioned the "strategic corporal" at the squad level as the central figure of such wars, rather than senior officers in their command centers. Subsequent events would prove the wisdom of Krulak's prophecy.

More recently another former Marine, Dr. Frank Hoffman, concluded from his study of contemporary battle that warfare had settled into a new and sinister middle ground between conventional and irregular war, what he termed "hybrid warfare." Hoffman first observed evidence of this new style of war in the Russian battle for Chechnya in 1996. He chronicled the same characteristic later in the 2006 Israeli war in Lebanon. Of course, his hybrid-war thesis is now accepted as a universal theory that connects wars in Iraq, Afghanistan, and, most recently, the Ukraine. Other authors, like Dr. David Johnson from RAND Corporation, have added new evidence to showcase this new non-Western approach to fighting Western enemies. According to Hoffman, this new style of warfare is adopted by an "adversary that simultaneously and adaptively employs a fused mix of conventional weapons, irregular tactics, terrorism and criminal behavior in the battle space to obtain [its] political objectives."[1]

The central connecting tissue behind all of our ideas is that, since the end of World War II, a host of adaptive enemies has emerged from turbulent but technologically unsophisticated regions of the world, intent on challenging Western militaries using their own methods. The laboratory of contemporary battle provides ample evidence to demonstrate that the emerging new age of infantry (or hybrid, or fourth-generation, wars) all share the exact same provenance: whenever former colonial states choose to fight Western armies, Western style, they lose. Four blitzkrieg-style Arab-Israeli wars (1948, 1956, 1967, 1973) ended well for the Israelis and badly for the Arabs; five American wars (Panama, 1989; Desert Storm, 1991; Kosovo, 1999; Afghanistan, 2002; the march to Baghdad, 2003) proved conclusively the dominance of U.S. techno-centric warfare. In contrast, whenever many of these same antagonists choose to fight Western armies their own ways, the outcomes are reversed: against us in Vietnam, Korea, Somalia, Afghanistan, and Iraq; against the French in Indochina and Algeria; twice against the Israelis in Lebanon; and against the Soviets in Afghanistan.

What are the consequences of this emerging new age of infantry? Also, perhaps more importantly, what should our military do to accommodate this new primal shift in the art of war? The recasting of warfare in the new age of infantry is manifested in numerous ways. Militaries are undergoing "demechanization" in all dimensions of war: air, land, and sea. By some accounts, the armies of the world have shed tens of thousands of fighting vehicles since the end of the Cold War. To be sure, much of this diminution is due to the collapse of the Soviet army. But a similar reduction has occurred in other militaries as well. It is interesting to note that today the German and British armies cannot assemble five hundred tanks between them. European armies now exercise companies of mounted forces, rather than brigades and divisions as in the past. The entire modern German army, the Bundeswehr, fields only four artillery battalions. Similarly, European militaries have given up their ability to transport armies overseas. All the meager European combat forces deployed to Afghanistan today rely on the U.S. Air Force for sustainment. The recent examples of wars fought in Georgia and Libya suggest that only the United States can project power to all corners of the globe in all three dimensions. Other militaries simply do not have the strategic reach to match us.

The downside of global demechanization has been a marked increase in the number and quality of close-combat forces worldwide. For friend and foe alike, small units are more useful in today's multidimensional hybrid conflicts that stretch from low-key insurgencies to high-end conventional warfare between Western-style militaries and unconventional opponents. For two millennia, the shift between mounted forces and infantry has been caused principally by changes in technology. The same is true today. Just as gunpowder weapons ended the dominance of the mounted knight, so too have long-range precision missiles practically ended large-scale armored shock formations of tanks supported by infantry fighting vehicles.

Connect the dots from the viewpoint of successful actions by our enemies during the past half-century, and the argument for a return of infantry dominance goes from obvious to compelling. The imperative to renew U.S. infantry forces comes from the enemy's ability to offset our big-machine advantage with advantages of their own: masses of regular and irregular foot Soldiers, with enthusiasm to sacrifice that offsets skill at arms; and an ability to learn quickly and adapt so that technological innovation can be offset by clever adaptations of existing technologies. His is a global scheme in which the strategic object is merely to kill Americans until we lose the will to carry on. His geostrategy is founded on the principle of distance: find a battlefield least conducive to long-term commitment, in inhospitable places such as cities, jungles, and mountains, where he can reduce the effectiveness of our machines and thereby increase the odds of defeating us with infantry alone.

ADJUSTING TO A NEW AGE: A UNIQUELY AMERICAN PROBLEM

The United States cannot fight fair, because a fair fight costs too many lives. This conundrum leads to the core of the greatest challenge of twenty-first-century U.S. warfare: How will the armed forces of the United States prevail in this new age of infantry if the cost of infantry fighting is too high? Let's begin by confessing how high the cost of the close fight really is. During wars in the American era, infantry, principally dismounted (foot) infantry, suffered four out of five combat deaths. In practical terms, this means that an overwhelming preponderance of deaths occur among a population that constitutes less than 4 percent of all the uniformed population of the Defense Department. Anyone not an infantryman in contact stands a far greater chance of dying from disease or accidents than from an enemy bullet.

Of particular interest is how these close-combat Soldiers die. Virtually all deaths at the hands of the enemy are suffered within a mile from contact with the enemy. About 52 percent of those who die do so trying to find the enemy, either as scouts, on point, or in ambushes. Once in contact, the close fight generally goes in our favor if the enemy can be engaged far enough away to employ superior U.S. firepower. Put a close-combat Soldier in a fighting vehicle of any sort, and his chance of surviving contact with the enemy increases about an order of magnitude. This fact flies in the face of popular perceptions drawn from battlefield footage in places such as Chechnya showing Soldiers roasting in burning panzers. Most of our Cold War armor was designed to take a head-on shot from a Soviet tank. Thus, most of a U.S. tank's armor protection is concentrated in its front 60 percent of obliquity. Again, the irony of real combat takes over the story—all of this frontal armor has saved few lives, because armor has never faced a serious enemy tank threat. Since the beginning of the American era, only ten tank crewmen have been killed by enemy tanks—all of them in the Korean War.

In contrast to mounted combat, the statistics for infantry deaths in close combat are troubling. A comparison of kill ratios between infantry and air-to-air combat is instructive. In World War II, the kill ratio in the Pacific campaign was about thirteen enemies to one American; in Europe against the Germans, the ratio was about eleven to one; in Korea, thirteen to one. Since the end of the Cold War, the kill ratio for the F-15 series of fighter aircraft flown by U.S. and Israeli pilots is about 107 to one. During the second battle of Fallujah, in November 2004, the ratio between enemy and U.S. infantry deaths was about nine to one within fifty meters. For Soldiers and Marines fighting inside buildings, the ratios were, tragically, much closer to parity.

INFANTRY AS A FUNCTION

During a month-long sojourn as a guest of Special Operations Command (SOCOM) in 2009, I roamed across Iraq and Afghanistan communing with many exceptional young men (yes, men—there were virtually no women). During breakfast in the huge Kandahar Mess Hall, I noticed an amazing variety of uniforms and accents. It looked like the bar scene in the movie *Star Wars;* sitting at tables all around were Special Forces, Marines, and Army Soldiers with their M4 rifles slung on the backs of their chairs. Next to them were infantrymen from

Australia, New Zealand, Poland, Great Britain, and France. Included in the menagerie were FBI agents in Army camouflage, along with sailors in their weird blue-pattern camouflage—if blue could be camouflage in Afghanistan. (I found out later these men belonged to a Navy Emergency Ordnance Disposal outfit whose mission was to defuse IEDs.)

To an outsider like me, the dynamics were remarkable. Looking around, I was struck that virtually everyone, to one degree or another, was either infantry or performing an infantry-like function. The message was clear: the practical exigencies of war in the American era have convinced the U.S. military that the centerpiece of tomorrow's warfare is the infantry. The mess-hall scene was convincing evidence that infantry had become a function, not a service or branch of service. The infantry function includes Army, Marine Corps, and Special Forces troops who occasionally share the close-combat space with like-minded specialists such as tankers, military police, and artillerymen.

The mess-hall scene was not a new one, by any means. In fact, America has practiced the infantry arts in peace and war since the American Revolution, but only recently has the art taken center stage. Now, the dominance of infantry has created the "great tactical dilemma." The enemy knows that dead Soldiers are our greatest vulnerability; so, for us, winning quickly while incurring the least cost becomes more than a moral necessity. It is now a national strategic imperative. The challenge for the future is to win quickly at less cost in human life. We are culturally averse to getting better at infantry warfare; we do not like to fight this way. We would prefer to kill from a distance. But our enemies will not let us off the hook. They are leading us where we are reluctant to go. Contemporary history and the shrewd actions of our enemies now compel us to change our priorities; our presence in this new age of infantry demands that making better infantry is no longer an Army or a Marine Corps problem. It is a national problem. And the challenge is not just to get incrementally better but to dominate the enemy in the close fight. We must achieve the same overwhelming kill ratios on the ground that we achieved in air-to-air combat.

The question is: How can the United States make infantry not just better but dominant on tomorrow's battlefields? The next chapter offers some new ideas.

[7]

Small-Unit Dominance

Veterans know the difference between being in a dangerous combat zone and being in close combat, seeking out and killing the enemy. Close combat is tough. Much of the rest of war is boring if hard work.
—Gen. James Mattis, USMC (Ret.)

The Right Stuff: Viking

I owe my life to Viking. In 1969, I was a battery commander on Firebase Berchtesgaden during the battle of Dong Ap Bia, better known to moviegoers as "Hamburger Hill." We were good Soldiers, but most of us were amateurs hoping to stay alive during what could only be described as a hellacious period in the nation's history. One Soldier was not an amateur. His name was Capt. Harold Erikson, his call sign was "Viking," and he commanded B Company, 1st Battalion, 506th Airborne Infantry. He was from Mississippi, had played quarterback for Georgia Tech, and had done a brief stint in the National Football League before being commissioned.

As his "handle" suggests, he was a big, blond, blue-eyed Soldier. He rarely spoke and never above a whisper. He was not a leader in the Pattonesque tradition. He did not swear often, and he avoided the limelight as much as possible. Yet when the bullets began to fly, when close combat became very close and killing became intimate, Viking came alive. When he was in charge many enemies died, and very few of his Soldiers suffered similar fates.

I watched him in action one night in August 1969, when a very large force of North Vietnamese regulars attacked us. He crouched in a foxhole that doubled as his command post. Occasionally, he would say something on the radio or whisper a command to one of his runners. Outside, things just happened. The artillery came in, close and deadly. The machine guns seemed to open up at just the right times and places. Troops always found creases in the enemy's flanks and scattered them with a few tightly disciplined volleys. Remarkably, Viking's company really never fired that much, but when they did, bad guys died in profusion. The troops would talk about Viking in hushed tones as if he were a god. They knew an assignment to B Company probably meant a ticket home, because Viking had the right stuff and would keep them alive.

In June 1969, his company came out of the field to spend some downtime protecting my battery at Firebase Berchtesgaden. The night after his arrival, early in the morning of June 13, the North Vietnamese 29th Regiment decided to pay both of us a visit. Nineteen of my fifty-five Soldiers were either killed or wounded severely enough to warrant evacuation. The loss was mainly my fault. It was not that I was new at the job. This was my fourth command, so I thought I knew what I was doing.

I remember very distinctly sitting on a stack of artillery boxes surrounded by the bloody flotsam of my devastated unit, my head in my hands, feeling sorry for both my men and myself. Viking sauntered up behind me as cool as if he had just finished a leisurely morning breakfast. He had this odd habit of constantly wiping his CAR-15 carbine with a toothbrush as he spoke. There was no love or comfort for me from Viking.

"So, what the fuck are you going to do now, Scales?" he mumbled behind my back.

To this day I remember every word of my reply: "Well, Viking, to be honest, lately I've been giving serious thought to law school."

"No, you moron, I meant what are you going to do *now*?"

"Frankly, Viking, I haven't a clue." I said, burying my head again in my hands.

"Well, you're probably going to die anyway but take a minute and come with me. . . ."

What followed saved my life in the months to come. Viking strolled about my area, pointing out such revealingly new concepts as "dead ground" (hidden from observation) and gaps in approaches and siting trip flares and limit stakes for my machine guns. He then went into some graduate-level work, detailing observation-post (OP) rotations and how to maintain alertness so as to detect subtle movements by an enemy crawling up to our perimeter. (Viking's means of maintaining alertness in his company was to call an OP twice on the radio and, if no answer, fire on it with his own mortars—seemed to work.)

But after four decades, I still remember how badly I failed. A much smarter and better-trained and better-equipped enemy taught me that I did not have the right stuff. The event made me promise that I would never again go to war number-two in a two-sided contest. It also burned into the depths of my soul several questions that have lingered, festered, ever since. I asked why the most technologically advanced country on the planet was unable make better weapons and equipment than the enemy. I asked why my Soldiers were so poorly prepared physically, intellectually, and emotionally for this fight. I asked why I could gain experience as a combat leader only by spilling their blood.

BETTER BUT NOT DOMINANT

We are better now. But occasional incidents in places like Fallujah and Sadr City in Iraq and Forward Operating Base Keating and Wanat in Afghanistan make it perfectly evident that the U.S. military has not come as far as it should have in its ability to dominate in the tactical fight. Failure to dominate at the tactical level to the degree of which we are capable is all the more incongruous because success in today's "hybrid" wars is achieved by the patient and often dangerous application of force by thousands of (mostly Army and Marine) squads, platoons, and teams. These small units patrol and operate principally from isolated outposts and forward operating bases, along primitive roads and trails, and among the people within villages and towns.

The final incongruity comes with the realization that Soldiers and Marines, those most likely to die are—when compared to their colleagues of other services—still often the very ones least well equipped, trained, and selected for their very dangerous calling. So why don't we do better at lessening our strategic vulnerabilities by doing a better job of preserving the lives of those most likely to die? The answers are numerous and complex.

INTIMATE KILLING

Intimate killing is a primal aspect of warfare, unchanged since the beginning of civilization. In the most basic sense it involves a clash of two warriors, one on one, armed with virtually identical weapons. The decision goes to the Soldier with the right stuff, the one with the greater cunning, strength, guile, ruthlessness, and will to win.

For a moment, put yourself in the place of a young Soldier or Marine fighting house to house in the mean streets of an Afghan village. Burdened with more than sixty pounds of gear, sweat dripping constantly into your face, you cannot stop shaking from the fear of what the enemy has in store for you around the next corner. Just ahead is a darkened house, its doors and windows closed and shuttered. The only sound is the crunching of your boots on trash and broken glass as you move in slow motion to surround the dwelling. You see the sergeant signal you to cover a side entrance. Through the faint haze, you watch your buddy kick in the door and immediately come face to face with an insurgent, who greets him with a burst of AK-47 fire that tears a hole in his chest. Your buddy does not die. The terrorist wants him to live just long enough for his buddies to rush in to the rescue and become additional trophies to be laid at the altar of heaven.

Now, it is your turn. You use your superior discipline and skill to approach the insurgent in such a way that you are detected only at the last second. Both of you raise your weapons simultaneously and open fire in a crushing tear of bullets that scatter and ricochet wildly across the room. One bullet finds the bad guy, and he falls in a bloody heap, just inches from your boots.

What exactly do you "feel" at this moment? Relief, to be sure, but you also feel something else that cannot be explained to anyone who has not committed an act of intimate killing. It is not joy, exactly, more like exhilaration and an enormous sense of self-satisfaction that in one of the most primal challenges—where all the satellites, drones, planes, ships, and smart weapons are of no use whatsoever—you prevailed, one on one, over an enemy Soldier.

One primal task defines the infantry: intimate killing. Killing close is the essence of what it means to be an infantryman. Others on the battlefield, such as pilots and artillerymen, kill, but they kill at a distance. Killing, to them, is detached, antiseptic. After a mission, a pilot may feel remorse at the realization that the bomb he dropped on some target below killed someone. But an infantryman sees his target die. He watches the life drain out of an enemy who chances across his sights. To be sure, Soldiers other than infantrymen may occasionally stumble upon the enemy. These are incidental fighters, occasional victims of war who die in ambushes, roadside bombings, and assassinations. But only an infantryman goes out every day with the intention of taking another human life in face-to-face, intimate combat. It is his skill at killing that wins contemporary wars.

While politicians and policy makers recognize the sacrifices of our men and women in uniform, they tend to turn a blind eye toward the harsh realities of close combat. Familiar Beltway concerns—such as winning against big-ticket adversaries, fighting in space and cyberspace, controlling the global commons, and facing the challenges of a "whole of government" approach to strategy—inevitably trump the bloodier and less comfortable matter of intimate killing. The lingering dissonance between the Beltway and the tactical battle has been pervasive for decades and spans every political party and administration from Truman to Obama.

Too often those who do not know war accept the industrial-age view that Soldiering is inherently more dangerous than other forms of combat. Likewise, policy makers tend to slight the tactical dimension by assuming that Iraq and Afghanistan are one-offs, mistakes that will never happen again: surely, the American people will never accept another unpopular ground war. The assumption misses the point. In today's wars the enemy chooses the time, place, duration, intensity, and the dimension in which future conflicts are to be fought.

THE TACTICAL DILEMMA

In order to feed the American domestic narrative with dead Soldiers, enemies have followed a consistent pattern of battlefield behavior. In Korea, the Chinese relied on nocturnal "human wave" attacks to kill our Soldiers. After two years of this punishment the Army began to withdraw behind a bunkered fortress that stretched 110 miles across the Korean Peninsula. Commanders turned to massive firepower to keep the enemy at bay. The result was a dramatic decrease in casualties. The price was the forfeiture of the tactical initiative. In Vietnam, after three years of war the pattern repeated. Losses to enemy ambushes and mines caused U.S. command to withdraw substantially inside protected firebases and engage with massive doses of firepower. (I recall vividly in 1969 firing more than seven hundred artillery rounds at a single sniper.)

After the Six Day War of 1967, the Israelis chose to reduce the cost of keeping the Egyptians at bay by constructing an elaborate string of fortresses on the east bank of the Suez. Over the next six years Egyptian guerrilla actions declined, but so too did Israeli awareness of Egyptian preparations to launch an assault across the canal in great force. Without question, a more aggressive approach to canal defense would have reduced considerably the cost of the 1973 war, if not precluding or preempting it entirely.

Until the arrival of Gen. David Petraeus as commander in Iraq, spiking casualties from IEDs and suicide bombings induced a similar pattern of reaction: U.S. forces withdrew inside contemporary versions of Vietnam-era firebases (forward operating bases) to reduce casualties. Increasingly, Soldiers moved about the countryside sequestered inside vehicles larded with armor to reduce the killing power of IEDs. In effect, these tactical withdrawals too often had the effect of substantially ceding control of critical areas and populations to the enemy. The price paid for protection was too high.

Hence the tactical dilemma. In every war in the American era that lasts too long, ground forces have faced two unacceptable alternatives: either fight the enemy on his terms in a fair and relatively even fight and suffer unacceptable casualties or seek protection at the cost of reducing casualties but losing the war. This dilemma, pitting Soldier protection against fighting effectiveness, is made all the more challenging by the fact that ground combat is fought in a very complex medium. The vagaries of terrain, the closeness of the enemy, and (in counterinsurgency) his ability to hide among the population makes the challenge of keeping Soldiers alive far more challenging than fighting in simpler media, like in the air and on the sea.

During my numerous visits to Iraq, I asked virtually every senior operational commander for his insights into how to solve the tactical dilemma. Their answers were unequivocal: Soldiers should not have to die to find the enemy. Thus the most important task for the future should be to avoid surprise, by seeing the enemy first. The nature of irregular war has exacerbated the challenge of finding the enemy. The enormity of the battlefield, the enemy's propensity to hide in urban areas, and his understanding of the benefits of collateral damage require that on tomorrow's battlefield the enemy must be watched and tracked reliably in real time. Today a commander gets only incidental glimpses of the enemy—much like a stop-action TV image limited in time and area. In the future, he must gain the perceptual high ground, by expanding his view in such a way that he is able to move from stop action to a continuous, uninterrupted "streaming video" image of the battlefield.

In order to dominate at the tactical level, the enemy must be fractured, his fighters dispersed, confused, and detached from their comrades and leaders before the close fight commences. To win the very-close-in war, we must change the very essence of how these battles are fought. An unfortunate consequence of urban fighting is that the deadly zone (the distance that separates two forces locked in a firefight) decreases from about 2,400 meters in open terrain to fifty meters or less. All too often in Afghanistan and elsewhere, the imperative to clear urban areas in which innocent civilians are present demands that a small unit must close well within the deadly zone against a hidden and prepared enemy. Inside the deadly zone, the "exchange ratio," or the relative cost of an engagement between friendly and enemy forces, no longer favors one side or the other. The fight becomes a fair one when small infantry must dismount from their vehicles and cross the deadly zone on foot. At close range the enemy's weapons, small arms, mortars, and explosive devices are as deadly as ours.

Soldiers in Iraq had a saying that the object of delivering fires was "to kill more enemies than you make." Killing power indiscriminately applied will shape the narrative to the enemy's advantage if it harms innocents, particularly if the media captures the destruction. Cold War–era firepower systems are designed to deliver masses of artillery and bombs across wide areas, with little ability to limit collateral damage. Hezbollah skillfully portrayed Israeli air strikes inside Lebanon as genocidal acts against innocent civilians. Western media repeated Hezbollah propaganda, greatly harming Israel's image abroad. Under mounting international pressure, the Israeli Defense Forces pulled their firepower punches, and the effectiveness of the aerial assault against Hezbollah targets diminished considerably. Without question, experiences such as these demonstrate that global exposure forces Western militaries to shift from massive area barrages to precise, discrete, immediate fires, particularly if the fires are delivered very close to Soldiers in contact.

Irregular enemies learned very early that rear-area Soldiers are the easiest to kill. In Iraq and Afghanistan, the lines of communications are long, poorly protected, and vulnerable to attack by ambush, snipers, and roadside bombs. The roads are also very crowded. Cold War–era matériel employed by conventional "mounted" (that is, in vehicles) units in Iraq and Afghanistan consumes enormous quantities of food, fuel, water, ammunition, and spare parts. The need to deliver the flotsam of machine war needlessly exposes support Soldiers to the tender mercies of the enemy along the lines of communications. Therefore, irregular wars of the future will demand that the vulnerable logistical tether tying isolated tactical units to their sources of supply be shrunk if not eliminated. Tomorrow's infantry must be able to fight supported by a much smaller and much less vulnerable logistical umbilical. The surest way to eliminate logistical vulnerabilities would be to supply the close fight predominantly by air. An aerial line of communication is possible if equipment and supplies can be delivered continuously and if the appetite for resupply is kept within the lifting limits of available aircraft. Today in Iraq and Afghanistan, no mounted fighting system can be completely supported from the air, and the enemy knows it.

Every professional Soldier who has seen close combat knows that armor, both personal and vehicular, protects Soldiers and saves lives. But it took the shock of seeing so many Soldiers die from roadside bombs for the Army finally to make its case for accelerating the production of first-rate body armor capable of stopping AK-47 rounds and for "up-armored" Humvees, and later the MRAPs (mine-resistant ambush-protected vehicles), to shield against explosive devices. Before the invasion of Iraq, one senior Army officer had made an impassioned appeal to civilian leaders inside the "acquisition agencies" of the Pentagon to accelerate the purchase of new individual fighting equipment. He was told that other big-ticket items took priority and that the Department of Defense was willing "to take risk in these areas." Unfortunately it is our Soldiers who are taking the real risk, not Pentagon civilians.

Finding better-quality close-combat Soldiers is the surest means for making our ground combat services dominant on tomorrow's battlefields. We expect these young men to perform tasks far more demanding than those of their "Willie and Joe" ancestors. They must be accomplished medical doctors, capable of keeping comrades alive for long periods using the most sophisticated medical equipment. They must be intelligence specialists, capable of entering an alien theater and immediately gaining an appreciation of the culture and combat capabilities of the enemy. They must be able to adapt on the fly to react to unexpected circumstances. They must be able to employ some of the most sophisticated precision weapons, while at the same time demonstrating patrolling, scouting, tracking, and tactical "fire and maneuver" skills that have not changed in millennia. Then, on a moment's notice, once the shooting stops, these men must change their entire skill set from warrior to humanitarian.

We should consider taking some pages from the special operations handbook and adapt their proven techniques to conventional Army and Marine Corps infantry units. Decades of research done within the special operations community validate the truism that older, smarter men make better close-combat Soldiers. Special operators have learned that an eighteen-year-old is still a kid, in close-combat terms. Youngsters just out of high school are brash and impetuous, and they tend to be reckless. Recklessness increases a young man's propensity for dangerous behavior. In combat, impetuousness too often gets him and his comrades needlessly killed.

Human research and anecdotal evidence prove that the optimum age for a close-combat infantryman is between twenty-eight and thirty-two. A man in this age bracket has a fully matured frontal cortex—the portion of the brain that regulates judgment. He has a smaller propensity for rash behavior. A mature close-combat Soldier is more likely to think before he acts. He is inherently more cautious, tends to pause to consider all alternatives before rushing forward. An older infantryman bonds better with his peers and traditionally acts more in concert with the group rather than as an individual when moving against an enemy. The Marines have certainly learned this lesson: Marines in close-combat units suffer proportionately more casualties, because Marine policy has been to recruit only the very young into infantry units. Most Marine close-combat infantrymen are in their first enlistments, and most of them are less than twenty years old.

One idea for creating a body of dominating infantrymen would be to accept infantry Soldiers and Marines only in their second enlistments. After four years in other arms, such young men would be more mature and closely committed to long-term service. More importantly, they would have some skill translatable to close-combat small teams. Second-term combat squads might contain Soldiers who know medical treatment, small-arms repair, communications, and intelligence. Mixing these skills in every small unit would make close-combat units multifunctional and capable of long-term, autonomous operations. More time in service would also give each small unit a leadership "bench" of understudies, ready to take command when leaders are incapacitated.

Of course the Army and Marine Corps would have to pay more for older and more senior candidates, but the potential reward would be well worth the investment. Older, smarter, and more skilled Soldiers and Marines not only fight better but are much less likely to become casualties. The long-term savings accrued from keeping more men alive alone would more than offset the initial investment. Only when we treat the selection, bonding, training, and leader development of our regular infantry with the same degree of time and resources used to make a special operations Soldier will we be able to create a new corps of close-combat Soldiers fully capable of fighting this new style of war.

WHAT NEEDS TO BE DONE

Experience in today's wars has taught the lesson that the actions of small combat units have national strategic consequences. Therefore, we must focus attention on how we fight at the tactical level of war as a national, not a service-specific, task. Department of Defense scientific communities have never made the small combat unit a priority for research and development at the national level.

In December 2014, Secretary of Defense Chuck Hagel, a Vietnam-era infantryman, created the Advanced Capability and Deterrence Panel (ACDP) as one of the core elements of his Defense Innovation Initiative, which he charged with pursuing creative ways to sustain and advance military dominance in the twenty-first century. Secretary Hagel said that we were entering an era where U.S. dominance in each of the key war-fighting domains could no longer be taken for granted. Today, though Hagel has left the department, the ACDP aims to identify offsets to competitors' military capabilities to establish a new era of American global power projection and operational advantage. The ACDP's tasking document is an outrage to Hagel's infantry heritage. Not once does it even mention the need to leverage technology to serve the ground Soldier or Marine. The tradition of neglect continues. In fact in its history, the Department of Defense has never attempted to achieve a "leap ahead" in technology in order to achieve dominance on the ground.

We must demand that the secretary of defense recognize and proclaim publicly that dominance on the tactical battlefield is an objective of importance to the nation . . . and pledge the human and fiscal resources necessary to make our military as dominant on the ground as it is today in the air, in space, and on the sea. The Department of Defense's leadership must develop the means to add a tactical perspective to strategic policy making, such that the needs of small units are exposed and addressed by its budgeting and policy-making staffs.

As a first priority, the secretary must establish a ground service board consisting of only the ground service chiefs, those of the Army and Marines, as well as the Special Operations Forces community. The recommendations of the chiefs would go directly to the secretary of defense for approval, bypassing all of the civilian bureaucracies that traditionally impede programs that support Soldiers and Marines. The board would select only weapons that are technologically possible—no space-based robots. They would fix on simple projects that have failed to appear after fourteen years of war, such as improved small arms, Soldier protection, Soldier sensors, squad drones, Soldier social networks (cell phones), and technologies to reduce the Soldier's load. A more radical solution would be to reserve all decisions on small-unit technology to SOCOM, so as best to ensure that new equipment gets to Soldiers quickly.

A national effort to achieve small-unit dominance should be expanded well beyond the Department of Defense to embrace a nationwide small-unit "community of practice." The best and brightest would be invited to join the effort—representatives from academia, industry, and the civilian law-enforcement sector, as well as public and private research and development institutions.

Further, fourteen years of failure have taught us that defense establishments focus on small units only if forced to do so. Thus, I strongly believe that Congress should establish a fiscally fenced "small unit" budget line that would be reserved for the ground services alone.

In July 2013 I watched the Afghanistan war documentary *Restrepo* and compared it to my experience decades ago: same division (the 101st), same lousy rifle (M16/4), same helicopter (CH-47), same machine gun (M2), same frightened young men trying to deal with the fear of violent death. Seared in my brain is the image of a young Soldier at Fire Base Restrepo, hacking away at hard clay and granite trying frantically to dig a fighting position. According to the open press, the United States is spending more than $300 billion on a new fighter plane. We have not lost a fighter pilot to enemy action since 1972. Why, after fourteen years of war, can't we give close-combat Soldiers a better way to dig a hole? For that matter, why do Soldiers exiting firebases today not have some means of looking over the next hill? Why doesn't every Soldier have his own means to talk to his comrades by radio? Why can't Soldiers on a remote firebase detect an approaching enemy by using sensors? Why can't Soldiers rely on robots to carry heavy loads and accomplish particularly dangerous tasks? I could go on, but you get the point.

These challenges can only be met by demanding that our national-level policy and planning staffs look at war from the ground up rather than the top down. What is missing is not a lack of empathy or concern but acknowledgment of the crushing imperative for our leaders to bridge the enormous cultural gap that has existed for two generations between the political and government elite, on one hand, and on the other the Soldiers they send to do the dirty task of intimate killing. Closing this cultural gap will take time, to be sure. But if we are involved in a long period of persistent conflict, we have an obligation to start now to change the culture. The Army and Marine leadership have done just about all they can within the narrow confines of their budgeting and weapons-buying authorities. It is time now for the country to pay attention and act. Our close-combat Soldiers and leaders deserve nothing less.

[8]

WAR IN TWO EPOCHS

McCHRYSTAL AND PATTON

In wars then let our great object be victory, not lengthy campaigns.
—Sun Tzu, *The Art of War*

No two generals could possibly be more diametrically opposite than George Patton and Stanley McChrystal. Both graduated from West Point and shared a passion for reading military history, but similarities end there. Patton was an acerbic, bombastic, narcissistic self-promoter whose skill as a warrior made him immortal. In contrast, McChrystal's personal life and active service accentuated the motto of his special warfare clan: the "silent professionals." As different as they are in time and temperament, both generals symbolize transformational epochs of the U.S. military art. Patton is the past; McChrystal represents the new age. For decades, McChrystal labored in the shadowy corners of Iraq and Afghanistan to evolve, through practical trial and error, a model of war that will shape for generations how America fights.[1]

Gen. George Patton's breakout from the Normandy beachhead in July 1944 and his dash across France signaled that the United States had at last mastered mechanized warfare. The "Patton method" subsequently became the doctrine for fighting the Soviet army in Europe throughout the Cold War. The method consisted of a mechanized-war doctrine, stolen from the Germans and melded with the uniquely American skill for applying air- and land-delivered firepower in support of tanks on the move. Some semblance of Patton's tank-heavy, firepower-intensive dash would be replicated twice against a single enemy: Iraq, once with the "Great Wheel" in Desert Storm and once with the "March to Baghdad" in 2003. Only the Israelis would conduct similar armored maneuvers, against Arab enemies in 1967 and 1973. Otherwise Patton's method no longer defines modern wars.

Patton's genius was well fitted to the last war of the European era. McChrystal represents the latest war of the American era. Patton represented the apex of twentieth-century mechanized warfare. McChrystal's legion of elite warriors is the highest embodiment of the art of warfare in the new age of infantry.

However, Patton's ghost still haunts the U.S. Army. He is embedded in our Cold War culture of machine-driven ground combat. It is perpetuated by the euphoria that came from twice crushing the incompetent Iraqi Republican Guard in the blowing sands of Iraq. Unfortunately, the utility of big-machine warfare began to fade as soon as U.S. military power took center stage. Patton's war was a crusade for national survival. Wars in the American era are limited wars. Throughout the American era, most efforts to apply the Patton method have been frustrated by huge shifts in the dynamics of war. One is the loss of the strategic initiative. Patton enjoyed the initiative. The German military danced to his tune. To be sure, Hitler surprised the allies by initiating the Battle of the Bulge, but within days the initiative returned to Eisenhower, not Hitler.

The United States fights its wars today at a disadvantage. The enemy holds the initiative, and we must fight without the ability to anticipate the place, time, duration, and circumstance of war. Loss of the initiative in the American era has led too often to miscalculation on both sides. Harry Truman never imagined that a 2-division commitment in 1950 would result in 38,000 dead Americans. Lyndon Johnson surely would never have sent troops to Vietnam if he had ever thought this act would kill 58,000 Americans and more than a million Vietnamese. Secretary of Defense Donald Rumsfeld never anticipated a protracted counterinsurgency when he sent armored forces into Baghdad. The succession of enemies guilty of miscalculating U.S. intent are many, and they include Manuel Noriega, Mohamed Farah Aideed, Slobodan Milosevic, Saddam Hussein (twice), the Taliban, Muammar Kaddafi, and, missing by just a hair, Bashar al Assad.

Patton fought a complicated war with pyramidal, linear structures. His Third Army was an enormous clockwork mechanism that moved in response to a detailed set of orders. Detailed, exhaustive planning put this giant mechanism on the road and orchestrated all its parts in a form of operatic synergy. The plan fed fuel, food, and ammunition from depots to attacking units at prescribed times and places. Subordinate officers briefed their pieces of the plan to Soldiers before moving out to assembly areas. Planning annexes and precise tables dictated exactly how fires were delivered, beginning with the Army Air Forces and proceeding to artillery, infantry mortars, and finally covering machine-gun fire at company and platoon levels. Many moving parts and complicated actions kept the mechanism running on time. This mechanism could only be put together over days or weeks dedicated to intense planning, rehearsal, and execution.

McChrystal fought a complex war. The elusive and ambiguous nature of the enemy and the need for immediate action forbade the old Cold War linear plans and top-down orders of the past. He discovered that complexity demanded shortcuts, anticipation, and the ability to conceptualize, plan, and execute on the move. The enemy had to be found in the creases, hidden in the shadows, and dispersed among the people. McChrystal fought against complex enemy networks whose tribal associations, amorphous connections, and hydra-headed leadership forced him to devise competing networks of his own. A networked force was impossible to create unless the pyramid was crushed and traditional command chains flattened and turned into a networked organization that matched that of the enemy.[2]

Patton willingly sacrificed his men to maintain the momentum of his armored phalanx. McChrystal's enemies know that the United States will stop fighting when the butcher's bill grows too large. Patton rolled across the northern European plain, an expanse of ground that does not rise more than three hundred feet from Brittany to the Urals. McChrystal's enemies fight in distant places in complex terrain, such as mountains and jungles. McChrystal fights "among the people," while Patton fought *through* the people in a rush to conquer Nazism.

Patton was the first to leverage properly U.S. dominance in the air to support troops on the ground. As he advanced across France, swarms of Army Air Forces "Jabos" (a German nickname for ground-support fighter planes) flew overhead, ready to strafe immediately any German target that impeded Patton's armored advance. McChrystal's enemies hide from airplanes. Successful avoidance is dependent on the enemy's ability to disperse, dig in, and hide among the people in order to use our rules of engagement to his own advantage.

The Germans occasionally fought Patton to a standstill, because they possessed superior tanks and antitank weapons. McChrystal's enemies have few tanks; instead, they employ primitive weapons in imaginative ways. The simple mortar remains the weapon of choice, and it is the most effective killer of Americans. Small arms and roadside bombs come in a dreadful second. As the Israelis learned to their sorrow in Lebanon, a semiskilled enemy Soldier can kill a Patton-era tank at great range using decades-old antitank missiles, supplied by our former Cold War enemies. McChrystal's wars will continue for generations. Patton's style of war, with its attendant intensity, mass, and massive application of killing power, is a thing of the past.

THE MCCHRYSTAL METHOD

In the fall of 2008 Lt. Gen. Charles Cleveland, then commander of all Special Forces in Iraq and Afghanistan, asked me to visit units under his command and report back on what I observed. I traveled on board the Special Forces "black" fleet of aircraft from Tikrit and Taji in Iraq, then on to Fire Support Base Ripley in Helmand Province, on the southern tip of Afghanistan. Very early one morning, I sat before consoles inside the Group Operations Center and watched flat-screen downlinks from orbiting drones follow one set of friendly black dots as they systematically killed dozens of enemy black dots.

I spent four exhilarating days living with these Soldiers at Fire Base Ripley. We convoyed outside the wire on patrols. I ate really bad goat as I watched Soldiers conduct a *jura* (an Afghan town hall meeting) with angry- and hostile-looking tribesmen. It took a very special group of Soldiers to play governor, police chief, and counselor to tribesmen who only a few months earlier had been killing Americans. I sat on the stoop of my "hootch" as a Special Forces team returned from a medical mission to a group of mountain villages. An abundance of the villagers had never seen a Western doctor before. On board one Humvee was a young woman with a uterine tumor she had carried since she was thirteen. The medics operated immediately and saved her life. A few days later, her family lifted her on top of a mule to take her home. They begged us never to mention her operation. If her village elders learned that she had been naked on an operating table, they would have her stoned to death.

Juxtapose Patton's massive phalanx of tanks roaring across France with the shaky solemnity of Fire Base Ripley and you see how far the American art of war has come in seventy years. Patton's mission was to crush the Wehrmacht; McChrystal's mission is unclear. Patton's enemy was a wounded but ferociously evil military with only ten months to live. McChrystal's enemy is diabolical, driven by an equally evil ideology amplified by the insanity of religious zeal. Patton fought across the north German plain; McChrystal's battlefield is global.

McChrystal's enemies have no talent at large-scale industrial age warfare. The 1973 Yom Kippur War was the last instance in which Middle Eastern armies tried with some success to mimic the Western style of machine warfare. Today, the large, mechanized formations that Middle Eastern potentates assembled against Western armies are gone: the Mahdi, Gamal Abdel Nasser, Saddam, and Assad the First and Second. Middle Eastern fighting forces like ISIS are still large but aggregated in small units, built mostly around tribal and clan affiliations. They may be poor at mimicking the Western way of war, but they are very good at applying a countervailing style of war and improving it incrementally as they learn and adapt. The North Vietnamese became adept at using shoulder-fired rockets to knock out U.S. armor. Chechen fighters defeated Russian mechanized advances into Grozny in 1996. Hezbollah's use of antitank missiles stalled Israeli advances in Lebanon. Al Qaeda's locally improvised explosives and detonators were the greatest killers of Americans traveling in vehicles. ISIS fighters have given up employing captured U.S. equipment on a large scale and have returned to the distributed style of war that made them successful in 2014.

Patton made corps, McChrystal made teams and, later, teams of teams. To Patton, small teams were merely building blocks to be stacked into very large phalanxes consisting of hundreds of thousands of men. To McChrystal, the team—superbly selected and patiently crafted—is the centerpiece of his method of war. Each team fights autonomously but in concert with others to achieve a greater strategic end. When he took command of Joint Special Operations Command in 2003, McChrystal understood the exquisite competence of his teams and how well they had performed in past wars. JSOC actions in Panama, Somalia, Kosovo, and Desert Storm were legendary. But McChrystal realized that large, dispersed, and long wars demanded more than just teams operating independently.

He knitted together "teams of teams" to achieve a collective strategic end. McChrystal's task in Iraq and Afghanistan was to destroy the enemy's network. To take down a huge, complex, adaptive, and sophisticated network like Al Qaeda demanded the creation of an opposing network that shared data and strategic consciousness among all fighting elements. He needed to include in his collective team of teams special operations entities out of his direct control, such as Central Intelligence Agency operatives and Marine special operations units. It took time to remove "tribal" and doctrinal barriers, but he succeeded. By the time he left command of JSOC McChrystal had placed a strategic, coordinating hand on the shoulder of the organization without affecting the initiative and individuality of his teams. The results speak for themselves: no army has ever before produced teams selected and trained well enough to fight such a precise and demanding kind of war—but we have.

The success of the McChrystal method begins with a complex and uniquely human process of preparation for war. Preparing the battlefield requires patience and often takes decades. In the late nineteenth century, the British Army "seconded" bright officers to various corners of the world and immersed them in the cultures of the empire. They became intimates with potentates from Egypt to Malaya. Names like "China" Gordon and T. E. Lawrence testify to the wisdom of such a custom. Even today, the British Army possesses officers with the ability to move comfortably between and within the inner circles of foreign militaries.

The U.S. Army's version of Lawrence of Arabia lives in McChrystal's world. Special Forces Soldiers spend time overseas deeply immersed in foreign cultures, particularly those cultures most likely to become engaged in conflicts of strategic importance to the United States. These are global scouts, well educated, with a penchant for languages and comfort with strange and distant places. The Army has given them time to immerse themselves in single cultures and to establish trust with those willing to trust them. They are a national treasure.

Fourteen years of war in Iraq and Afghanistan have taught the recurrent lesson that war is inherently a human rather than a technological enterprise. Patton's close-combat Soldiers came from the dregs of the recruiting pool. Before they arrived in Europe, they were poorly trained and led by mediocre commissioned and noncommissioned officers. Patton's massed-produced army had to learn to fight by fighting, and unfortunately their teachers were the Germans.

By war's end, Patton's army was superb—but the human cost of creating this great army was far too high to be repeated today. Patton's army became a fearsome fighting force, but not until the weak, cowardly, unlucky, and stupid had been eliminated in the deadly, Darwinian filter of close-combat fighting.

In contrast to Patton, McChrystal's unique "band of brothers" is recruited and selected from the best and brightest. Incompetence and weakness are discovered and eliminated though harsh, brutal, and uncompromising field-testing that takes months—in some cases, years. Patton's wastage was so great that Soldiers, rushed into combat, often died alone among strangers. McChrystal's close-combat teams are collections of individuals made far more lethal through mutual trust and long association. Think of these men as you would a professional sports team, but one where losing means death instead of defeat. They are trained like athletes, their offense, defense, and special teams raised to a level of competence unmatched in our history.

McChrystal's success proves that small units of superbly selected, trained, educated, led, and bonded Soldiers can kill much larger aggregations of enemy while keeping friendly and innocent deaths to a minimum. Make no mistake, the McChrystal method is about killing, but killing of a different sort. The president at one time joked about "whack-a-mole" tactics in Afghanistan. Whack-a-mole tactics work when the moles are enemies who occupy critical positions within terrorist networks, essentially the middle management of leaders, communicators, transporters, financiers, technicians, and enforcers. In many ways, the McChrystal method is the opposite of shock and awe. It is often painfully deliberate, fed by the patient collection of intelligence wrung from sources as disparate as turned informers and the big ears of the National Security Agency. Nothing happens without repetitive, realistic planning and rehearsals.

McChrystal's precision replaces Patton's mass. Over the past twenty years, McChrystal's teams of special operators have evolved another uniquely American method, one that substitutes exquisite skill, information, and precision for mass, maneuver, and weight of shell. We first watched the McChrystal method at work in Afghanistan immediately after 9/11, when small Special Forces units mounted on horseback and teamed with the Afghan Northern Alliance destroyed the Taliban using precision strikes delivered from aircraft orbiting high overhead.

As we have seen in any number of Hollywood re-creations, these teams execute with precision, violence, and surprise. No operation goes down without involving many layers of "enablers." Intelligence officers feed information constantly to teams as they move to the fight. Armed and unarmed drones of many sorts follow and feed video pictures of enemy movements below. Some of the killing is done up close, to be sure, but most by aerial precision weapons that obliterate the enemy in the dead of night.

McChrystal's capabilities match the shape and character of today's battlefields. Patton's battlefield was densely packed with masses of men and machines backed by huge logistical tent cities that provided all of the amenities of home. McChrystal's battlefield appears empty by comparison. His Soldiers operate in small groups, supplied mostly from the air. A ground force reshaped in the McChrystal image dominates in combat through knowledge rather than mass. In tomorrow's wars a galaxy of armed and reconnaissance drones will orbit overhead 24/7. Soldiers will be connected to each other over a ubiquitous combat Wi-Fi network in which small units rather than generals in command posts are the centerpiece. In such an environment, Soldiers may be dispersed, but the intimacy that comes from electronic "touch" will never allow them to fight alone.

Patton's army and its enemy fought like two boxers in a darkened room. His tanks and artillery flushed the enemy though contact, often paying in blood to discover the enemy's location. McChrystal's Soldiers never go into combat blind. Rather than reacting to the enemy's initiative, they "see" what is about to happen by way of sensors loitering overhead. During his time as commander of Special Operations Forces in Iraq and Afghanistan, McChrystal succeeded in tearing out the "green door" that separated national strategic intelligence from the Soldier in combat. Armed with an open aperture of intelligence linked to an "unblinking eye" overhead, Soldiers will rarely be surprised. They will always be prepared for combat before combat begins, thanks to simulation technologies that will permit them to walk through every maneuver and to kill every target literally hundreds of times bloodlessly, using real-time computer-driven rehearsals.

The McChrystal method will never succeed unless every small unit is capable of killing at a distance with overwhelming force. Drones and Soldier-mounted ground sensors will allow small units to detect the enemy long before the enemy's ambush is sprung. The Soldier will rely on precision fires delivered from great distances to kill well outside the ranges of the enemy's small arms, missiles, and artillery.

Patton would never fight at night. McChrystal's force is best known for its use of night raids in Iraq and Afghanistan. Think for a moment of this same concept applied on an enormous scale. Soldiers in small units move with stealth about the battlefield. They swoop in unseen to strike with discretion and precision, then depart, leaving behind a stunned and demoralized enemy. The mass killing power of such Cold War leftovers as fighter jets, ship missiles, tanks, and artillery will still be present to be sure, but they will be used only sparingly should the enemy be dumb enough to mass.

"Fair fights" occurred in Afghanistan and Iraq too often, when the enemy managed to get too close. On tomorrow's battlefields, Soldiers will be able to win every "intimate" fight decisively. Technology to achieve dominance in the close fight is cheap: better, lighter, and impenetrable body armor; shoulder-carried precision missiles that can kill tanks and bunkers at long range; and "smart" small arms that can "home" on to individual targets without aiming. These technologies are cheap and available, more *Popular Mechanics* than *Star Wars*.

During the Civil War, Abraham Lincoln wrote about the sad "arithmetic" of war. Once the first shot is fired, the arithmetic begins the attrition that reduces fighting power even when not in battle. Nothing has changed. Disease, accidents, and psychological stress all contribute to the wearing away of not only numbers but also the physical and emotional sharpness that every close-combat unit needs to survive. Unfortunately, in an all-volunteer force, the rate of replenishment never overcomes the arithmetic. In the American era, combat prowess reaches a peak rather quickly then diminishes slowly over time.

Short of a draft, nothing can be done to reduce the corrosive effects of the arithmetic once war begins. Thus, the greatest shortcoming of the McChrystal method is time . . . and people. The making of dominant small units, like that of fine wines, cannot be hurried. Two years are needed to train and acculturate a team or squad, more for larger close-combat forces. Thus, the force the nation has at the beginning of a conflict cannot be increased substantially during the conflict without risking catastrophic losses. The only alternative is to win quickly and go to war with many more high-quality Soldiers than the nation thinks it needs in peacetime. Lenin is thought to have written, "Quantity has a quality of its own." In the American context, he meant that wars are won more quickly when overwhelming force is applied. Experience during the early days in Iraq also taught that underwhelming force gives the enemy time to regain momentum and change the dynamics of the battlefield. Get more Soldiers into the fight quickly and win. Take too long and face defeat. It is that simple. The ground services must face the problem of the arithmetic by "overmanning" every close-combat unit by about a third, to ensure that these units do not atrophy though lack of numbers.

The McChrystal method is working against ISIS. However, killing ISIS will require a scaling of the method never attempted before. ISIS is huge. Sadly, the men and machines within SOCOM necessary to do the job are too few and are terribly overused. To succeed over time, the McChrystal method must be cloned and amplified within conventional Army and Marine forces to a degree as yet unimagined within the Department of Defense.

Obstacles to expanding the McChrystal method outside the narrow confines of the U.S. SOCOM clan are many. SOCOM may be the most intractable obstacle to proliferating the McChrystal method. Special operations leaders argue that such elite forces can only be made in small batches. Truth is that there are more than enough men to expand the McChrystal method fully if all Army and Marine close-combat forces are made more "SOF-like." By no means does this concept mean that SOCOM's teams will be subsumed in "Big Army" or that their proficiency will be diminished in any way. On the contrary, the purpose of such a reform would be to push all Marine and Army infantrymen up the scale of proficiency toward the Tier I SOF standard as far as resources, availability of skilled manpower, and time will allow.

Think of a conventional infantry selection program that mimics the best of McChrystal's teams of teams. Imagine a conventional close-combat training program just as tough and eliminative as, say, Army Ranger School is today. Those enlisted infantrymen who pass selection would begin unit buddy-bonding in basic training, where they are met by the same officers and noncommissioned officers (NCOs) who will lead them for their entire terms of enlistment. Perhaps the Army would change its Cold War personnel policies to allow infantry NCOs and officers to remain in command of these same small units for at least seven years or more. Conventional infantry units should receive exactly the same high-tech equipment as their Special Forces brethren, to include organic drones, dedicated satellites, and first priority for vehicles, weapons, aircraft, and protective equipment. Of course, such a transformation would take time. Building a conventional "elite" force would require a ruthless culling of the ranks to allow only the best and brightest to be selected, trained, and bonded, in a manner proven by decades of past successes in the special operations community. But make no mistake: elevating the fighting power of U.S. Army and Marine small units from superior to dominant is cheap by the standards of contemporary big-ticket programs.

U.S. close-combat forces would require changes in recruiting laws, administrative policies, and budgeting—a small price to pay for a new U.S. force that will be absolutely unbeatable in combat. To ensure that they remain robust, all close-combat Soldiers should be given special treatment by the Department of Defense in proportion to their value to the nation. They should be paid more—much more. There is no reason that a computer programmer in the Pentagon should make the same as an infantryman humping a 120-pound rucksack under fire on his fifth tour in Afghanistan. They should be retired as soon as the physical and emotional toll of close combat makes them no longer effective. They should be exempted from the routine distractions that all too often dull the fighting abilities of garrison Soldiers. Rank and station assignment should be more a function of a Soldier's skill and experience rather than his place in some unit-manning roster.

IMPLICATIONS FOR THE FUTURE

Our past, present, and future enemies have a plan proven from a well-thumbed and bloody game book. The U.S. military has the workings of a long-term response, well started by recent experience in war. In fact, our forces today are remarkably well positioned to move into the future with only modest changes in structure, weapons, and operational concepts. To shift from Patton to McChrystal does not imply that the Defense Department must scrap its legacy collection of planes, ships, and tanks. The nation needs a varied toolbox of capabilities to confront enemies we cannot anticipate. Our air and sea forces will continue to provide absolute dominance against any conventional enemy. The McChrystal method simply seeks to achieve the same degree of dominance for ground forces that our sea and air forces now enjoy. A larger and more robust close-combat force will ensure preservation of the one capability that the country seems to use most often to exhaustion. Tomorrow's close-combat units must be husbanded like the irreplaceable national treasures they are.

Our enemies are watching, and they read history. From the examples of Mao Zedong, Ho Chi Minh, Al Qaeda, ISIS, and the Taliban, future enemies are increasingly convinced that the United States can be bested though a strategy that succeeds principally by killing U.S. Soldiers. The road to miscalculation is open for traffic. It is only a matter of time before we collide with another enemy filled with the hubris that comes from past successes. If past is prologue, a thin line of close-combat Marines, Soldiers, and special operators will be called upon to end it. We must have the numbers and the quality to ensure that we do not run out of high-performing ground forces before we run out of time.

[9]

FEEDING THE NARRATIVE

What we needed was to ask of each operation contemplated:
"Will this operation create more bad guys than it takes off the
streets by its implementation?"

—Gen. David Petraeus, USA (Ret.)

Wars in the American era will be won by changing perceptions rather than by just killing men. I had this truism driven home to me one evening in November 2007 while having dinner with Gen. David Petraeus at his headquarters in Baghdad. It was his birthday, but before joining his staff for a cake-cutting ceremony, we talked at length about war.[1]

It was a good time for him. The success of the "surge" begun the previous year was no longer in doubt. Casualties, both U.S. and Iraqi, were down enormously. Convoys could drive along roads previously laced with killing IEDs. Petraeus and his commanders felt confident enough to walk about Baghdad without body armor. For the moment, he was winning the war.

The subject of our conversation was far broader than just the day's wartime events. We spoke at length about military history and the nature and character of the war. As the evening progressed, our discourse was interrupted periodically by a string of staff officers bringing to the dinner table the details of the next day's operations. I was struck by the uniqueness of the moment. Here was a strategic leader interrupting an interchange on the subject of military philosophy to approve what seemed to me to be mundane operational decisions. These were decisions being made in a manner that previous generations of higher-level commander would not have comprehended. Petraeus' tactical intercessions were few, to be sure, but they came whenever a military operation was bound to influence the narrative. He was particularly focused on the unintended consequences of sensitive special operations night raids into Sadr City against Shia militia leaders. He wanted these men dead. However, he also wanted support from more moderate Shia leaders in Sadr City and acquiescence of Shia citizens of Baghdad for these intrusive and violent operations.

To understand the significance of the moment, it is necessary to understand the difference between decisions made at the strategic and operational levels of war. Strategic-level commanders like Petraeus make decisions that link operations in the field with the president's broad national security policies and objectives. The operational level of war ties the employment of tactical forces to achievement of the president's strategic end state. Strategy wins wars. Operations win campaigns. Tactics win battles. Petraeus contributed to the Pentagon's strategic war plan, and he superintended the implementation of that strategy though his immediate control of the fighting forces in the field. He left the vast majority of the details of fighting battles to tactical commanders, who sense, track, and kill or capture the enemy every day at the brigade, battalion, and company levels.

The Army's focus on (some would say obsession with) the operational level of war began in earnest after the Israeli performance in the 1973 Yom Kippur campaign. The Army realized then that the tactical focus of Vietnam had become too narrow, given the larger-scale demands for fighting a very broad, deep, fast-moving, and enormously lethal campaign against conventional forces like those of the Egyptians in the Sinai, the Syrians on the Golan, and, by inference, the Soviets on the north German plain.

The Army's discovery of war at the operational level led to an intellectual renaissance among the officer corps and its eventual embrace of AirLand Battle—the doctrinal concept that codified a renewal of massive, mounted big-machine warfare, essentially the ultimate embodiment of blitzkrieg. Saddam provided this generation of officers the opportunity for vindication during

Desert Storm when five division-sized "big arrows on the map" wheeled across the sands of Kuwait and Iraq in a classic hundred-hour operational maneuver to crush the Republican Guard. Saddam repeated the favor twelve years later, when he opened the door for two division-sized large arrows to conduct a classic operational maneuver, this time linearly and in parallel from Kuwait to Baghdad in three weeks.

The big-arrow school of operational art began to lose its luster somewhere along the march to Baghdad. Gradually, the spontaneous actions of small bands of irregular forces, the "Fedayeen Saddam," began to make themselves felt. Armed with automatic weapons and rocket-propelled grenade launchers, this pickup team of fighters continually attacked U.S. armored columns on the march. Had U.S. commanders been more observant, they would have seen an enemy in the process of adapting to a technologically dominant force—a phenomenon they should have recognized from their service in Vietnam.

The object of an operational maneuver is to exploit the advantages of fire and maneuver, in order to strike at the enemy's "brain," with the intent of collapsing his operational centers of gravity. The collapse of the enemy commander's ability to control his units in the field would cause a collapse of will—a psychological and emotional meltdown among those in power resulting inevitably in the collapse of the state. During Desert Storm, Gen. Colin Powell was thinking about the link between operational success, the defeat of the Republican Guard, and the cutting-off of the head of the strategic snake (figuratively speaking). It worked then, and it worked momentarily on the march to Baghdad, because the snake had a head—Saddam and his henchmen. Success at the tactical level by winning a succession of battles allowed the achievement of operational success. Victory followed. It is just that the enemy had a vote; on the march to Baghdad, he changed the nature of the war by redefining war at the operational level.

Today, the Islamic terrorist snake has no head. Or maybe better put, it has many heads, each Hydra-like with the capacity to regrow after decapitation. Shortly after the capture of Baghdad Petraeus saw the operational level seem to disappear. Suddenly tactical successes no longer guaranteed strategic success, because there was no operational tissue connecting them. Soldiers did well in places like Najaf and Fallujah; they killed enemies in profusion, but strategic ends continually slipped further away with each perceived success.

Petraeus postulated that maybe the operational level had not disappeared. Maybe it had changed form. Maybe the tenets that ensured success in blitzkrieg-style wars are different in wars fought against irregular enemies who have no heads. To be sure, the end state of war is still the same as it has been for millennia: the moral collapse of the enemy. War will always be a test of will, but this war suggests that the operational means for transferring tactical success to moral dominance has morphed into a shape that was becoming clear enough to perceive and define.

Operational success in blitzkrieg warfare was gained through speed and destructiveness. Embrace the technological power of the internal combustion engine and the wireless to control the clock by committing violent acts of killing that so shock an enemy that he becomes paralyzed, unable to recover his composure before capitulation. But speed of movement and destructiveness are no longer guarantors of success in today's wars; the clock has stalled. Nearly seven thousand dead Americans testify to the truism that violence is still an ingredient in our wars. However, the connection between tactical and strategic success is no longer direct and immediate. Something else is impeding the translation of one to the other. Some new source of friction keeps killing from being enough.

Just before we left the dinner table, Petraeus looked briefly at each of the next day's tactical plans submitted by his combat commanders. He attended to his commander's kinetic plan, but he also filtered the next day's plan through an intellectual image of the "narrative." His interest was not in the plan so much as its consequences. After a few moments of reflection he though deeply about the effect each operation would have on the four "audiences" that would be influenced by his decisions: the Iraqis, the enemy, the Arab community, and the American people. Like any strategic leader, he considered the context of these tactical engagements. Would the perceptual consequences of tomorrow's tactical operation properly feed his intended perceptual outcome? What would all four audiences think if it failed? As I watched him deliberately trace through the details of each intended tactical action, I could not help thinking about the paradoxical juxtaposition between Norman Schwarzkopf's hand waving across the arrows on a big map during one of his televised briefings and that quiet moment of reflection when Petraeus leaned over the dinner table, stared at each plan, and turned over in his mind the global consequences of even the smallest tactical engagement.

I realized at that moment that the operational context of tomorrow's wars had changed fundamentally. During the dinner, Petraeus demonstrated a sense that the operational level of war in the American era was now defined by two opponents, each trying to capture and control the "narrative." The winning side would be the one best able to translate tactical actions, kinetic and non-kinetic, into the most convincing story of the conflict in progress. Petraeus' four audiences, rather than the enemy's operational brain, would be the strategic focus of all of tomorrow's action. The internal combustion engine and the wireless of the industrial era of warfare have given way to the microchip and the video camera as the primary instruments for achieving operational success.

In effect, Petraeus understood that the technological means for winning at the operational level of war had leveled the playing field. The enemy has as good (or perhaps even better) access to the global information network as do the Western powers. Our technological skill in broadcasting information is matched by the enemy's ability to create distrust within sympathetic cultures concerning our intentions. The enemy's unique skill at manipulating the narrative serves to create uncertainty and discomfort among the Iraqis, the American population, and our allies.

During his years in command of U.S. forces in Iraq and later in Afghanistan, Petraeus matured his vision on how to translate successful small-unit tactical successes into lasting strategic ends through the use of operational "amplifiers" that feed the narrative. The first amplifier is truth. The enemy's narrative cannot compete with ours as long as we are not afraid to tell the truth, trusting that the asymmetry of truth-telling inherent in a democracy at war must eventually favor our side to a decisive degree. When done right, speed in truthfulness is analogous to being the first unit to reach the objective in a conventional war. We cannot pause long enough to spin the truth through the cultural filters of the military's turgid public-affairs bureaucracies. The purpose of getting the truth out first should not be to impress our political ideology or methods on the population but to present ourselves as the only practical alternative for restoring civility to a war-ravaged society. Even among alien populations, such as the Sunnis in Iraq today, the truth about the vile nature of ISIS killers, broadcast repeatedly and witnessed firsthand in places like Mosul, Ramadi, and in small Sunni villages in Anbar Province, can turn the course of the narrative stream and increase its acceptance among the local population. Since the exit of U.S. forces in Iraq, we have discovered to our peril that among the Sunnis this is a fragile task—usually accomplished only when ISIS and Al Qaeda alienate the people through very public and horrific excesses.

The second narrative amplifier, therefore, is speed. Before Petraeus arrived, truth would have to wait until the Pentagon and White House bureaucracies staffed every tactical action captured on video to decide if it was worthy and politically acceptable for the Iraqis and the global media. Today the task of lifting the fog of war depends not on the ability to observe the enemy's actions but on the ability to be first with the information. With the arrival of global social media, the interval from observation to broadcast has accelerated from days or weeks to hours, in some cases minutes. To compete, Petraeus realized, all intermediaries between tactical units and the media had to be eliminated. Washington had to trust its Soldiers to tell the truth in order to compete with terrorist and anti-American outlets.

Video cameras in the hands of close-combat units is the surest guarantee of speed. Video technologies have become so inexpensive that the U.S. command should equip every small unit on patrol with helmet-mounted cameras linked to a single media clearing-and-collection point. U.S. reporters embedded with close-combat units used to be a common sight in Iraq and Afghanistan. Not so anymore . . . and the American narrative is suffering from the media exit. In the future, we must begin to re-embed media, perhaps by using more reporters from regional countries whose views are more in tune with the culture of the region and whose opinions are more likely to be trusted. Native-speaking witnesses can be harsh in their criticisms, but their messages have great power when they chronicle far more horrific—and common—actions by a diabolical and cruel enemy like ISIS.

The third amplifier is clarity. A "whole of government" approach to fighting an irregular war is a good idea, as long as there are not too many hands on the throttle. The Defense Department often sees an event in somewhat different contexts than the State Department or the Central Intelligence Agency. Too often, the facts become too stilted and prescriptive when filtered through an overly bureaucratic and layered process. The greatest credibility comes from young leaders and Soldiers who tell their own stories. Even if not terribly articulate, a young infantryman's breathless description of a firefight is far more believable than the same story sanitized and filtered by the White House Press Corps.

The fourth narrative amplifier is the offensive. Soldiers take great pride in their will to close with the enemy on the battlefield, but they tend to be less aggressive when closing with the enemy on the global media stage. Our fear of being wrong often allows the enemy to be first when he has no concern about being right. Commanders in Afghanistan today have learned to question first reports but show latitude for second reports. Again, video images of firefights and other incidents tend to confirm second reports. Some senior commanders are still reluctant to release sources and means of observation, but the Cold War is over. It is better to give the enemy a hint of the power of our sources and means than to allow him to get away with a lie that can easily be refuted. Sadly, even after fourteen years of war in the Middle East, U.S. policy makers and commanders still fail to place into context the absolute centrality of the narrative in planning for and executing future warfare. The presumption is that the information campaign should support the combat phase of an operation. In fact, global media attention on any war the United States contemplates reverses this tenet: in the future, the kinetic fight must support the narrative.

Looking back over our past experiences in Iraq, it is interesting to contrast the first and second battles of Fallujah. They collectively provide an interesting example of the real-war consequences of narratives preceding kinetics. Prior to the first attempt by the Marines to take the city, in April 2004, the enemy occupied the Fallujah General Hospital—located in the extreme northwest corner of the city, near the Euphrates River bridge. There Sunni insurgents hanged four Blackwater contractors. The hospital director provided safe passage to the hospital for the international media, which immediately started spouting false stories about the "atrocities" being committed by the Marines. As the battle progressed, the hospital filled with the dead and wounded. The media fed the narrative to the enemy's advantage, and soon the global outcry over the carnage became so overwhelming that administration pressure forced a premature termination of the battle of Fallujah. The enemy's propaganda war succeeded in beating the Marine kinetic war.

On the second try to take Fallujah, in November 2004, the Marines changed their operational plan to put the narrative first. The hospital became the first objective to be taken. The media never made it into the hospital this time, and the public was denied images of civilian suffering in the city. Sadly, the total cost in life would have been less had the Marines won the narrative battle the first time.

If perception is the end, then the means to achieve that end is discourse with those we seek to influence. In contemporary irregular conflicts there are competing, perhaps even warring, narratives. Each seeks to sway, through discourse, a very broad and eclectic audience. In an age in which this stream of discourse cannot be easily deflected, the narrative that leads to the fulfillment of the will of the population is given credence. The perception is that battlefield successes (or failures) can be interpreted as signposts pointing toward the side most likely to achieve victory or defeat. The narrative battle is not an even match. We may have truth on our side, but enemies like ISIS have the advantage of proximity, cultural affinity with the people, and a freedom to dramatize the brutalities of today's irregular conflicts from their perspectives.

Populations will inevitably receive evidence through a series of social, cultural, and ethnic filters. For example, we saw efforts to provide humanitarian relief to the Kurds stranded in ISIS-held territory as a satisfying part of our narrative. ISIS saw it as a very dangerous intrusion that had to be curtailed by escalating the violence to the point where innocent women, children, and the elderly were executed with extreme, and very public, violence. One event, using two separate cultural filters, can feed two dueling narratives. Violence, too, influences the narrative but in a different way. On American television we saw Iraqi military and Syrian civilians blown to bits or gassed, and we were as horrified as the narrator. On ISIS media, the same violent images were filtered through a different cultural lens, and insurgent sympathizers throughout the world agreed with the righteousness of the outcome. Conversely, when we see optical or infrared video feeds from fighter aircraft or aerial drones showing the destruction of enemy insurgents the reaction is not horror for those inside destroyed vehicles but our own brand of righteousness.

Often, tactical action viewed from the perspective of the narrative has outcomes at odds with a blitzkrieg-era perspective. For example, an infantry platoon may destroy a particularly troublesome enemy terrorist cell that is using a mosque as its base by calling for a precision bombing mission, then by delivering an assault to kill or capture those remaining alive inside. However, the narrative may turn against this tactical action when an enemy team arrives shortly after the assault to remove weapons and explosives and distribute bloody Korans to suggest that the target was actually young men at prayer. Of course, most of the population in the immediate vicinity of the attack would realize that the whole thing was a setup. They would also be perfectly glad that the enemy cell was gone. But the weight of evidence, when transmitted and interpreted through the cultural lens across the entire population, is not favorable in this instance to our version of the narrative.

Consideration of the narrative's influence must be the most important factor for determining whether or not the effort will succeed—or whether it should be conducted at all. How differently history would have played out if Lyndon B. Johnson and the Joint Chiefs had understood the impact of the global media's coverage of the Vietnam War on a Petraeus-like set of key audiences. General Westmoreland's early search-and-destroy strategy prior to the Tet Offensive was the proper course of action for destroying Viet Cong and North Vietnamese army main-force units efficiently and in large numbers. Yet, the psychological impact of our Soldiers burning villages created a "David and Goliath" perspective that made subsequent images of Tet all the more debilitating to the psyche of the American people. Media images can be just as important as traditional factors such as logistics, command and control, intelligence, fire, and maneuver. Most critical will be the enemy's psychological strength and his potential to adapt his narrative to overcome battlefield reverses.

Thus, today's challenge is to develop another generation of Soldiers equally skilled in the narrative arts. Skill at feeding the narrative is no longer a contributor to achieving strategic success in irregular war. It is in fact the principal determinant, the psychological center of gravity, for shaping the perceptions and influencing the will of the population. We must always remember that the narrative stream is neutral but that who occupies and exploits it is not. In the end, "ground truth" or actual battlefield conditions will prevail. In this new American era of warfare, the art of feeding the operational narrative requires skill at maneuvering across the expanse of human perception rather than an expanse of territory.

At present the enemy's ability to preempt and dominate the narrative seems to be ascendant. Petraeus once commented that while ISIS has far fewer social media outlets and less network sophistication than the West, it does have command of messaging. Its leaders are able to link religion and cultural bonds to their war aims. They understand Islamic youth and how to touch those most disaffected in the West. They shape the narrative based on the targeted audience: for Muslims in the West, a seductive and romantic view of an ISIS fighter's life on the front, the prospects of a willing mate, a good salary, and a fast track to Allah for those who die for the Prophet; for Muslims in the region, a celebration of the bloody, brutal, humiliating savagery against apostates beheaded or burned to death on video. Perhaps the greatest advantage ISIS possesses in controlling the narrative is their success on the battlefield. We learned long ago that it is very hard for the losing side to be convincing—and at this writing the Western coalition and the Iraqi government are perceived to be and are losing to ISIS. After more than a year of success, even the Obama State Department seems to have concluded that our ability to win the narrative (or, to use "State Speak," our "counter-messaging") is far inferior to the messaging of ISIS. They admit that ISIS is far more nimble in spreading its message than we are in blunting it.[2]

REMOVE HOPE, WIN THE NARRATIVE

Sadly, today Petraeus is seeing his brainchild, the 2007 "surge," go into reverse after Obama's precipitous withdrawal of U.S. troops in 2011. ISIS victories have also reversed the narrative; coming in second in the narrative can only lead to defeat. The question is: How to regain dominance in the narrative? The only sure way to turn the tide is to take the offensive and attack the ISIS narrative at its core, to convince the audience that ISIS is no longer winning. A sense of loss for such a fragile entity will inevitably erode the narrative and cause the believers to lose hope that ISIS will succeed.

Hope drives the narrative. Hope for the extremist comes from the belief that ISIS's harsh brand of theology and rabid ideology will prevail. Hope drives trying—or a "response initiation," in the psychologist's jargon. To the extent hope is present, a terrorist will translate belief into action. As hope is removed even the most ideologically attuned enemy will become passive and inert. Think for a moment of hope filling a fragile crucible; an ISIS defeat in Iraq and Syria cracks the crucible. The question is how to do it with enough drama and speed that terrorists all over the world lose hope and become passive. From any perspective, the ISIS enclave in Syria is militarily unassailable. Iraq, however, is a different story.

Arab cultures seem particularly vulnerable to the mercurial collapse of hope though decisive military action. The cosmic swings in hope among Arab Soldiers before and after defeats in Arab Israeli wars in 1948 and 1967 and our victory in the Gulf War against Saddam's army in 1991 are instructive. The apathy that followed Osama bin Laden's killing also suggests that hopelessness among terrorists can result from the death of a single terrorist icon. Think for a moment of hope as a crucible that is filled over the years by successful terrorist offensive action against the West and Western-affiliated countries in the Middle East. If hope fills the crucible through violent actions, then only a counter-violent, military response can crack the crucible and empty it of hope. The object of a campaign against hope is not necessarily to kill in large numbers but to find the most vulnerable piece of the crucible and break it dramatically, decisively . . . and quickly.

A campaign against hope, a war to regain the narrative, must start from Baghdad and move northward up the Tigris and Euphrates Rivers. The vulnerabilities for ISIS rest in the disconnectedness of its garrisons, spotted astride the rivers like a string of pearls. Thanks to recent U.S. bombing, ISIS cannot move between these enclaves. Thus a series of patient, sequential ground assaults against ISIS garrisons in cities like Taji, Hit, Tal Afar, and eventually Mosul will create momentum sufficient to push ISIS back to the Syrian border. These will not be victories so much as very public humiliations, the antidote to hope, signaling a decisive swing in the narrative that favors the legitimate government of Iraq.

Can the Iraqis do it? If so, can they do it soon, before ISIS solidifies its grip on the river cities? One thing is certain: the last best hope for an offensive outcome against the hopefulness of these killers rests with the Iraqi army and the Americans who are trying to turn them into a viable fighting force, or at least a force competent enough to turn the enemy's hubris into hopelessness. When hopelessness prevails, no slick, social media–driven narrative can prevail. If ISIS is perceived by their audience to be losing in its war against the infidel, the war of the narrative shifts to our side. Loss of hope leads to loss of fighting will; a will to win is the strongest weapon in the ISIS arsenal. Once will is eroded by a loss of confidence in the narrative message, its quest to establish a caliphate is doomed.

[10]

THE HUMAN DIMENSION

Courage is a moral quality; it is not a chance gift of nature like an aptitude for games. It is a cold choice between two alternatives, the fixed resolve not to quit; an act of renunciation which must be made not once but many times by the power of the will. Courage is willpower.
—Charles McMoran Wilson, 1st Baron Moran, *The Anatomy of Courage*

The essence of every profession is expressed in the writings of its unifying theorists: Freud for psychology, Adam Smith on economics, Justice Marshall on law, and—depending on one's political preferences—Marx or Jefferson on governance. War is no exception.

The nineteenth-century Prussian writer Carl von Clausewitz is still regarded as the master prophet, whose views on the character and nature of war have held up best over the past two centuries. Periodically, changes in the culture, technology, economics, or demographics induce movements to revise the classic masters. After the Great Depression, John Maynard Keynes amended Adam Smith, behavioralists supplanted Sigmund Freud, and John Marshall gave way to Oliver Holmes, who eventually surrendered to the revisionist doctrines of Hugo Black and Earl Warren. The profession of arms has been subject to intrusion by intellectual revisionists more frequently than any other profession, perhaps because armed conflict is the most complex, changeable, and unpredictable of all human endeavors. And history has shown, tragically, that failure to amend theories of conflict in time has had catastrophic consequences for the human race.

Changes in theories of war come most often during periods of historical discontinuity. Events after 9/11 offer clear evidence that we are in such a period now. Unfortunately, contemporary revisionists to Clausewitz have not been well treated in today's practical laboratory of real war. In the moment before 9/11, the great hope was that technology would permit the creation of new theories of war. This view, influenced by the historical successes of the United States in exploiting technology, has been carried to extremes by some proponents of "shock and awe," followed closely by such silly techno-concepts as "effects-based" and "net-centric" operations. Their true believers visualized a future in which sensors, computers, and telecommunications networks would "lift the fog of war." They postulated that victory would be ensured when admirals and generals could sit on lofty perches and use networks to see, sense, and kill anything that moved about the battlefield. Actions of the enemy in Iraq and Afghanistan have made these techno-warriors about as credible today as stock brokers after the Great Depression.

Theory abhors a vacuum as much as nature does, and so newer revisionists have popped up in profusion to fill the void left by the collapse of techno-centric theories of war. One philosophy proposes to build a new theory of war around organizational and bureaucratic efficiency. Build two armies, so the proponents argue, one to fight and the other to administer, and the new age of more flexible and adaptive military action will begin. Another group of theorists seeks to fit the facts of history into a pattern bringing us to a "fourth generation" of warfare, one that makes all of Clausewitzian theories of state-on-state warfare obsolete. Thus Western states are threatened by an amorphous, globally based insurgent movement. The inconvenience of Middle Eastern states collapsing and reforming in the midst of a state-dependent terrorist environment makes this fourth-generationalist assault on the master difficult to sustain, if not actually embarrassing.

To be generous, we can acknowledge that each of these revisions contains some elements of truth, but none satisfies sufficiently to give confidence that

Clausewitz can be amended, much less discarded. To be sure, networks and sensors are useful even against terrorists, particularly in ground warfare at the tactical level. Armies should be reorganized to fight irregular wars more efficiently. The influence of the state in irregular war must be revised to accommodate the realities of nonstate threats or, perhaps more accurately, not-yet-state threats; Osama bin Laden's first desire was for his own caliphate, or even emirate. But at the end of the day—and in light of the bitter experiences of recent years—it is clear that none of these rudimentary attempts at revision possess the intellectual heft or durability to challenge the tenets of the classic master of conflict theory.

THE AGE OF "AMPLIFIERS"

Enter Alan Beyerchen, distinguished historian at Ohio State University. He's adopted a fundamentally different approach and by doing so has captured the intellectual high ground in the battle to amend theory in light of modern war's realities: Beyerchen would embrace rather than replace the master. Beyerchen has developed a taxonomy of war in the modern era in terms of four world wars. Each war was shaped by what he calls "amplifying factors." Amplifiers are not "multipliers" or "enablers," in that their influence on the course of war is nonlinear rather than linear; amplifiers do not simply accelerate the trends of the past, they make war different.

For example, World War I was a chemists' war, in that the decisive strategic advantage on the battlefield was driven in large measure by new applications of chemistry and chemical engineering. The war should have ended for the Germans in 1915, when their supplies of gunpowder nitrates were exhausted, but the synthesis of nitrates by German scientists allowed the war to continue for another three horrific years. World War II was a physicists' war. To paraphrase Churchill, the atom bomb ended the conflict, but exploitation of the electromagnetic spectrum in the form of the wireless and radar won it for the Allies. "World War III" was the "information researchers'" war, a war in which intelligence and knowledge of the enemy and the ability to exploit fully that knowledge allowed the United States to defeat the Soviet Union with relatively small loss of life.

Most strikingly, Beyerchen places what is popularly known as "transformation" at the end rather than the beginning of an epoch in which the microchip accelerated the technology of the information age, but only after the culmination point of the information age had been reached and the war substantially won. In other words, the value of "net-centrism" as an amplifier—a factor that fundamentally shapes the nature of conflict—has passed; its formative influence on the course of war is over. ISIS and Al Qaeda's success in Iraq simply drives the last nail in its coffin.

Think of the shifts between world wars as tectonic, rather than volcanic, events. The physicists' war did not simply erupt to supplant the chemists' war. Their respective influences as amplifiers simply diminished over time. Amplifiers still retain influence: armies still use chemistry and physics (and most certainly networks) to gain advantage on the battlefield. The danger is that a military force will remain devoted to an amplifier long after it can no longer offer truly decisive returns. Thus by Beyerchen's logic, we may be spending trillions on old amplifiers—on better chemistry, better physics, and better information technologies—to gain only marginal improvements, a few additional knots of speed, bits of bandwidth, and centimeters of precision. In doing so, the question that arises is: Are we ignoring the amplifying factor that promises to be truly decisive, that might win World War IV at very little cost?

THE HUMAN BATTLEFIELD

In searching for this "emerging amplifier," Beyerchen returns to Clausewitz's basic insight: that war is influenced primarily by human beings rather than by technology or bureaucracy. The problem in the past has been that the human factor could never be a significant amplifier, simply because its influence was relatively fixed and very difficult to exploit. Humans have been considered constants more than variables. Yes, Soldiers could be made better through conditioning, selection, psychological tuning, and—since the last century—through education, but ultimately, the human factor has usually come down to numbers. Bigger battalions make better armies. Clausewitz did allow for the amplifying factor of genius in war—he fought repeatedly against Napoleon. However, he conceded that human frailties made the identification and nurturing of genius very problematical.

Beyerchen's idea is that the human and social sciences will change Clausewitz's perception of the constancy of the human influence in war. In effect, he argues that we are beginning the tectonic shift into World War IV, the epoch when the controlling amplifier will be human and behavioral rather than organizational or technological. From his theory we can postulate a new vision of the battlefield, one that shifts from the traditional "linear" construct to a battlefield that is amoebic in shape; it is distributed, dispersed, nonlinear, and essentially formless in space and unbounded in time. This war and all to follow will in fact be what I would call "psychocultural" wars.

Let us come down from the clouds a bit: experience in Iraq and Afghanistan has convinced many in the military intellectual community of the value of psychocultural factors in war, but the idea that these factors are now decisive, that indeed they constitute and dominate the battlefield, may be a tough sell. After all, U.S. forces have won three world wars through the efficient application of technology. We have grown generations of generals who have been taught and have learned by their own experience that victories come from building better things. Our fixation on technology—our very technological success—has led us to believe that the Soldier is a system and the enemy a target. Soldiers are now viewed, especially by the Defense Department, as an "overhead expense," not a source of investment. Viewing war too much as a contest of technologies, we have become impatient of and detached from those forms of war that do not fit our paradigms. Techno-centric solutions are in our "strategic cultural DNA."

WINNING WORLD WAR IV

Moreover, even if we were not burdened with the baggage of our past successes, trying to divine the depths of the coming human, biological, and behavioral era of war would be as problematical today as anticipating the arrival of the digital age was immediately after World War II. Wars, blessedly, are fought infrequently, and epoch-defining conflicts are even more rare. Our base of experience for anticipating future events is limited to experimenting in the laboratory of war; we discover that tectonic plates are moving only when we feel the ground shake. We can perhaps say that Korea and the 1979–89 Soviet War in Afghanistan are the alpha and omega of World War III, but we can only dimly begin to feel the plates of our new world war shifting, almost imperceptibly. So let us stipulate that Iraq and the present Afghan war are the beginnings of a new era, but let us also be extremely cautious not to forecast so energetically as to anticipate what these wars portend from the human and cultural perspectives. Let us not look for a level of precision or prediction that we cannot achieve and is likely to lead us astray.

Building on Beyerchen, here's what I anticipate current conflicts in the Middle East and elsewhere are telling us about what is to come. In a nutshell: World War IV will cause a shift in classical centers of gravity from the will of governments and armies to the perceptions of populations. Victory will be defined more in terms of capturing the psychocultural, rather than the geographical, high ground. Understanding and empathy will be important weapons of war. Soldier conduct will be as important as skill at arms. Culture awareness and the ability to build ties of trust will offer protection to our troops more effectively than body armor can. Leaders will seek wisdom and quick but reflective thinking rather than operational and planning skills as essential intellectual tools for future victories.

As in all past world wars, clashes of arms will occur, but future combat will be tactical, isolated, precise, most likely geographically remote, unexpected, and often terribly brutal and intimate. Strategic success will come not from grand, sweeping maneuvers but rather from a stacking of local successes the sum of which will be a shift in the perceptual advantage—the tactical *schwerpunkt,* the point of decision, will be very difficult to see and especially to predict. As seems to be happening in Iraq today, the enemy may as well own the psychocultural high ground and hold it effectively against U.S. technological dominance. Perceptions and trust are built among people, and people live on the ground. Thus ground forces—specifically the Army, Marine Corps, Special Forces, and the various reserve formations that support them—will decide the course of future wars.

Clausewitz tells us that the side that holds the initiative will ultimately prevail. In this new era, the initiative will be owned by the side that controls time. As Lt. Gen. David Barno, now retired, former commander of U.S. and coalition forces in Afghanistan, is fond of saying, "In Afghanistan, Americans have all the wristwatches but Afghans have all the time." The enemy will attempt to control the clock, with the strategic intent of winning by not losing. He will use the clock to wear down American resolve. Management of the clock will allow him to use patience as a means to offset U.S. superiority in killing power. His hope is to leverage our impatience so as to cause us to overreact with inappropriate use of physical violence. Perception control will be achieved and opinions shaped by the side that best exploits the global media, particularly social media. Also, there is another sense of the clock important to appreciate: we are in a race between the rogue states' or nonstate terrorists' acquiring and using nuclear weapons versus our acquiring and deploying enough psychocultural armament to beat them on the ground. Yet even without nukes, the enemy has a natural advantage. He presents a paradox that plays to his intrinsic strengths. You must support us, he tells the population, in spite of our brutality, or support the outsider who may be more humane but who is not part of our religion, culture, clan, tribe, or ethnicity. And, he can say, I will always be here; will the Americans?

THE ELEMENTS OF VICTORIES

How can we discover the path to victory in these future wars? Chemistry had little practical wartime utility when the irreducible elements of knowledge were earth, air, fire, and water. During World War I, chemists learned to analyze and design molecules for desired functions. Applications quickly emerged for explosives, propulsion, and poison gas. Only in the last few decades have the foundations of the social sciences advanced to the point that they might become the elements for victory. Until the military intellectual community acknowledges that virtually all failures in Afghanistan and Iraq were human rather than technological—perhaps still an open question—will the social sciences attract much interest as amplifiers? Can we yet say, after fourteen years of war, that we understand the enemy's culture and intent? The evidence thus far is that we have been intellectually, culturally, sociologically, and psychologically unprepared for this kind of war. To me, the bottom line is clear: if the single most important objective for the first three world wars was to make better machines, then surely the fourth-world-war corollary will be to make better Soldiers, more effective humans. To become so, Soldiers need improved social science in nine areas.

CULTURAL AWARENESS

In our Middle Eastern wars, a curtain of cultural ignorance continues to separate the good intentions of the U.S. Soldier from indigenous peoples of good will. Inability to speak the language and insensitivity in conduct become real combat vulnerabilities that the enemy has exploited to his advantage. The military of the future must be able to go to war with enough cultural knowledge to thrive in an alien environment. Empathy will become a weapon. Soldiers must gain the ability to move comfortably among alien cultures to establish trust and cement solid relationships that can be exploited in battle. Not all are fit for this kind of work. Some will remain committed to fighting the kinetic battle, but others will come to the task with intuitive "cultural court sense," an innate ability to connect with other cultures. These Soldiers must be identified and nurtured just as surely as the Army selects those with innate operational court sense.

Social science can help select, very early, Soldiers who possess the requisite social and cultural intelligence. Likewise, scientific psychology can assist in designing and running cultural immersion programs that will hasten the development of culturally adept Soldiers and intelligence agents. Cultural psychology can teach us to understand better both common elements of human culture and how they differ. An understanding of these commonalities and differences can help gain local allies, fracture enemy subgroups, avoid conflicts among allies, promote beneficial alliances, and undermine enemy alliances.

BUILDING ALIEN ARMIES AND ALLIANCES

World War IV will be manpower intensive. The United States cannot hope to field enough Soldiers to be effective wherever the enemy appears. Effective surrogates are needed to help us fight our wars. The Army has a long tradition of creating effective indigenous armies in such remote places as Greece, Korea, Vietnam, El Salvador, and Colombia, but almost without exception, the unique skills required to perform this very complex task have never been valued, and those who practice them are rarely rewarded. Today's Soldiers would prefer to be recognized as operators than as advisers. This must change. If our strategic success on a future battlefield will depend on our ability to create armies from whole cloth—or, as in Iraq, to remove an army that has been part of the problem and make it a part of the solution—then we must select, promote, and put into positions of authority those who know how to build armies. We must cultivate, amplify, research, and inculcate these skills in educational institutions reserved specifically for that purpose. We must also do this preemptively or prophylactically, by building the most suitable psychocultural infrastructures both in the theater of war and at home.

PERCEPTION SHAPING AS ART, NOT SCIENCE

People in many regions of the world hate us. They have been led to do so by enemies whose perception shaping is as brilliant as it is diabolical. If the center of gravity in World War IV is the perception of the people, then perhaps we should learn how the enemy manipulates the people; information technology will be of little use in this effort. Damage is only amplified when inappropriate, culturally insensitive, or false messages are sent, however sophisticated the information networks that carry them. Recent advances in the social psychology of leadership and persuasion can help train Soldiers to win acceptance of local populations and obtain better intelligence from them. Recent cognitive behavioral therapy has documented remarkably effective techniques for countering fear and abiding hatred such as we see in the Middle East; our challenge is to create a human science intended specifically for shaping opinions, particularly among alien peoples. This task is too large for a single service or even for the Department of Defense. It must be a national effort, superintended by distinguished academics and practitioners in the human sciences who understand such things, rather than by policy makers who have proven in Iraq that they do not.

INCULCATE KNOWLEDGE AND TEACH WISDOM

In our latest wars, junior Soldiers and Marines have been asked to make decisions that in previous wars were reserved for far more senior officers. A corporal standing guard in Kabul can commit an act that might well affect the strategic outcome of an entire campaign. Yet the intellectual preparation of these very junior leaders is no more advanced today than it was during World War III. Thankfully, the native creativity, innovativeness, and initiative exhibited by these very young men and women belie their woeful lack of psychosocial preparation.

Learning to deal with the human and cultural complexities of this era of war will take time. Leaders, intelligence officers, and Soldiers must be given the time to immerse themselves in alien cultures and reflect on their professions. Yet in our haste to put more Soldiers and Marines in the field, we risk breaking the very intellectual institutions that create opportunities to learn. Today, we are contracting out our need for wisdom by hiring civilians to teach in military schools and colleges. Educational science has long understood that reading and listening are the least effective means for retaining or increasing knowledge. Teaching is at least an order of magnitude more effective, while researching and writing are far better still.

TACTICAL INTELLIGENCE

The value of tactical intelligence—knowledge of the enemy's actions or intentions sufficiently precise and timely to kill him—has been demonstrated in hybrid wars. Killing power is of no use unless a Soldier on patrol knows whom to kill. We should extract from our combat experience a commitment to leverage human sciences to make the tactical view of the enemy clearer and more certain, to be able to differentiate between the innocents and the enemy by reading actions to discern intentions.

The essential tools necessary to make a Soldier a superb intelligence gatherer must be embedded in his brain rather than placed in his rucksack. He must be taught to perceive his surroundings in such a way that he can make immediate intuitive decisions about the intentions of those about him. His commanders must be taught to see the battlefield through the eyes of their Soldiers. The Soldier must make decisions based on the "gut feel" and developed intuition that comes from an intelligence gatherer's ability to see what others cannot. While profiling is abhorrent in civil society, it is essential for Soldiers. The intuitive ability to look into a village and pick out those most likely to do harm is a skill that can be sharpened by studying unique behaviors among alien cultures. There is a growing science of intuition and gut feeling, and these capabilities might be enhanced by this new capability and its allied technology. Machines and processes might make intelligence easier to parse and read, but knowing the enemy better than he knows us is inherently a psychocultural rather than a technological, organizational, or procedural challenge.

PSYCHOLOGICAL AND PHYSIOLOGICAL TUNING

Life sciences offer a promise that older, more mature Soldiers will be able to endure the physical stresses of close combat for longer periods. This is important, because experience strongly supports the conclusion that older men make better close-combat Soldiers; scientific research also suggests that social intelligence and diplomatic skills increase with age. Older Soldiers are more stable in crisis situations, are less likely to be killed or wounded, and are far more effective in performing the essential tasks that attend to close-in killing. Experience within special operations units also suggests that more mature Soldiers are better suited for fighting in complex human environments. Science can help determine when Soldiers are at their cognitive peaks. Psychological instruments are available today to increase endurance and sustained attention on the battlefield. Today, conditioning science has succeeded in keeping professional athletes competitive much longer than even a decade ago. These methods should be adapted to prepare ground Soldiers as well, for the physical and psychological stresses of close combat.

From another, more sinister perspective, we realize that too often individual bad Soldiers acting badly in a strategically visible fashion can cause perceptual damage that years and thousands of good Soldiers cannot undo. The horrible actions of a few Soldiers at Abu Ghraib prison in 2004 set back the American narrative for years. The shadow of their malfeasance is with us still and can be seen in terrorist videos and online chat rooms. Today, some technologies exist to find the sociopaths before they do such inestimable harm. We must make aggressive use of these tools to select them out of service and send them home.

LEADERSHIP

World War IV will demand intellectually ambidextrous leaders, people capable of facing a conventional enemy one moment, shifting to an irregular threat the next moment, and then transitioning to the task of providing humanitarian solace to the innocent. All of these missions may have to be performed by the same commander simultaneously. Developing leaders with such a varied menu of skills takes time. Unfortunately, World War IV will be long and will occupy ground leaders to the extent that time available to sharpen leadership skills will be at a premium.

There are precedents for developing these skills. In Vietnam, the air services developed "Top Gun" and "Red Flag" exercises as a means of improving the flying skills of new pilots bloodlessly before they faced real and skilled opponents. Recent advances in the science of intuitive decision making will give the ground services a similar ability to improve the close-combat decision-making skills of young leaders; senior commanders will be able to use these tools to select those leaders with the intuitive "right stuff." Over time, leaders will be able to measure and assess improvements in their subordinates' ability to make the right decisions in ever more complex and demanding combat situations. They will have access to coaches and mentors who will pass on newly learned experiences, with an exceptional degree of accountability and scientific precision.

INTUITIVE DECISION MAKING

The Army and Marine Corps learned in Afghanistan and Iraq that operational planning systems inherited from World War III would no longer work against an elusive and adaptive enemy. They were forced to improvise a new way of campaign planning that emphasized the human component in war. Gut feel and intuition replaced hierarchical, linear processes. They learned to command by discourse rather than formal orders. Information sharing became ubiquitous among even the most junior leaders, who were now able to communicate in real time with each other and with their seniors. Dedicated Soldier networks have fundamentally altered the relationship between leaders and have forever changed how the Army and Marine Corps command Soldiers in battle.

THE CRUCIBLE OF COURAGE

The lives of Soldiers in small units depend on the ability to fight and win in the close fight. Their fight is a very human one, a test of skill nurtured by personal, intimate gifts and the will to win. Long before Alan Beyerchen, the icon of the human and behavioral approach to World War IV was Lord Moran. Moran was a field surgeon in World War I, and in World War II he was Winston Churchill's personal physician. He authored the seminal work on Soldiers in battle: *The Anatomy of Courage*. Lord Moran was the first to explain the emotional side of intimate killing; he described a "crucible of courage" that every infantryman carries with him as he enters battle. The crucible is filled with courage, to be sure, but also "grit," or the substance that keeps a Soldier on task regardless of the hardships endured, as well as "resilience," different from grit in that resilience is an emotional antibody that delays or inhibits the onset of post-traumatic stress.

A Soldier's emotional crucible empties quickly in combat. The rate of discharge is driven by many causes other than fear: first among them of course is fatigue, but there are also hunger, thirst, palliation or combat isolation, and distrust of comrades and leaders. The crucible empties once the shooting starts. The courage remaining in a Soldier's crucible shifts the balance between the two forces that pull on him as he advances against the enemy: one is to do his duty and not let his buddies down. The other is more primal: it is simply to run away, an act that any normal civilian would understand. When the crucible empties, the Soldier's emotions fall flat, and he ceases to function.

Maybe the science of World War IV may help to slow or possibly even forestall the draining of a Soldier's emotional crucible. For a moment place yourself in a small unit, about to engage in the horrific experience of "in extremis" combat in World War IV. Imagine how the psychological, behavioral, and emotional strength of Soldiers in this moment might be amplified by better understanding of the human dynamics that make Soldiers and leaders into superbly competent small units. Then imagine how little investment in the human, cultural, behavioral, psychological, and physiological sciences would be needed to make close-combat Soldiers far better at the deadly chore of "intimate killing."

Soldiers must see and sense in such a way that there are no surprises. Every psychological advantage on the battlefield—courage, cohesion, audacity, and the ability to maneuver without caution or friction—is enhanced by knowledge of the enemy. In fact, experience in wars shows that the overwhelming reason why Soldiers dominate in the close fight is an ability to see the enemy while remaining unseen. We must exploit the human sciences to heighten a Soldier's ability to "see" the battlefield. Some Soldiers and leaders possess an intuitive ability to see the battlefield. Part of this skill, of course, comes from familiarity with physical surroundings. Others gain the advantage by exercising an extraordinary ability to "read" emotions of the indigenous population. Some can actually sense the presence of the enemy and "smell out" particularly dangerous situations. The sensing of these "native scouts" must be enhanced with onboard or remote electronic sensors to see well ahead, deeply beyond their immediate surroundings.

While in the close fight, Soldiers must possess the psychological hardness to maintain stability short of the emotional breaking point. War is a test of will. Even the best-trained small units break when stressed beyond their emotional breaking points. When a unit goes beyond this point, it can no longer remain cohesive and effective and must be removed from the battlefield to be rebuilt, physically and emotionally. The key to long-term fighting power is for commanders to anticipate breaking points in the heat of battle and remove units from direct combat immediately before they collapse.

Small units must possess "group resilience" in the face of sudden death. Resilience is a collective trait that defines the ability of a unit to "snap back" from emotional, psychological, or physical erosion after a close-combat engagement. This emotional elasticity is present in a unit that has a reserve of traits that make a unit able to be stretched and returned to full combat capability in a very short time. Physical fitness is key. So also is the ability of each Soldier and leader to "shake off" quickly the trauma of initial contact.

Once the shooting starts, the small unit must be able to degrade gracefully to maintain collective resolve. The ability to moderate the "rate" of emotional decline in combat is essential. Anecdotal evidence from previous close-combat engagements strongly suggests that the ability to flatten the sine curve of collective emotion in the close fight is a key component of staying effective and avoiding moral collapse throughout the engagement.

Small-unit leaders must possess "cognitive clarity." Seeing is not enough. Commanders must be able to deaden their emotional highs and lows, such that they retain the ability to make decisions intuitively with less than perfect information and often alone and under extreme stress. Cognitive clarity comes with the ability to trust emotion over reason, to develop a finely tuned ability to decide under pressure and ignore the caution that urges waiting for more information or wasting time with traditional decision-making processes.

Soldiers cannot lose the trust of their leaders. At the small-unit level, trust comes from confidence among Soldiers that a leader's decision-making skills will give them the greatest chance of surviving contact with the enemy. Thus a Soldier's trust at the small-unit level is less sensitive to other factors traditionally important at the operational or strategic level, such as intelligence or rank. Soldiers will always follow a leader who braves the crack of the first round and reacts in a manner that will get the mission done at the least cost in blood.

Soldiers must be able to "morally suppress" the fear of violent death. Those familiar with the dynamics of close combat will attest to the phenomenon of moral authority in the close fight. When units enter the deadly zone, both sides are usually aware of who will win. Past performance and reputation are powerful forces that often make one side assume a position of inferiority. Conversely, Soldiers who are confident in their abilities and the abilities of their buddies and leaders generally cannot be beaten. Suppressing an enemy's will to fight can be done only by achieving a long-term, sustained level of moral dominance through extraordinary battle skill and audacity demonstrated over time. Conversely, in today's networked environment, subject to exposure by the global media, a single incident of poor performance or substantial loss in a single engagement will have an inordinate effect on the performance of the entire ground effort.

Soldiers must be made comfortable with killing. Destroying a life is, thankfully, not a natural act. As we have seen in the alleged acts of a single rogue infantryman in Afghanistan, mindless killing is an act of psycho-pathological behavior and cannot be tolerated in combat. Thus an effective small unit must possess a delicate emotional balance between restraint and ultimate aggression in close combat. Most experienced combat veterans will testify that the hardest kill is always the first. More often than not, first kills have to be experienced against enemies to whom killing is an art, frequently practiced. Thus one of the most difficult leadership tasks in the human dimension is for a commander to inure his team emotionally to killing from the very beginning of an operation, with no psychological "workup."

Soldiers must be taught to lessen the fear of spatial and temporal isolation. The greatest single source of psychological friction on the battlefield is "palliation," or the fear of dying alone. Fear of violent death permeates a Soldier's being, and long isolation saps all of his senses. Palliation is reduced by constant reinforcement by leaders and by "touch" with a nearby buddy. As the fight begins, the noise and confusion of the close fight amplifies the need for reinforcement and "touch" at the very time when both are very difficult to achieve.

WINNING WORLD WAR IV

Cognitive sciences can be leveraged to enhance small-unit training in many ways, from speeding the acquisition and enhancing the retention of foreign languages to training Soldiers in command-decision simulators to sharpen the ability to make decisions in complex tactical situations. Cognitive sciences can be employed in the creation of highly efficient and flexible training programs that can respond to ever-changing problems. Models of human cognition can also be used to diagnose performance failures during simulated exercises. These measures can assist in training Soldiers to attend to hidden variables and to weigh and filter properly the many factors that determine optimal performance in complex decision-making tasks.

However, the social sciences can accelerate the process for building great small units only so much. The one ingredient necessary for creating a closely bonded unit is time. The aging of a good unit, like that of a good wine, cannot be hurried. Platoons need at least a year to develop full body and character. Since the pipeline will be so long and the probability of death so great, the ground services must create many more close-combat units than conventional logic would demand. The lesson from Iraq and Afghanistan is clear: in future wars, we can never have too many close-combat units.

As the Army and Marine Corps downsize in the years ahead, the number of close-combat Soldiers will certainly (and unfortunately) be reduced in proportion. Fourteen years of war have been the catalyst that accelerated the modernization of Soldiers' weapons and equipment. Now that peace is near and money grows short, matériel modernization will surely slow or even stop. After years of study, lecturing, and prodding, I believe now more than ever that the best investment we can make of our diminishing human and capital resources would be to leverage the human sciences—to improve the fighting power of close-combat Soldiers, to focus on what goes *in* the Soldier as much as on what goes *on* the Soldier.

[11]

INTENT AND INTUITION

I am not afraid of an army of lions led by a sheep; I am afraid of
an army of sheep led by a lion.
—Alexander the Great

Good Soldiers perform best under good leaders. The future combat environment, so challenging for Soldiers, will be even more stressful for those who command them. It is hard to imagine today how strange and fearsome this battlefield will appear to a young infantry leader. He may find himself and his unit transported literally overnight to a distant and inhospitable spot on the globe. Time from notification to deployment may be so short that the leader will have to do planning, rehearsals, and troop briefings while flying to the objective area. Once on the ground, he will find himself fighting an enemy who has been waiting for him, dug in, camouflaged, and arrayed for combat, hidden from the killing effects of airpower. The battlefield will be not only hostile and unfamiliar but empty as well. The leader may be located many miles from his higher headquarters, and his Soldiers will be out of sight and scattered in small groups over a vast area.

When close combat begins, this young man, perhaps only months out of college, will be expected to orchestrate a panoply of weapons and sensors in a very complex and ambiguous environment. He will have to maneuver his subordinate units to converge on the target at precisely the right time and place.

While the leader may have a sizable information advantage over the enemy, the rush of real-time information will force him to make life-or-death decisions within a decision cycle measured in minutes, if not seconds. The standards against which his performance will be measured will be high. The media will be everywhere on the battlefield, and he may well face the emotional trauma of seeing a video of his unit—and perhaps pictures of his dead Soldiers—on global social media immediately after the battle. This new "climate" of warfare will demand that a young maneuver leader learn and practice a different style of leadership—a style reserved in past wars for officers of much greater maturity and experience.

During the Civil War, many generals, Union generals in particular—Joseph Hooker, John Pope, Irwin McDowell, and most sadly, George B. McClellan— performed well at the division and corps levels but failed miserably when elevated to army command. Ironically, after failing as army commanders, many of them later redeemed themselves by returning to command at lower levels, performing well until war's end. One reason for this phenomenon was the geometry and dynamics of Civil War battlefields. An infantry corps stretched across a front of about a mile. A corps commander could quite literally see his unit from one end to the other. He was close enough to the action and had time enough during the battle to see the enemy's actions, make decisions, and order Soldiers about by direct contact in real time.

Earlier in the nineteenth century, the corps was the highest level of command to require the skills of a practical operator, a war-fighting "mechanic." A corps commander was able to see a problem develop and to dispatch Soldiers or artillery to solve it on the spot. At the army level of command, the dynamics of war were different. The army commander was much more distant from the battle and consequently had no ability to act immediately or to control Soldiers he could not see. The distance of the army commander from the action slowed responses to orders and created friction such that the commander was obliged to make decisions before the enemy's actions were observed.

Civil War army commanders were now suddenly required to exhibit a different set of skills. For the first time, they had to think in terms of time and command formations by inculcating their "intent" in the minds of subordinates with whom they could not communicate directly. Very few of the generals were able to make the transition from direct to indirect leadership, particularly in the heat of combat. Most were very talented men who simply were never given the time or opportunity to learn to lead indirectly. Some, like the two generals George Meade and Ambrose Burnside, found themselves forced to make the transition in the midst of battle. Gen. Robert E. Lee succeeded in part because, as military adviser to Jefferson Davis, he had been able to watch the war first-hand and to form his leadership style before he took command. Gen. Ulysses S. Grant was particularly fortunate to have the luck of learning his craft in the Western theater, where the press and the politicians were more distant; their absence allowed him more time to learn from his mistakes. From the battle of Shiloh to that of Vicksburg, Grant was largely left alone to learn the art of indirect leadership through trial and error and periodic failure without getting fired for his mistakes.

The implications of this phase of military history for the future development of close-combat leaders are at once simple, stark, and self-evident. As the battlefield of the future expands and battle becomes more chaotic, complex, and inhospitable, the line that divides the indirect leader from the direct leader will continue to shift to lower levels of command. The circumstances of future wars will demand that much younger and less experienced officers be able to practice indirect command and leadership by intent. The space that held 2 Civil War armies of 200,000 men at Gettysburg in 1863 would have been controlled by a reinforced mechanized battalion of about 1,000 Soldiers in Desert Storm, and in remote Afghan provinces maybe by only a company or platoon, fewer than 100 Soldiers. This means that younger commanders will have to command Soldiers they cannot see and make decisions without the senior leader's hand directly on their shoulders. Distances between all the elements that provide support, such as artillery, aircraft, and supplies, will demand that young commanders develop the skill to anticipate and think in time. Tomorrow's tacticians will have to think at the operational level of war. They will have to make the transition from "doers" to thinkers, from commanders who react to what they see to leaders who anticipate what they will see.

To do all this to the exacting standards imposed by future wars, new leaders must learn the art of commanding by intent very early in their stewardship. The concept of "intent" forms the very essence of decentralized, indirect command. A senior commander must be assured that, in his absence, subordinates will make decisions he would make were he on the spot; inculcating the commander's intent involves more than giving and receiving orders. If they are to act in concert and to adhere to the will of the senior commander, subordinates must understand the commander's bias, his personality, and how he thinks. They must be able to understand intuitively how an operation will be executed. There must exist between seniors and subordinates such a bond of trust and mutual understanding that detailed conversations are not necessary. Actions need to become instinctive and follow a general line of direction rather than a narrow path. In the heat of combat, the situation will change so fast that assumptions that prompted an order hours before might no longer be valid. A commander will know he has been successful when subordinates believe they are free to selectively disobey.

The Army and Marine Corps must begin very early to find and prepare the young leaders who exhibit the ability to command by intent and move them very quickly along the track to higher command. Time is short; the brigade commander of 2030 was commissioned two years ago. The process can be made very selective without harming the readiness of close-combat units, because the Army needs relatively few with the special talents—the "right stuff"—of close-combat command. In a U.S. Army the size of today's, perhaps no more than two hundred will be needed to lead at battalion level and above.

The immediate challenge will be to identify those characteristics that will provide the highest probability that leaders chosen will be up to the task. The measured judgment of superiors is useful but no longer enough. Initial selection for command must not be left solely to chance or to the subjective opinions of senior officers—or even, for that matter, to the individual desires of the aspiring close-combat officer. The system of command selection must reinforce subjective observations with the addition of more objective factors. The first essential ingredients are intelligence and the ability to apply the gifts of intellect to achieving success in war. Actual experience in past wars suggests that the candidates most likely to succeed at the art of indirect command will be officers who are intelligent, self-confident, self-reliant, and comfortable with uncertainty and ambiguity. Given enough time and patience, those less gifted can be trained to perform in a predictable fashion when exposed to familiar circumstances, but only those who are highly intelligent and well educated can be relied upon to demonstrate consistently the creativity and the capacity to act, or the independence of thought essential to acting, under pressure in the presence of uncertainty and ambiguity.

While the relationship between intelligence and performance is a tenuous one to prove empirically, no one would deny that smart officers tend not to get their Soldiers killed. Yet at a time when intellectual credentialing has become essential for professional certification within the teaching, legal, and medical professions, the U.S. Army remains one of the few major military organizations in the world that does not require accountability in the form of certifying examinations. Officer education has been a subject of endless debate and deserves a volume of its own. To be sure, U.S. Army officers today devote a significant portion of their time in service to schooling, but the schools lack both rigor and accountability. School attendance should not be the principal means for measuring the quality of an officer's intellect. The brightest can best be identified and nurtured by being given a first-class education, honed continuously through a lifetime of learning and assessed periodically by rigorous, objective examinations that measure their knowledge of the art and science of war and their ability to think clearly under the stress of combat.

Intelligence cannot be the sole factor used to select the best and the brightest. Military history is replete with examples of intellectually gifted officers who simply lacked the other attributes necessary to be successful in combat command—such as courage, integrity, charisma, or (rarest of all) the ability to sense terrain and anticipate intuitively the pace and tempo of battle. The Special Forces method of screening candidates using physically and emotionally rigorous selection programs could be adapted as a general means for identifying those who possess these special attributes. Such a system would go a long way toward eliminating subjectivity and bias from the selection process. Rejection rates would most certainly be high, and it is probable that those who did "survive" the process would not meet today's accepted profile of a model combat-arms officer.

Breaking the cultural mold in order to select officers with just the right qualifications and credentials to lead by intent will require a significant change in U.S. Army "culture." Experience with the quality of close-combat officers in previous wars tells us that past practices have allowed too many unsuitable officers to assume command in combat. Often, the inadequacies of these commanders have become evident only when they had failed in actual battle. The ground services can no longer afford the luxury of shedding Soldiers' blood to find the right man for the job. What is now required is capacity for intuitive battle command. Command in combat is not only demanding and at times dangerous; it can be lonely as well.[1] Commanders are expected to maintain distance from their subordinates. Yet a glance at the lives of great commanders suggests that most of them established a relationship with a peer—with someone whose opinions and counsel they knew to be genuine and not self-serving. Global social media would allow field commanders to establish long-term and continuous working relationships with senior mentors, perhaps retired senior officers whom they could consult before making key operational decisions. A mentor located far from the terror, confusion, and discomfort of the battlefield, with access to all the analytical tools, records, and lessons learned—and perhaps linked via the Soldier's cell-phone network with a larger colloquium of peers possessing expertise in various aspects of the operational environment—might be able to add calm wisdom and secure counsel at the time when a commander in combat needs it most.

The argument for keeping small units together for long periods applies even more strongly to command teams and operational staffs. In the past, certain successful command relationships were so close that military historians have indicated the bonding by hyphens. The Lee-Jackson, Grant-Sherman, and Hindenberg-Ludendorf phenomena, for example, illustrate the synergy gained when understanding and communication between commander and principal deputy are in perfect alignment. Science and service personnel systems simply cannot anticipate such effective personal combinations; when they do emerge and prove themselves in battle, however, they should be recognized at the earliest possible command level and respected and utilized as the particular team rises in rank and authority.

The combat experience of Special Forces operators suggests that there is a "sweet spot" in age when indirect leaders, both enlisted and officer, are at their best. It begins at about twenty-eight, when the prefrontal cortex (which regulates judgment in the brain) is fully developed, and ends at about forty, when physical and emotional resilience for this type of work begins to fade. Perhaps the idea of a brigade commander leading a major operation in his or her thirties might be offensive to today's generation of generals, but the science is solid. Gifted, creative, and physically driven leaders fit into this very limited time box: war, like, for that matter, virtually every creative enterprise, is the preserve of the young. Albert Einstein and Isaac Newton were in their twenties when each changed the nature of physics. Alexander was of a similar age when he conquered the known world. Napoleon was a postadolescent artillery captain when he destroyed the defenses of Toulon.

The popular science-fiction book *Ender's Game,* written by Orson Scott Card in 1984, gets to the issue of intuitive, indirect command and youth. In the book, the leaders of the International Fleet, facing a world-ending threat, devise a unique method for selecting a very special leader possessed of a futuristic version of the "right stuff." The leader is a young boy, Ender Wiggin, who becomes such a gifted intuitive warrior that he saves the universe.

Ender is truly a metaphor for a leader many of us have sought to create for many decades. A small-unit tactical leader like Ender leads by intuition. Only recently have the physical sciences discovered that intuitive leadership is real. Professor Gary Klein's now-iconic book *Sources of Power* was the first to profess that intuition, or "gut feel," was a motive force in decision making. Klein discovered that intuition is just as legitimate as more deliberate decision making by business and military leaders. Klein went so far as to contend that many leaders who say they properly follow a decision cycle actually ignore it and decide what to do based on gut feel alone . . . and that many of them were quite successful. Col. Tom Kolditz, head of the Behavioral Science and Leadership Department at West Point, followed Klein's research closely. After five years of studying the wars in Iraq and Afghanistan, Kolditz concluded that "we have been intellectually, culturally, sociologically, and psychologically unprepared" for the kind of war we face today. "Now we must commit resources to improve how the military thinks and acts in an effort to create a parallel transformational universe based on cognition and cultural awareness."[2]

Kolditz postulated that perhaps Klein's theories of intuitive decision making might be preferable to the Army's "Military Decision Making Process," left over from World War II. He interviewed firefighters and policemen after they had experienced traumatic situations. Almost inevitably, when asked about "what just happened," they would answer Kolditz with blank stares. After some prodding the leaders would say words to the effect of "I followed my instincts," or "I followed my gut feelings," all signs that Klein's theories about intuitive decision making might be useful for combat leaders as well as firemen and police.

Kolditz theorized that good sergeants and lieutenants had been making themselves into Enders for some time. The process usually began with the rip of a machine gun in an ambush or the explosion of an IED within a convoy; everyone goes to ground and searches for the leader. The leader has only seconds to react before being overrun. He begins to shout orders: set up a base of fire, charge through the beaten zone, assault the enemy under covering fire. He turns to his artillery forward observer and orders supporting fires. He looks around to take a mental head count to see who's dead, wounded, or too shocked to continue. He reports his status to higher authorities and repeats the process all over again.

Klein and Kolditz saw actions like these as part of a legitimate process that could be sharpened with research and further study. They believed that intuition and gut feel were the true ingredients of Soldier proficiency in the heat of battle. They concluded from their studies that indeed there are actually two types of decision makers: those who follow a process and those who could instantly recognize stored mental patterns, sort through them in milliseconds, and select the one that seems to fit best the situation at hand.

In 2007 Professor Martin Seligman of the University of Pennsylvania, the founder of the study of positive leadership, parsed Kolditz's and Klein's data to develop a series of regression equations in an effort to find those few people with the innate ability to think intuitively. The results were nothing short of amazing. These equations predicted success to a "fair degree of certainty" in finding those with innate intuitive abilities. In fact, Marty gave it a name, "Eagles and Turkeys," referring, respectively, to those who can think intuitively under pressure and those who can only devise and follow a plan.

Enders, Vikings (recalling my savior in Vietnam), and Eagles, whatever you want to call them, have that special quality, the "right stuff." Of course Soldiers in battle know who the turkeys are and usually find ways to avoid them when the shooting starts. Gen. Jim Mattis told me of an incident during the Fallujah battle, when he came across several squads whose assigned squad leaders, staff sergeants, were missing. When he demanded the leaders' presence a young post-adolescent, usually a steely-eyed lance corporal, would talk for the squad. "Sir, the chief is . . . [fill in the blank: going back for mail, reporting to platoon headquarters, getting ammo]." Mattis got the point and remarked to me after the battle that the one thing that makes U.S. close-combat forces so great in battle is their ability to suborn the chain of command on occasion in order to give authority to the eagles as soon as the first shot is fired. Soldiers and Marines want to live, so they instinctively turn to the ones they have known all along would keep them alive. Mattis asked me one night in his office if he could "bottle this." Well, maybe we can.

It would not be easy. For a time, I and a few of my colleagues, like retired colonel Jack Pryor, became consultants to the Marine Corps and oversaw a research and testing regimen in the human and cognitive sciences with the objective to reshape the Marine Corps learning environment for small units by exploiting the work of Klein, Seligman, and Kolditz. Mattis and I hoped that once he took over Joint Forces Command, we could turn selection and training for intuitive leaders into a national-level enterprise. We envisioned virtual immersions, small-unit "Top Gun" exercises that would find the turkeys and eliminate them before they got Marines killed. We would change the world and save thousands of young lives.

Of course, as they have with so many Soldier-focused ideas, the bureaucracy, politicians, bean counters, lawyers, and media killed our effort. To their credit, the Marines under General Mattis applied the human sciences as much as they could. They built a virtual tactical-engagement environment (a primitive virtual, instrumented shoot house) in an abandoned tomato factory at Camp Pendleton, California. They established very rigorous human-science laboratories to exploit Kolditz's, Klein's, and Seligman's cutting-edge human-science work. Sadly, it was all too little, too late. The Army was not interested at the time. Without the Army's fiscal heft, none of these amazing projects would go anywhere.

To this day, General Mattis and I still contend that "exquisite preparation and selection" of a very few men and women of superb intelligence, courage, and imagination would make them virtually undefeatable against even the most diabolical, distant, and well prepared enemy. Creating Enders and Vikings cannot become a growth industry unless the Army is convinced of its efficacy. So far, it has been a hard sell. By 2020, the Army will have gone down to only 32 close-combat brigades, each of about 3,000 Soldiers. To make the most of these very few, the Army should develop its own version of *Ender's Game*. The Army would need to select no more than about 2,000 Enders as tactical small-unit leaders and no more than about 350 Viking clones as future company commanders. To make future Enders, close-combat sergeants and lieutenants would be immersed in the tenets of intuitive leadership and sent through a virtual Top

Gun school before leading squads and platoons. More senior officers would be educated at America's most prestigious graduate schools and spend virtually all of the rest of their professional lives competing to be among the thirty-two colonels chosen to command combat brigades. They would stay in command for as long as they remain at the "Ender" or "Viking" level. Eventually, like the Heisman Trophy quarterback who begins to miss passes and throw more interceptions than touchdowns, these great commanders would go on to positions of greater strategic responsibility but would never command close-combat Soldiers again.

Thirty-two brigades, that's it. Thanks to the parsimony of the Congress and the strategic ignorance of the administration, the thirty-two brigades of brothers and sisters is the only force available to the world's only true superpower to maintain dominance in the American era for perhaps generations to come. To be sure, thirty-two is not enough. If we are to win in future wars, we must demand that this very thin red line be winnowed from a very large bench, that it mercilessly hold accountable those who make the cut. We must create a body of officers who lead and follow by intent, who fight with intuition, who can "see" the battlefield before battle begins, and who can operate alone without equivocation or uncertainty. All the ground services, particularly the Army, must be willing to spend whatever is necessary to make them Enders and Vikings, not McClellans.

[12]

TOUCH

Wars may be fought with weapons but they are won by men.
—Gen. George S. Patton Jr.

Fear grips every Soldier's heart as he closes on the enemy. Once bullets start whacking over his head, he is pulled by two opposing psychological forces. One is fear of violent death and the prospect of dying alone; psychologists call this phenomenon "palliation." The other is the imperative for a Soldier to follow orders, advance, and not let his buddies down. A Soldier chooses the latter when he has confidence in his leaders and when he is in touch with those around him. A Soldier chooses the former when his sense of isolation and detachment forces him to go to ground and huddle in fear.

This "touch" phenomenon, or the sense of a trusted buddy nearby, is the key psychological accelerant that induces a small unit to advance against the enemy. History is replete with examples. No sooner had Soldiers crossed the bloody Norman beaches than they ran into Germans defending behind "hedgerows." These were thick, impenetrable lines of hedges, some higher than a tank. The Normans had lined their square farming plots with hedges on all sides. The effect of fighting in hedgerows was horrific. Outside, waiting to attack, every Soldier experienced extreme sound deadening. Once he advanced inside these hedgerow "boxes," he found himself in a maddening acoustical sound chamber, with the horrific staccato of machine-gun fire and the shouts of wounded men resounding all around and amplified many times.

The defending Germans dug in behind these dense walls of foliage and punched holes through them to create protected fields of fire, from one hedgerow to the next. U.S. Soldiers had been trained to listen for orders from their leaders, scan to the next hedgerow, and shoot any German who showed his head. The Germans had developed other habits after four years on the Eastern Front. As soon as a lookout spotted the Americans, the Germans began ripping the opposite hedgerows with a steady fusillade of machine-gun fire. To senior U.S. commanders, the German pattern of fire was indiscriminate and seemingly wasteful for an army so short of ammunition. The Germans' intent was not to hit anything but to make noise and intimidate by fire. In the dark, they talked and shouted incessantly, oblivious of the stunned Americans only a few yards away. Sometimes they whistled and sang to each other. Of course, later in the Normandy campaign the U.S. command came to realize that the German actions made sense. Their boisterous antics were simply a means for keeping in touch in the dark. Their "team chatter" dispelled their own personal anxiety and struck fear into the U.S. infantry, who hugged the dirt and huddled silently in the open looking for targets they could not see and listening silently for orders from sergeants who were probably already dead.

A Soldier's greatest fear is to die alone, separated from his comrades. The sound of his comrade's voice steels him and gives him assurance that his buddies—although they cannot be seen in the darkness—are only an elbow's length away. The Germans later testified that the sound of comrades sustained them more than the sound of their weapons. We should take a page from the Wehrmacht. Experience in recent wars tells us that Soldiers are far more effective if they can maintain voice and visual contact with their buddies. In fact, research done by the Army after World War II and Korea strongly suggests that "palliation" is a far greater inhibitor to unit cohesion and effectiveness than casualties, lack of leadership, fatigue, hunger, or thirst. These studies showed that Soldiers were more likely to break contact and run when they lost contact with their leaders in the close fight or when they witnessed a key leader running to the rear, even if his purpose was merely to reposition to better observe the enemy. Isolation, loss of "touch," and ignorance of surroundings causes Soldiers to falter and lose the will to fight on.

In Afghanistan, narrow streets and dark alleys have replaced hedgerows but the need for Soldiers to maintain contact with their buddies and immediate leaders has not changed. Telecommunications technology has advanced far enough to enable every Soldier to "see" and "talk" to everyone in his squad using an individual audio and video connection. Yet for reasons that only the vagaries of the Army's acquisition system can explain after fourteen years of war, too many Soldiers in Afghanistan still must rely on hand and arm signals to maintain small-unit cohesion in the close fight . . . just like their great grandfathers did in the Norman hedgerows.

The incongruity of a Soldier's forced digital isolation is all the more difficult to understand given the fact that today's Soldiers have been literally raised with texting and with cell phones at their ears. They go from giving and sending thousands of tweets and texts a day to total isolation in the most dangerous place on the planet . . . the battlefield, a place where a Soldier is in most need of human contact. There is simply no excuse for the members of the world's best ground force's not having the same digital devices to maintain intimate contact with their buddies that they left behind in high school.

Part of the problem with Soldier "touch" is that the military is wired from top down and not bottom up; for most of our fighting force, this is a good thing. Think of it this way: the Navy moves in tens. When the conning officer on the bridge says "Hard right rudder!" everyone turns right—heroes, cowards, and everything in between. Sailors are all quite literally in the same boat. Therefore, a pyramidal telecommunications system works best for the sea services. All information travels from below to the bridge, and commanders at the top make all the decisions.

Air forces move in hundreds. While the air services are manned by hundreds of thousands of dedicated young men and women, the fighting, killing and dying is done by a select few who require years and millions of dollars to train. Pilots operate in an uncluttered environment: radar beams follow them and aerial "touch" is just a radio button away. So when a strike group streaks toward the target, the generals on the ground are able to follow the action with a unity of effort, a level of control, and visibility that is virtually absolute.

Soldiers and Marines are, of course, different. They move by the hundreds of thousands, like ungimbaled gyros, crashing across a landscape that is cluttered, often unmarked and filled with terror and dread. Every Soldier is different. The heroes move forward under fire, and the cowards, well, cower and lag behind, and every shade of character in between operates according to their inner compasses. Even with today's global positioning systems and enormously complex telecommunications, often the generals are out of touch with combat forces in contact with the enemy. More often than not, land battle is a test of the leadership of small-unit leaders: the sergeants and lieutenants, out of touch with the generals, who have to push, cajole, and lead their charges from the front. Thus, a ground communications system friendly to Soldiers would connect buddies to each other and to the outside world.

The problem is that most of the communications executives within the Department of Defense have been raised to feed the top, not expand or enrich the information moving about the bottom. Sadly, the military's version of information-technology executives have learned from experience to please the bosses first, to make sure the admiral on the bridge knows all. So how can we provide our Soldiers in combat with the "touch" they so desperately need? Short answer: look at communications from the bottom up . . . not the top down. In other words, reverse the traditional communications pyramid.

In his remarks to Captain Swenson during Swenson's Medal of Honor ceremony in the White House, President Obama noted that the helmet-cam video taken of Swenson carrying his wounded comrade to the medevac helicopter was the first to record a Medal of Honor recipient in action. Did you happen to notice in the video the bulky radio stuffed in Swenson's backpack? This battle was fought in 2009, when ragpickers in Mumbai had cell phones. Why can't our fighting men and women have cell phones in combat? Swenson's remarkable helmet cam was like a military version of commercial "GoPro" cameras we see mounted on scuba divers, cliff jumpers, and police patrolmen.

Radios are cheap. Virtually every cop on the beat has a handheld "brick" to keep in touch with his partner. Cameras are cheap. After the Ferguson and Baltimore riots in 2015, many state and local police began to attach them to officers on the beat. Soldiers should be similarly equipped. Every member of a squad should possess a communications device (think of a Soldier's cell phone with camera and Internet connectivity) sophisticated enough to allow every Soldier to remain connected to every other Soldier in his squad. If possible, the device should provide data as well as voice. Likewise, small-unit leaders at squad level should be able to "see" their Soldiers, in some virtual sense. Individual video monitors attached to every Soldier might be scooped up by a leader's cell phone to bring him audio, video, and GPS linkage, which, collected and fused, would tell the leader where every Soldier in his squad is.

GoPro-like cameras embedded on a Soldier's rifle or machine gun could be linked to a higher-level commander to assist him in determining whether the target is enemy or an innocent. Data collected from hundreds of small arms would offer a mosaic of the battlefield that would give intelligence officers a real-time view of the action. This micro view would then be fused with images from drones and other viewing sources to paint a panorama of a huge expanse of battlefield, a view that would come close to a leader's dream of finding "ground truth" in an unambiguous and intimate fashion.

Recall that loss of touch among Soldiers in the close fight often results in a paralytic impulse to go to ground, paralyzed by fear and isolation. Modern sports psychologists have found that athletes give off physiological "markers" that if properly measured can tell precisely their physical and psychological state when running or playing on the field. This same technology can be applied to monitor a Soldier's emotional state and provide a commander with the opportunity to intervene before palliation sets in.

To explain the consequences of such a capability, let us look inside the dynamics of a small unit in extremis (at the point of death). Units in combat break first psychologically, often long before they break physically. Army manuals suggest that units are no longer combat-effective after suffering 30 percent casualties. But elite German units on the Eastern Front kept together and fought ferociously with fewer than 10 percent effectives remaining in the fight. The same resilience was apparent among elite U.S. units, such as the Airborne and Ranger units in Normandy.

These units avoided palliation because—through superior training and selection, as well as superb leadership—they avoided or forestalled what Soldiers call "the tactical culminating point." This point occurs when a unit can go no farther. The unit quite literally runs out of momentum and freezes on the battlefield. Once culmination occurs, that unit can no longer fight as a cohesive entity and must be removed from combat. Most such units cannot return until complete refurbishment in the rear, a process that often takes weeks or months. Some units have become so badly spent emotionally that they had to be disbanded completely.

What if commanders could track palliation? What if every commander in contact had in front of him a small iPad-sized "emotional dashboard" that collected the psychological condition of every Soldier in the fight? These "combat polygraphs" would help a leader decide which of his Soldiers was best prepared emotionally to perform a specific combat task. Collective data would tell higher commanders when a small unit had reached its emotional, physical, or psychological point of exhaustion. The dashboard might transmit such easily measured indicators as heart rate, respiration, and galvanic skin response (or body sweat). What if every Soldier's helmet contained a field MRI that tracked critical functions in certain parts of the brain, like fear response, visual acuity, and emotional exhaustion?

Think for a moment of a company commander who watches his battle unfold and sees the emotional indicators begin to reach culmination. Perhaps he could send in the reserve, slow the momentum, or call in heavier supporting fires to slow down the group palliation. Think of how many lives would be saved and how much more effective tactical combat would be in U.S. small units. None of this is science fiction.

Cell phones are ubiquitous. Every teenager has one and uses it insatiably. The Army could just as easily buy and employ cell phones and other personal devices, much like most teenagers do . . . as throwaway devices. A multi-billion-dollar contract would pay for replacements as new technologies or more current "apps" become available. Like many commercial varieties, Soldier cell phones would have a kill switch so that the enemy would not be able to use the data. It would use commercial encryption like any other advanced cell phone. Such a solution would take the National Security Agency (NSA) out of the development of Soldier technology and save years and billions in development. A cell-phone camera linked to a body and weapon camera would cost less than a hundred dollars. Images fused from every Soldier device on the battlefield would give higher-level commanders a view of the real battlefield, instantaneously and from a perspective previously unknown in battle.

A local military social network could be established immediately on arrival in the combat zone by using drones as virtual "cell towers." An ad hoc network over the battlefield would tie together all of the information-gathering systems and link them to external sources of information, giving the commander and his staff as clear a picture of the battle as possible, and in real time. Every Soldier would be linked to his commander as part of the network. The lowest-ranking infantryman on patrol would have much the same access to combat "WiFi" as higher commanders. He will be able to "listen in" as his chain of command makes decisions. He will know his commander's thought processes, the various tactical options discussed, and the intelligence and operational "big picture" long before his unit receives explicit orders. From such an intimate connection, he will understand the "why" of the mission as well as the "how." A Soldier's cell phone will tell him exactly where each of his buddies is. He will sustain his moral strength by constant "team chatter" with his buddies. Should the Soldier get wounded, his cell phone would "read" his condition and automatically send it and his location to nearby medics. Likewise, a Soldier cell phone could tell a medic not to bother, that the Soldier's vital signs had suddenly ended.

We live in a world with six billion cell phones, but our Soldiers still do not have them. It is inexplicable that after fourteen years of war and two decades into the social media generation, a Soldier cannot e-mail, tweet, or text a comrade at a time when "touch" is vital to the Soldier's very existence. Soldiers are denied proper "touch" for two reasons. First, sadly, senior combat commanders do not want their Soldiers talking. One combat-experienced colonel was horrified when I suggested the Soldier cell phone. "My God, sir," he replied, "what if they're listening to me? What if they're talking about me?"

"Well, maybe the fact that you're afraid of your Soldier's chatter should tell you something about the quality of your leadership," I replied.

The second impediment to issuing Soldiers a cell phone is the military's communications and security bureaucracies. Remember, those civilians, the G-6 or C4ISR (command, control, computers, communications, intelligence, surveillance, reconnaissance) executives are officials who made their ranks by making their bosses happy. They were the ones who made sure the admiral in the command center and the general in his headquarters could talk to everyone below him. They were never rewarded for making sure Soldiers in combat could talk to their buddies. So it is no wonder the military information-technology community is willing to waste more than ten billion on JITRS, the Joint Integrated Tactical Radio System, which, sadly, never worked and was never fielded. A cell phone today costs about a hundred bucks.

Another bureaucracy that impedes Soldier communications is the communications security services like NSA, where security concerns often approach levels of paranoia, such that they would rather deny a Soldier his cell phone than take the chance that an alien power could listen in. Of course, at the tactical level a Soldier can get by with only primitive encoding software, because his conversations are, well, tactical and useful to an enemy for only a few moments. Instead, the bureaucrats will not allow a Soldier to talk until his level of security is at least as high as the president's.

The bottom line is that while our policy makers, scientists, and defense bureaucrats profess that their purpose in life is to support the "war fighter," the truth of that profession is dependent on who they consider the war fighter to be: if it is an admiral or general, the sentiment is perfectly correct. If it is some poor Soldier facing intimate death, contemporary evidence suggests that they do not care.

[13]

RIPLEY'S GHOST

Want to know what's good enough for our Soldiers? I'll tell you.
The best, that's what's good enough.
—Lt. Gen. David Grange, USA (Ret.)

Abraham Lincoln knew he was a politician, not a Soldier. Yet he often possessed wisdom and instincts for war that escaped his military advisers and commanders. Intuitively he knew that the Civil War would be won or lost on the battlefield. It was his duty to ensure that the huge industrial advantage of the North would be translated into decisive advantage, as two great masses of armed men met in mortal combat.

Lincoln was too close to history to understand that the Civil War was fought at the cusp of the first "precision revolution" in warfare, a period that combined industrialization with gun technology. Within three decades the invention of smokeless powder, the repeating rifle, and the machine gun would amplify the precision, range, and rate of fire of military small arms by three orders of magnitude. Nevertheless, he sensed that new "repeating" rifle designs would give Union Soldiers a tenfold advantage in the close fight. These rifles could also be loaded and fired from the prone, thus presenting a very small target to the enemy.

One afternoon just a month and a half after the battle of Gettysburg, Christopher Spencer, the creator of a seven-shot repeating rifle, walked Abraham Lincoln out to a grassy field near where the Washington Monument now stands in order to demonstrate the amazing potential of his new gun. Lincoln had heard about the mystical powers of repeating rifles at Gettysburg and other battles where some Union troops already had them. He wanted to test them for the rest of his Soldiers. The president quickly put seven rounds inside a small target forty yards away. He was sold.

The dynamic and indomitable Gen. John Buford commanded the Union cavalry at Gettysburg. His men had been armed with the new Sharps repeater. On the morning of the first day, Buford's thin line of troopers had lain on their bellies under cover behind McPherson's Ridge and opened a rapid fusillade on the advancing Confederates, holding them off for three hours until infantry reinforcements arrived. Buford's repeaters might well have decided the day and perhaps even the battle. On the second day of battle the Berdan Rifles, a small regiment of carefully selected and trained "sharpshooters" armed with the Sharps long-barrel repeating rifle, caused enormous damage to Gen. James Longstreet's advance against Little Round Top.

To Army bureaucrats, repeaters were an expensive, ammunition-wasting nuisance. Ignorant, unimaginative, vain, and disloyal to the point of criminality, the Army's chief of ordnance, Gen. James Wolfe Ripley, refused to equip Union infantry with repeating rifles at a time when the Confederacy was getting them in large numbers from Europe. The Civil War historian Robert V. Bruce has speculated that, had such rifles been widely distributed to the Union army by 1862, the Civil War would have been shortened by years, saving hundreds of thousands of lives.

Ripley's ghost is with us still. More than a century and a half ago General Ripley crafted the argument against repeaters that has so deeply ingrained resistance to change in the Army that, amazingly, it persists to this day. The Ripley argument goes: "Give the Soldiers a fast-firing gun and they will just waste ammunition; do not give a Soldier a machine too complex for him to master; too many calibers of ammunition cannot be supported by the ammunition supply train; the troops are satisfied with what they have and it is 'good enough'; and most persistent of all, so many machined parts makes repeating rifles too expensive to issue to every Soldier."

Ripley's bureaucratic victory over Lincoln was the beginning of a long, drawn-out defense scandal that did the Army—and the nation—no favors. I should know. I was almost one of Ripley's victims. In June 1969, in the mountains of South Vietnam, the battery I commanded at Firebase Berchtesgaden had spent the day firing artillery in support of infantry forces dug into "Hamburger Hill." Every person and object in the unit was coated with reddish-brown clay blown upward by rotor wash from Chinook helicopters delivering ammunition. By evening, we were sleeping beside our M16 rifles. I was too inexperienced— or perhaps too lazy—to demand that my Soldiers take a moment to clean their guns, even though we had heard disturbing rumors about the consequences of shooting a dirty M16.

At three o'clock in the morning, the enemy struck. They were armed with the amazingly reliable and rugged Soviet AK-47; after climbing up our hill for hours, dragging their guns through the mud, they had no problems unleashing devastating automatic fire. Not so my men. To this day, I am haunted by the sight of three of my dead Soldiers lying atop rifles they had broken open in frantic attempts to clear jams.

With a few modifications, the weapon that killed my Soldiers almost fifty years ago is killing our Soldiers today in Afghanistan. During my thirty-five years in the Army, it became clear to me that from Gettysburg to Hamburger Hill to the streets of Baghdad, the American penchant for arming troops with lousy rifles has been responsible for a staggering number of unnecessary deaths. Over the next few decades, the Department of Defense will spend more than a trillion dollars on F-35 stealth fighter jets that after nearly ten years of testing have yet to be deployed to a single combat zone. Bad rifles are in Soldiers' hands in every combat zone.

In the wars fought since World War II, the vast majority of men and women in uniform have not engaged in the intimate act of killing. Their work is much the same as that of their civilian counterparts. It is the infantryman's job to seek out and kill the enemy, intentionally, at the risk of violent death. The Army and Marine Corps infantry, joined by a very small band of special operations forces, comprises roughly 100,000 Soldiers, some 5 percent of uniformed Defense Department employees. During World War II, 70 percent of all Soldiers killed at the hands of the enemy were infantry. In the wars since, that proportion has grown to about 80 percent. These are the (mostly) men whose survival depends on their rifles and ammunition.

In combat, an infantryman lives an animal's life. The primal laws of tooth and fang determine whether he will live or die. Killing is quick. Combat in Afghanistan and Iraq reinforces the lesson that there is no such thing in small-arms combat as a fair fight. Infantrymen advance into the killing zone grimy, tired, confused, hungry, and scared; their equipment is dirty, dented, or worn. They die on patrol from ambushes, from sniper attacks, from booby traps and improvised explosive devices. They may have only a split second to lift, aim, and pull the trigger before the enemy fires. Survival depends on the ability to deliver more killing power at longer ranges and with greater precision than the enemy.

Any lost edge, however small, means death. A jammed weapon, an enemy too swift and elusive to be engaged with aimed fire, an enemy out of range yet capable of delivering a larger volume of return fire—any of these cancel out all the wonderfully superior and expensive U.S. air- and sea-based weapons that may be fired in support of ground troops. A Soldier in basic training is told that his rifle is his best friend and his ticket home. If the lives of so many depend on the development of a thousand-dollar, six-pound composite of steel and plastic, why can't the richest country in the world give it to them?

The answer is both complex and simple. The M4, the standard carbine in use by the infantry today, is a lighter version of the M16 rifle that killed so many of the Soldiers who carried it in Vietnam. (The M16 is still also in wide use today.) In the early morning of July 13, 2008, nine infantrymen died fighting off a Taliban attack at a combat outpost near the village of Wanat, in Afghanistan's Nuristan Province. Some of the Soldiers present later reported that in the midst of battle their rifles overheated and jammed. The Wanat story is reminiscent of experiences in Vietnam; in fact, as noted above, other than a few cosmetic changes, the rifles from both wars are virtually the same. Also the M4's shorter barrel makes it less effective at long ranges than the older M16—an especially serious disadvantage in modern combat, which is increasingly taking place over long ranges.

The M16 started out as a stroke of genius by one of the world's most famous firearms designers. In the 1950s, an engineer named Eugene Stoner used space-age materials to improve the Army's then-standard infantry rifle, the M14. The 5.56-mm cartridge Stoner chose for his rifle was a modification not of the M14's cartridge but of a commercial Remington rifle cartridge that had been designed to kill small varmints. His invention, the AR-15, was light, handy, and capable of controlled automatic fire. It outclassed the heavier, harder-recoiling M14. Yet, the Army was again reluctant to change. As James Fallows observed in 1981, it took the "strong support" of President John F. Kennedy and Defense Secretary Robert McNamara to make the Army consider breaking its love affair with the large-caliber M14. In 1963, it slowly began adopting Stoner's invention.

The "militarized" adaptation of the AR-15 was the M16. Militarization—more than a hundred proposed alterations supposed to make the rifle combat-ready—ruined the first batch to arrive at the front lines; the cost in dead Soldiers was horrific. A propellant ordered by the Army left a powder residue that clogged the rifle. Finely machined parts made the M16 a "maintenance queen" that required constant cleaning in the moisture, dust, and mud of Vietnam. In time, the Army improved the weapon—but not before many U.S. troops died.

Not all the problems with the M16 can be blamed on the Army. Buried in the M16's, and now the M4's, operating system is a flaw that no amount of militarizing and tinkering has ever erased. Stoner's gun cycles cartridges from the magazine into the chamber using gas pressure vented off as the bullet passes through the barrel. Gases traveling down a very narrow aluminum tube produce an intense "puff" that throws the bolt assembly to the rear, making the bolt assembly a freely moving object in the body of the rifle. Any dust or dirt or residue from the cartridge might cause the bolt assembly, and thus the rifle, to jam.

In contrast, the Soviet AK-47 cycles rounds using a solid operating rod attached to the bolt assembly. The gas action of the AK-47 throws the rod and the bolt assembly back as one unit; the solid attachment means that mud or dust will not prevent the gun from functioning. Fearing the deadly consequences of a "failure to feed" in a fight, some top-tier special operations units like Delta Force and SEAL Team 6 use a more modern and effective rifle with a more reliable operating-rod mechanism. Yet frontline Army and Marine riflemen still fire weapons much more likely to jam than the AK-47. Failure to feed affects every aspect of a fight. A Russian infantryman can fire about 140 rounds a minute without stopping. The M4 fires at roughly half that rate.

During the Civil War General Ripley argued, among other things, that infantry Soldiers would have trouble handling the complexity of new repeating weapons. We hear similarly unconvincing arguments now. Today's grunt has shown in fourteen years of war that he can handle complexity. He's an experienced, long-service professional who deserves the same excellent firearm as the more "elite" special operations forces.

What should a next-generation, all-purpose infantry rifle look like? It should be modular. Multiple weapons can now be assembled from a single chassis. A squad member can customize his weapon by attaching different barrels, buttstocks, forearms, feed systems, and accessories to make, say, a light machine gun, a carbine, a rifle, or an infantry automatic rifle.

The military must change the caliber and cartridge of the guns it gives infantry Soldiers. Stoner's little 5.56-mm cartridge was ideal for softening the recoil of World War II infantry calibers, in order to allow fully automatic fire. Today's cartridge, however, is simply too small for modern combat. Its small mass limits its range to less than four hundred meters. The optimum caliber for tomorrow's rifle is between 6.5 and 7 millimeters. The cartridge could be made almost as light as the older brass-cased 5.56 mm by using a plastic shell casing, which is now in final development by the Marine Corps.

The Army can achieve an infantry version of stealth by attaching newly developed sound suppressors to every rifle. Instead of merely muffling the sound of firing by trapping gases, this new technology redirects the firing gases forward, capturing most of the blast and flash well inside the muzzle. Of course, an enemy under fire would hear the muted sounds of an engagement. But much as with other stealth technology, the enemy Soldier would be at a decisive disadvantage in trying to determine the exact location of the weapons firing at him.

Computer miniaturization now allows precision to be squeezed into a rifle sight. All an infantryman using a rifle equipped with a new-model sight need do is place a red dot on his target and push a button at the front of his trigger guard; a computer on his rifle will take into account data like range and "lead angle" to compensate for the movement of his target and then automatically fire when the hit is guaranteed. This rifle sight can "see" the enemy Soldier day or night at ranges well beyond six hundred meters. An enemy caught in that sight will die long before he could know he was seen, much less before he could effectively return fire.

But infantrymen today do not use rifles equipped with these new sights. Hunters do. In fact, new rifles and ammunition are readily available. They are made by many manufacturers—civilian gun makers and foreign military suppliers that equip the most elite special operations units. Unlike conventional infantry units, top-tier special operations units are virtually unrestricted by cumbersome acquisition protocols and have had ample funding and a free hand to solicit new gun designs from private industry. These units test new guns in combat, often with dramatic results: greater precision, greater reliability, greater killing power.

The Army has argued that in an era of declining resources, a new rifle will cost more than two billion dollars. But let us say the Army and Marine Corps buy new rifles only for those who will use them most, namely the infantry. The cost, for about 100,000 infantrymen at $1,000 each, is then reduced to roughly $100 million, less than that of a single F-35 fighter jet. The Army and the Marine Corps can keep the current stocks of M4s and M16s in reserve for use by non-infantry personnel in the unlikely event that they find themselves in combat.

From the time of Gen. James Ripley to today, the Army has found reasons to deny its Soldiers in the line of fire the safest and most efficient firearms. It does not have to be this way. A few dollars invested now will save the lives of legions of brave infantrymen and women for generations to come.

[14]

THE UNBLINKING EYE

Brutality and injustice made us raise our hands towards the sky for years;
God didn't respond to us, but drones came to our rescue.
— M. F. Moonzajer, Afghan citizen

From the beginning of recorded history to just a few hundred years ago, armies fought with primitive muscle-powered instruments, usually variations of farm implements or beasts of burden. For the most part, armies won or lost based on the concentrated muscle power of converging lines of infantry. Gunpowder would make the mounted knight obsolete, to be sure. Even until the American Civil War, generals still maneuvered their armies by muscle power and considered the push of the bayonet to be decisive in battle.

Technology in the early days of the Industrial Revolution improved slowly. Thus, it comes as no surprise that the infantry muskets used by Gen. Robert E. Lee as a young captain in the Mexican War of 1846–48 were no different from those used by the British redcoats at the battle of Breitenfeld in 1631. In a similar manner, Lord Nelson felt no technological inferiority sailing his flagship *Victory* into the French fleet at Trafalgar in 1805, even though *Victory* was more than a hundred years old.

Later in the nineteenth century, the pace of technological change accelerated rapidly and in the course of this change altered war fundamentally. Generals of the period failed to understand the implications of change on the battlefield . . . and they paid a horrible price in blood. Lee knew that his Soldiers were firing rifles capable of killing out to ranges ten times greater than the smoothbore muskets his Soldiers had carried in Mexico. He was aware that rifling allowed artillery to shoot with precision out to four miles or more. Yet, on the third day at Gettysburg he sent 13,000 men across 980 yards of open wheat fields. Even though historians consider Lee to be America's greatest combat general, he was still the victim of his past experience in Mexico. He knew technology had changed the character of warfare, but as so often happens in warfare, even he, one of the best and brightest of generals, could not escape the visceral, firsthand experiences of his past.

THE MACHINE-GUN DISEASE

Fast-forward fifty years to 1914 and the beginning of World War I. British, French, and German generals—all of whom had read accounts of Gettysburg— similarly sent their Soldiers across open fields in the face of rifles improved to fire smokeless powder and small-caliber bullets. These same bullets were strung together in belts to be fed into Hiram Maxim's invention, the "machine gun," which mowed down a generation of young men. It took almost seven million dead to teach the generals how to deal with this first "precision revolution" in accuracy, range, explosive power, and mass.

In 1915 after the tragic battle of Loos, the British general staff collected at Salisbury Plain to discuss how many autofiring devices a regiment needed to support an attack across the trenches. Should the standard complement of 18 machine guns be increased to, maybe, 24? Actually, the right answer has turned out to be 1,800, enough to make every rifleman a machine gunner. The Germans came to this conclusion 30 years later on the Eastern Front during World War II. The Russians learned the proper number in 1947 with the invention of the AK-47. The U.S. Army decided on automatic fire for all infantrymen in 2012.

In 1995 I created the "Army After Next" Project, an extraordinary group of very young Soldiers and civilians tasked to find the technology that might usher in the next shift in the course of war. Certainly, future gazing is a perfidious craft, and war is the most complex of all human endeavors to anticipate. The primary conclusion of our group was that the next transformational technology to change the nature and character of war—in effect, the "machine gun" of the twenty-first century—would be the armed drone.

We studied the Gulf War carefully, and we concluded that early drones used in that war would someday be capable enough to see, track, and eventually "stare" at the enemy below, and with such clarity as to create an opaque battlefield. Several high-level war games at the Army War College in 1997 confirmed that the creation of what we then called an "unblinking eye" would also change the enemy's behavior. An overhead perch would reduce his aggressiveness, cause him to hide and go to ground without having had the opportunity to mass his forces. We had discovered the new "machine gun" that would ensure future victories.

At the time we postulated all sorts of futuristic drone-like technologies that might perform the staring function. We thought about very-high-flying balloons, space-based telescopes capable of watching tactical movements by small units thousands of miles below. The games strongly suggested that the technology of choice was the drone; in our virtual experiments, we armed them with precision missiles, because we realized that it took too long for one machine to find a target and another to kill it.

Our drone of choice in the nineties was Global Hawk, a huge Air Force unmanned drone that carried a large payload and could loiter over a single point for hours. In subsequent literature we forecasted the transformational impact of a true "unblinking eye" and pushed the Air Force to get on board. Fast-forward six years. We watched on television as huge Air Force B-52 bombers made lazy eights in the sky over the Taliban in Afghanistan. There it was: small Special Forces units mounted on horseback were sending up precision targeting data to the circling bombers with cell phones and laptops. There was our unblinking eye. Later, we learned that the Air Force and CIA had codeveloped a smaller killer-drone, the Predator . . . and the race was on. We were right after all.

Sadly, it did not take long before our military fell victim to the machine-gun problem. We saw the same phenomenon play out again with aerial surveillance using drones. It reminded us of how long it had taken for armies to embrace autofiring infantry weapons fully. The machine-gun disease is with us still, and the impediments are many: the Army and Air Force have a bad habit of building units around machines and overstuffing them with staff officers, crews, support groups, and other excessive and expensive overhead. By 2005, newly formed Air Force drone squadrons were manned with more than a hundred airmen. Soon, the cost of proliferation became too high in human capital. Thus rapid proliferation, enough drones to secure the safety of Soldiers on the ground, became too expensive.

Since its inception, the Air Force has demanded control of everything that flies. The idea of drones being proliferated widely to everyone (like machine guns in World War I) is anathema to radical proponents of a centrally controlled Air Force. Likewise, bean counters in the Pentagon decry the costs inherent in a huge proliferation of different types of drones dispersed among many different services and functions . . . the bean counters want efficiency, standardization, rationalization, and economies of scale. The needs of Soldiers like Sergeant Giunta and Captain Swenson, who might have found some use in an orbiting drone that warned them of danger, simply is not a factor in a bureaucrat's short list of important things. Finally, the military's turgid weapon-buying bureaucracy cannot keep up with rapid advances in drone technologies, particularly since civilian companies, not defense agencies, make most such advances. While today the Army struggles to launch a next-generation "hand thrown" drone, such a simple battery-powered device is sold at Walmart.

During my visits to combat units in Iraq and Afghanistan, I watched how the military coped with the promise of the unblinking eye. Every commander was vociferous and unequivocal about one fact: Soldiers should never have to die to find information about the enemy. Thus the most important task for the future should be to avoid surprise by acquiring the ability to see the enemy first. In wars within the American era 52 percent of close-combat deaths have been suffered trying to find the enemy. Today in Afghanistan that proportion has grown to 84 percent.

I gained a glimpse of how decisive a truly effective unblinking eye might be in combat when, in the fall of 2008, I was the guest of the 5th Special Forces Group, based then at Taji Airfield, just outside Baghdad. It was two in the morning. The small confines of the Special Forces Command Center were sparsely manned and deathly quiet. Spaced evenly across the ceiling were six flat-screen televisions, each projecting sharp images—downloads from Predator drones. Each screen followed a night raid in progress in real time. I watched, transfixed, as a dozen small black dots scattered across each screen; clearly, they were Special Forces "direct action" teams closing in on sleeping Al Qaeda terrorists. Occasionally the group commander, Col. Darcie Rogers, sitting next to me, would note when the collective groups of black dots started to converge. The feed was soundless, but we could see the moment very clearly. A flash of black momentarily blanked out a portion of the screen, and then we watched the frantic scattering of the few black dots lucky enough to rush away from the kill zone.

As these six small raids played out nearly simultaneously, Colonel Rogers noted dryly that after three years of night raids Al Qaeda knew about the drones. He found it interesting that, over time, the presence of these fearful aerial eyes was forcing Al Qaeda to change its behavior. Its fighters avoided windows. They tried to disperse and hide under sheds and thick trees. They rarely fought back when surprised by the raids. Some tried to run; their panic came across the screens as staccato, jerky rushes and darts that the maneuvering Soldiers below watched on their (still classified) handheld sensors, linked to the drones orbiting above. Death came instantly and from a place they could not see. In effect, the presence of drones and ground sensors in the hands of these elite small units decided the outcome far before battle began.

Then, as today, no special unit—Special Forces, Delta Force, SEALs, or Rangers—would dare go into such inhospitable places without a drone overhead. I wondered what would have happened had Sergeant Giunta and Captain Swenson had the same capability overhead during their horrific fights. Why isn't it possible for every close-combat unit in harm's way to have exactly the same life-saving unblinking eye overhead?

Sadly, the Air Force is today's machine-gun corps. In April 2015 the Air Force reduced the number of Predator and Reaper drone sorties it was able to fly from sixty-five to sixty, citing the stress that a sixty-five-sortie "mission tempo" was having on drone pilots . . . pilots flying from Creech Air Force Base just outside Las Vegas, Nevada. Just a few years ago, in 2008, the Air Force was content with flying thirty-three missions per day until Secretary of Defense Gates forced them to push toward meeting the needs of ground commanders. The Air Force leadership complains now that the demand for drones is insatiable and cannot be met. Of course, the real question, like the question never asked in World War I, is, "How many does the war fighter need?" Is it sixty or six hundred? If it takes six hundred to keep Soldiers and Marines alive, then why doesn't the Air Force just do it? Now you see the problem.

With such disappointing support from the Air Force, the Army has been forced to get into the armed-drone business in spite of huge fiscal problems. To its credit, the conventional Army in Iraq and Afghanistan has made some progress with new drone technologies. In 2008 Task Force Odin, a manned and unmanned aviation brigade stationed at Balad Airfield in Iraq, offered the promise of such a capability. However, the view provided by Task Force Odin's aerial systems was limited in time (a few hours) and space (a few square kilometers) at an exorbitant cost. The hope, never realized in Iraq, was to deploy a system capable of staring across the battlefield constantly, 24/7. A staring drone would give commanders the ability to detect the enemy's behavior by watching, over time, his tempo, cycle of operating, and what Soldiers call "pattern of life." Armed with such information a commander would be able to anticipate the enemy's action perhaps days or weeks in advance.

Drones are particularly useful for fighting irregular wars, the sort of conflicts that dominate battles throughout the American era. The enormity of the battlefield, the enemy's propensity to hide among the people in urban areas, and his understanding of the benefits to be gained from collateral damage to the people require that on tomorrow's battlefield the enemy be watched constantly and tracked reliably in real time. Unfortunately, thanks to a modern-day corollary of machine-gun disease, our ground forces have far too few drones. Those few capable of seeing over great distances and staying airborne for very long periods are controlled by politicians and generals, often in distant places; some are even flown from bases in the United States. Too many are dedicated to "terrorist plinking" in Pakistan and Yemen, far too detached from real war to help the Giuntas and Swensons in their efforts to avoid ambushes and stay alive in the close fight.

Throughout history, a small-unit leader's greatest desire is to see the enemy from over the hill. This task can best be done bloodlessly, using unmanned aerial robots. When Soldiers are in contact, a tactical commander should be able to observe the action very closely, so as to intuit the most intimate of the enemy's thoughts and actions. He should also have a broad, complete, and uninterrupted macro view of his area of operations, such that the enemy would find it very difficult to hide or approach his position without detection. Such a capability should be sufficiently mobile and flexible to allow a tactical commander to employ it with a minimal transport and logistic burden. It must also belong to him, and him alone.

Thus speed of decision making and delivery are both essential for the task. Cold War doctrine was premised on the need to seize point objectives, in order to deny the enemy control of the high ground. This imperative to gain "positional advantage" also shaped every aspect of ground-force doctrine. Key terrain is still an important tenet in places like Iraq and Afghanistan, but it is defined differently. At times, points of terrain can be objectives worth fighting for: an insurgent hideout, a bomb-making factory, perhaps a cache hiding weapons or propaganda materials.

But irregular warfare is war among the people, and it requires the controlling of populations. Such wars are fought on distributed, dispersed battlefields. As the enemy spreads out to contest the countryside or urban areas, we must follow him there. But the challenge in distributed warfare is to do more than just "spread out." In fact, as units disperse they change their patterns of maneuver and behavior. They are forced through dispersion to forfeit their traditional advantages of mass, operational speed, and quick concentration of killing power.

DRONES IN FUTURE WAR

Wars of the future cannot be won without absolute domination of the air and cybersphere above our Soldiers. They must be protected by an "unblinking eye"—a constant, reliable, ubiquitous, and overwhelmingly dominant sphere of information. Think of this protective "cybersphere" as both an invisible barrier to blind the enemy and an eye that shifts, moves, and hovers to watch and track the enemy with great clarity, reliability, and precision. Experience in Kosovo, Iraq, and Afghanistan has shown dramatically that, to a great extent, today's technologies now permit air and naval forces to create a fairly impervious shield of information, one that protects them in their relatively uncluttered mediums of war. The complexities of terra firma make the task far more challenging for Soldiers and Marines fighting on the ground.

A cybersphere is needed that is robust, layered with redundant capabilities, and reliable enough to accommodate with an enormous bandwidth the rich calculus of ground warfare. Even the global Internet and satellite communications of 2030 will not be sufficient to provide the connectivity necessary to sustain a battlefield cybersphere. Therefore, ground forces in all probability will have to take their bandwidth with them into the battle area. Most of the unit's information systems and capabilities will be self-contained. Reliability and security will be ensured by a robust, layered system of sensors and communications that begin in space and descend down through the atmosphere to every variety of drones to ground sensors and sensors attached to Soldiers.

Dedicated tactical satellites in high earth orbit will tie the force to its support base in the United States. The next layer would consist of high-altitude, long-endurance, unmanned aerial vehicles flying in the stratosphere above the formation to provide continuous observation of the battle area. These superdrones would be stealthy and fly at altitudes above the reach of an enemy's antiaircraft missiles. They would be linked into the command centers, somewhere in the region and in the United States. Some might best be employed as high-altitude "cell towers" that connect together all of the Soldier cell phones in a single integrated network.

The medium drone layer would consist of improved versions of Predator and Reaper armed drones. A group of ten or twelve of these would be dedicated to a brigade in contact and linked directly to small units in a firefight. A small-unit leader, or a sergeant or lieutenant, would simply designate a close-in target with a handheld laser range finder. An Army or Air Force drone pilot in the United States would be cued to the sergeant's beam and would verify the target and release the missile to the target. Such an arrangement would put killing effects on a tactical target in less than a minute.

The small drone layer would consist of small, cheap, disposable, handheld drones, some the size of hummingbirds, carried into battle in each Soldier's rucksack. Whenever a unit in action came across an uncertain situation, the Soldier would release his drone to fly over roads and trails or hover inside buildings and bunkers. These silent, virtually invisible minibirds would lurk inside and provide video and infrared images to a small unit waiting to enter. Some of the devices in a Soldier's rucksack would be "suicide" drones, essentially very small drones with small explosive devices attached. Think how many of Captain Swenson's men might have been saved had Swenson flown an explosive drone into his target instead of throwing a hand grenade.

No reason exists for any ground action to be fought again without a drone overhead and sensors in the hands of every small unit involved. How many drones must be overhead to protect an infantry brigade in combat? Ask the same question about machine guns—I do not know. But I do know it is many,

many more than hover over a brigade in Afghanistan today. The technology to buy and build this constellation of drones is at hand. If the military is too hidebound and slow to build it, then the Army and Marines should be able to buy it from enterprising civilian technology firms. With an unblinking eye overhead, every future close engagement should be an unfair fight. Enemies under the gaze of hundreds of buzzing unmanned machines will assume they are defeated before the first shot is fired.

[15]

MOTHER SHIPS AND
BATTLESHIP BUREAUCRATS

In Afghanistan, a lieutenant led his patrol in hot pursuit of a Taliban band. . . . When the officer dismounted his troops and sent them after their quarry, they fell even further behind; for each man had to clamber upward encumbered with sixty pounds of body armor, and well as weapon, ammunition, communications and survival pack. The officer aborted the mission. . . .

—McClatchy Newspapers, January 11, 2009

During the decades between the world wars, a few farseeing admirals recognized that command of the seas would depend on the ability to command the air above the seas. Two admirals, William Simms and William Moffett, fought a campaign inside the Navy and in the halls of Congress to build a fleet of large-deck aircraft carriers, capable of destroying the Japanese fleet at a distance—from the air. Before Pearl Harbor, the "battleship barons" argued that carriers and aircraft were too vulnerable and that battleships too invincible to be destroyed from the air. The Japanese would be defeated by battleships possessed with a few more knots of speed, inches of armor, and longer-ranging guns than theirs. Of course, it took Pearl Harbor and a close-run battle of carrier-versus-carrier in the Pacific to prove the battleship barons wrong.

The Army is substantially in the same place today. A legion of battleship bureaucrats, most of them passionate, well connected Cold War–era retired officers, administration officials, congressmen, and Soldier-bureaucrats in the weapons-buying trade, are trolling the halls of Congress and filling trade journals with articles proclaiming that the Army's current fleet of battleships—five-decade-old, massive Cold War tanks, artillery pieces, and infantry carriers—are good enough. Just rearrange some of them into smaller, more agile units. Add some information technology and brand-new sensors and, by God, what was good for Patton and Schwartzkopf will be good enough to fight Russia and China, as well as ISIS and its spawn. Theirs is a seductive voice, particularly to a Congress reluctant to spend money on defense.[1]

The battleship bureaucrats are a dangerous lot, because they are as wrong today as the battleship barons were seven decades ago. Today's ground-fighting machines, particularly those intended to carry infantry, are too massive and immobile to be effective in a war against a distributed, dispersed, and elusive enemy. The Cold War–era Bradley Fighting Vehicle carries only six infantry. These are "dismounts," not a squad, intended only to protect the vehicle as it advanced its cannon and missiles. In irregular wars it is the infantry, not the carrier, that needs to be advanced, and with support from systems on board the vehicle. The changing nature of wars in the American era calls for a new generation of infantry carrier, each vehicle capable of "overwatching" an infantry squad as it ferrets out elusive enemies hiding in places an armored vehicle cannot reach . . . or see.

The Army has tried to defy the battleship bureaucrats before, by building a new fleet of fighting vehicles. Early in the Iraq war, the Army dedicated billions to the (awkwardly named) Future Combat Systems (FCS). Not a vestige of FCS is left. It died in Iraq, where the need to protect Soldiers against improvised explosive devices trumped the need for cutting-edge armored fighting vehicles. Now the Army is left with a fleet consisting of two obsolete carrier types: the Bradley and a wheeled "bus," or Mine Resistant Ambush Protected vehicle (MRAP), good only for protecting against IEDs. Only the Stryker armored squad carrier even begins to meet the needs of a future mounted force.

In the spring of 2015, the Army formally suspended the purchases of any new combat vehicles. The plan now is to get rid of the MRAPS as fast as possible and refurbish more than 1,600 Abrams tanks and 2,500 Bradley Infantry

Fighting Vehicles over the next decade. Other than a symbolic "ring job" to engines and transmissions, the Army will tie its long-standing superiority in armored warfare to a single technological improvement: the fitting of a single new-generation night sight . . . for the whole fleet. That is it.

Compare the Army's sad tale to that of the other services. The Air Force gets a trillion-dollar stealth fighter, the F-35; the Navy gets a new stealth fighter and a carrier, as well as a new high-tech submarine fleet. The Army gets a new sight . . . for a tank designed to fight on German highways and in open deserts. None of our Cold War fleet can be transported quickly to hot spots, nor can the huge tonnages of these behemoths or the fuel and parts they demand be sustained without creating a logistical tail so vulnerable that it, not the fighting vehicles, becomes the object of the enemy's attention. During one of my trips to Iraq in 2008, a general told me that he was conducting 42,700 round-trip truck runs per month to supply heavy tank forces in Baghdad. Trucks filled with gas and diesel are too many tragic, vulnerable targets that translate into too many needless deaths just to sustain a force that is too heavy and cumbersome to be maintained in an isolated and often primitive part of the world.

Why are these Cold War–era tanks so heavy, and why do they need so much fuel? Simply put, our seventy-two-ton Abrams tank is designed to kill other tanks. In tank-on-tank duels, the winner is usually the one with the thicker armor in the front and a main gun (cannon) large enough to penetrate the frontal armor of the enemy's tank. The only problem with this argument is that in the American era of war, our enemies do not fight our tanks with tanks. Increasingly, they do not have any. Instead, as the Israelis learned in Lebanon in 2006, an insurgent enemy kills tanks with rockets and long-range missiles. This explains the very curious fact that during the entire seventy years of wars fought in the American era, only ten—yes, that is ten—U.S. tank crewmen have been killed fighting enemy tanks. Compare this to the nearly 100,000 Soldiers and Marines killed by small-arms fire and mortars.

And yet, history tells us that Soldiers should fight mounted whenever possible. Sure, we have all seen the newsreels and videos from World War II and the Arab-Israeli wars that show burning iron monsters with dead Soldiers inside; the data, however, supports a different picture. In wars in the American era, an American close-combat Soldier transported by, or fighting in, any vehicle stands a 90 percent greater chance of living and a 50 percent greater chance of surviving wounds when mounted. The only question to be answered is what kind of fighting vehicle suits the nature and character of today's wars. The answer lies with understanding how the demands of today's wars differ from those of the Cold War. We begin with the foot Soldier.

Modern technology quite literally weighs down a modern foot Soldier and forces him to ride to battle rather than walk. In his iconic book *The Soldier's Load and the Mobility of the Nation*, the famed chronicler of infantry in battle S. L. A. Marshall observed that from the Roman to the Civil War Soldier, the load carried by an infantryman in combat remained about one-third of his body weight.[2] The weight carried on the march to battle was slightly heavier. Modern human and behavioral research reinforces the wisdom of the ancients by concluding from exhaustive studies that Soldiers who march into close combat with too heavy a load are less able to perform. Extreme exhaustion leads to inattention, sloppy decision making, and very poor marksmanship, particularly for machine gunners.

Yet in spite of proven wisdom to the contrary, our Soldiers and Marines in Iraq and Afghanistan carry enormous loads, mostly north of one hundred pounds, which for an average Soldier is about two-thirds of his body weight. Given the demands of modern combat, it is unlikely that this load can be reduced very much: in hot, high climates, Soldiers need at least a gallon of water per day—total weight, eight pounds. His weapon and ammunition weigh about twenty pounds. Modern Soldiers also carry stuff the ancients would never have contemplated, such as sensors, radios, signals detectors, and, of course, the batteries to power them. But the big difference between the loads of the ancients and today's infantryman is the enormous price a Soldier pays for protection. Even a Roman infantryman carried less than twenty ponds of metal covering, medieval Soldiers perhaps ten pounds of leather breast protection. A U.S. infantryman's body armor and helmet weigh more than forty pounds, roughly equivalent to the total load carried by infantrymen just a few decades ago. So infantrymen are pack animals. Even the largest and fittest among them cannot march very far and remain capable of effective combat. Yesterday's Soldiers could march to war. On today's battlefields, even "foot Soldiers" have to ride.

Walking to war is also dangerous. That is why today's infantry must be able to get quite close before dismounting, often well within the range of the enemy's small arms and rocket-propelled grenades. Success in engagements in places like Iraq and Afghanistan is often contingent on how long mounted small units can stay mounted before exposing themselves. In today's wars, numbers count, and success in the close fight is often contingent on how many infantry can be safely delivered next to the enemy before dismounting. The complexity inherent in finding and killing an enemy buried inside cities and villages in places like Afghanistan and Lebanon has shown that infantry fighting vehicles must be sized for the complexities of urban warfare. They must be small and very agile. They must be light enough to negotiate third-world bridges. In irregular wars, infantry vehicles must be able to maneuver in very tight places. Israeli Merkava tanks, with their wide stances and very long and protruding main guns, were at a disadvantage when forced to enter villages occupied by Hezbollah infantry. Because today's hybrid enemies hide among the people and remain in the shadows, fighting vehicles must possess unprecedented visibility even when crews are buttoned up. Urban maneuver demands frequent shifts from mounted to dismounted movement. Thus Soldiers must not lose protection, connection, or situational awareness when the vehicle ramp comes down.

The bottom line is that our experience in today's wars dictates that the traditional functions of fighting vehicles must change. Tomorrow's wars will be principally infantry centered and demand a new infantry carrier that is intended less as a weapons carrier than as a universal Soldier carrier capable of transporting at least an infantry squad over long distances, under armor, to arrive silently and unexpectedly right on top of the enemy. In other words, our infantry need a "mother ship."

MEETING THE MOTHER SHIP

In the fall of 2007 Gen. David Petraeus asked me to visit Iraq with the purpose of suggesting which cutting-edge technologies then in the field held the most promise for exploitation in the future. I visited ground combat units struggling to adapt new matériel to fit the unique circumstances of irregular warfare. The high point of my visit was the day I spent with the 4th Battalion, 9th Infantry "Manchus" at Taji. These Soldiers had been newly equipped with the Stryker wheeled, armored infantry carrier.

My visit happened on a very hot day. Two Soldiers waited to greet me. They stood alongside their Stryker, bent over by the crushing burden of more than one hundred pounds of gear. I walked around the vehicle, followed by one of the Soldiers. As I peered into the crew compartment, he leaned over and whispered, "Hey, sir, know what we call this thing?"

"No, what?" I asked.

"We call it the mother ship," he said, glancing at his buddy with a knowing grin.

The mother-ship analogy was in fact an unintended Soldier metaphor for how fundamentally irregular war experience was altering perceptions of mounted combat. After receiving the Stryker, the Manchus had what they called "an Apollo 13 moment" as they experimented with their newly issued kit to optimize it for a new kind of war. They adapted the Stryker to perform as a long-range, long-term transporter, a rally point, a rest center, and a command-and-control node at the squad level. It performed as a sensor and firepower platform and as a planning and organizing facility, among numerous other functions. During the Cold War, an infantry fighting vehicle was designed to approach a dismount point some distance from the objective. The ramp went down, and the squad continued the assault, supported by the vehicle's machine guns. The Manchu Soldiers in Iraq, however, approached the enemy at night, stealthily, and arrived at the enemy's doorstep before dismounting. The scene painted for me by these infantrymen was more of a SWAT team takedown than a traditional combined-arms mounted assault.

A UNIVERSAL CARRIER

My day with the Manchus and other subsequent visits to Iraq and Afghanistan reinforced the concept of the universal carrier capable of transporting any small team likely to be placed in harm's way, such as engineers, military police, psychological operations forces, and many others. Watching the Manchus in action also convinced me that the experience of contemporary wars strongly supports the argument that the dividing line between mounted and dismounted combat no longer exists. A Manchu Soldier equipped with modern communications and sensor gear is burdened by about 120 pounds. The Manchus' experience shows that to gain a significant advantage over the enemy, tomorrow's Soldier will require access to many technological devices, to include connection to networked sensors. The bottom line is that overburdened ground forces—whether heavy or light, Army, Marine, or SOF—fighting in a country as inhospitable and vast as Afghanistan must remain tied to a mounted tether. The challenge will be to determine how the tether should be designed to be optimally effective in contemporary wars.

The campaign to build a vehicle impervious to improvised explosive devices did not go well in Afghanistan. Our forces there relearned the immutable lesson of history: that the enemy will always improvise in order to find expedient means to destroy a vehicle. In fact, every vehicle deployed to Afghanistan, including MRAP and Stryker, is vulnerable to IED attack. Larding on too much armor to defeat an IED inevitably makes the vehicle too heavy and cumbersome to be an effective fighting machine, particularly in primitive places like Afghanistan. The lesson of contemporary wars is that designing a vehicle capable of avoiding IEDs is the best defense against them. In Afghanistan, virtually all casualties are suffered within five hundred meters of a road. The new universal carrier must be able to travel and maneuver off the roads, which today are studded with IEDs. It must be agile enough to maneuver across valleys and negotiate the narrow confines of village streets. The design must strike a balance between the need for protection and the need to traverse primitive bridges, cross planted fields, and negotiate narrow canals and tight urban passages.

FAST, QUIET, AND DEADLY

To perform the counterinsurgency role properly, an infantry carrier suitable for war in the American era must not only be fast but also quiet. The example of the Manchus' assaults on insurgent hideouts in Iraq points to the need for tactical units to approach insurgent positions undetected. To achieve absolute surprise, the vehicle must be linked to an overhead "unblinking eye," a small tactical drone, capable of sending a continuous image of the target.

Irregular wars require a fast and agile carrier. Engagements against insurgents are always fleeting. The dispersed nature of operations in primitive places demands that isolated tactical units—squads and platoons—collect together quickly from scattered locations to engage massed enemy attacks. The need in irregular warfare to mass spontaneously demands a vehicle capable of sustained speeds of seventy kilometers per hour over broken and undulating terrain. Only a tracked vehicle designed for stealth as well as speed and protection can meet this requirement.

Foreign analysts are observing a global trend toward beefier weapons. The Bradley Infantry Fighting Vehicle's 25-mm gun, for example, is seen as "falling behind" the 30-mm to 40-mm weapons mounted on comparable tracked or wheeled vehicles worldwide. Clearly, the .50-caliber machine gun on the Stryker is far behind its foreign counterparts. Any future infantry carrier should be armed with a cannon of at least 30 mm, capable of providing onboard support for its squad and able to destroy enemy infantry carriers at great range.

Speed of action should complement speed of movement. As we have seen in tragic places like Combat Outpost Wanat and Firebase Keating in Afghanistan, small units must be able to respond to enemy attacks immediately with over-powering, precise, discrete, intimate, and sustained killing power. Experience has shown that immediate reaction to enemy contact cannot be achieved by external systems, such as fixed- and rotary-wing aircraft. Artillery is more respon-sive and less vulnerable to atmospheric conditions, but the battlefield in Afghan-istan is too vast to allow all tactical maneuver inside the artillery-range "fan." Thus, the mother ship must have a self-contained onboard weapon for sensing and engaging a dismounted enemy directly with overwhelming firepower.

A new infantry carrier must possess the robust networking capability essen-tial for today's irregular wars. U.S. dominance on future battlefields will be guaranteed by dominance of sensing sciences and the ability to proliferate infor-mation over the network. Focusing the network on the Soldier will emphasize connectivity over capacity. The objective must be to give every Soldier the abil-ity to maintain virtual "touch" with his buddies. He should be well connected to the outside world continuously, whether inside or outside the carrier.

The mother-ship principle will demand a fighting vehicle optimized to operate in small units for prolonged periods in inhospitable terrain and climate. In the past, limitations induced by logistics and complexity allowed small units to sortie only from large bases and for limited periods. Experience in recent wars suggests that in the future, small units will have to operate away from for-ward operating bases for days or weeks, returning only periodically for supplies, fuel, and refit. Prolonged small-unit operations will also demand that all of the primal combat functions (fire, maneuver, intelligence, command and control, and logistics) be available within a small clutch of vehicles—no more than two or three, collected for sustained support in remote and dispersed villages and urban areas.

A sad fact of today's acquisition system is that all too often the operational environment changes faster than the weapons buying (acquisition) cycle. FCS was conceived during the 1990s, when the Army demanded a force capable of rapid strategic speed and tactical agility, but once the bullets start to fly, ground forces tend to shift from speed to killing power and protection. This is exactly what has happened after 9/11. The future might require that ground combat vehicles operate in more conventional environments. Therefore, it is imperative that the new mother-ship design be flexible enough to allow an increase in "strap on" armor to allow it to perform on a more lethal, denser, and higher-tempo battlefield.

THE SYSTEM THEY DESERVE

We are fourteen years into a war that might last a generation. Yet, the ground services still do not possess a fighting vehicle optimized for today's wars. This situation is all the more incongruous given the fact that Soldiers and Marines have paid a hugely disproportionate cost in Iraq and Afghanistan. They deserve the best but have yet to receive it.

A new armored vehicle must atone for almost a decade of neglect. To be successful, its development must be a national effort that embraces all ground services. It must be done quickly, yet avoid the tragic haste of the MRAP program. It will be expensive. But as one general told me recently, "Land warfare is no longer the cheap alternative." Time is short; we are still at war. The lives of our Soldiers and Marines are on the line. Let us get on with giving them the fighting system they deserve.

[16]

FIREPOWER

Artillery adds dignity to what would otherwise be an ugly brawl.
—Frederick the Great

The Civil War was the first American conflict professional European Soldiers observed. Beginning in 1862, members of the Greater Prussian General Staff, as well as representatives from Great Britain and France, visited Union and Confederate field commands. The views of these men were remarkably alike—and uniformly unkind. They were appalled by what appeared to be a singular lack of field discipline on both sides. One observer noted, "Neither was the fire of the Confederate infantry under the complete control of their officers, nor were their movements always characterized by order and regularity. It was seldom that men could be induced to refrain from answering shot for shot; there was an extraordinary waste of ammunition, there was much unnecessary noise, and the regiments were very apt to get out of hand."[1]

Observers noted that the Americans would rarely close with the enemy but chose instead to fight at ranges of a quarter-mile or more and throw enormous quantities of lead at each other, often for hours without end. What these observers witnessed first-hand has become immutably associated with the American style of warfare—the willingness of Americans to expend firepower freely to conserve human life.

Americans have routinely emphasized the value of firepower in their way of war for a number of reasons, some of them based on a continuing military practice that began in the Civil War, but others, more complex, arising from the essence of American national character. America's preoccupation with preserving the lives of its Soldiers is deeply rooted in its liberal democracy. Thomas Jefferson's elevation of *life* as one of the inalienable rights of an individual underscored the obligation felt by American political philosophers in the new republic to provide for the protection of its citizenry. The inherent value of human life has become a political and moral imperative, carried down and amplified through generations, and passed into the ethic of American military men. Throughout our history, from Antietam to Hamburger Hill, a victory won with too many lives was not considered a victory at all.

The proclivity to save lives in combat has been made all the more difficult by a parallel distinction highlighted in chapter 2—the distrust of large standing armies. Reliance on the citizen-soldier has customarily given the United States a strong militia—but a less strong military. It has meant that American armies have had to learn to fight by fighting. Firepower lessened the cost of this education. In its major wars the United States has been willing and rich enough to compensate in matériel what it lacked in preparation for war. Once mobilized, America's war industries overwhelmed enemies with weaponry. Artillery and aircraft have proven to be best suited for this purpose; bombing and shelling from great distances are the most cost-effective means for delivering killing power while avoiding direct, bloody contact with the enemy.

AIR AND GROUND FIREPOWER

Our enemies universally feared American artillery. Colonel Yahara knew that Okinawa would fall, because he had no answer for the industrial deluge of U.S. firepower. The Germans defending the beachhead in Normandy had little complimentary to say about American fighting methods . . . except for the ability of U.S. artillery to fire "TOTs" (time on targets, that is, rounds from multiple guns timed to strike at nearly the same moment) that massed many far-distant and dispersed artillery pieces on an single target with devastating consequences for any German unit caught in the open. After the Normandy breakout the Germans feared roving U.S. fighter planes, the hated "Jabos," which appeared out of the clouds to massacre convoys and troop positions.

Our copious use of air- and ground-delivered firepower in Korea again demonstrated that the U.S. military needed to substitute explosives for a very poorly performing close-combat force defending against the North Koreans and later the Chinese. This was the first "limited war" fought in the American era, and as in all similar wars to follow the American people had little heart for it. To lessen the human cost the U.S. command in Korea continually increased the dosages of artillery devoted to support each infantry attack. In one attack during April 1951, along what was known as the "No Name Line," the 38th Infantry was supported by thirty-five battalions of artillery that fired more than two thousand rounds in less than two minutes. Unfortunately, as the firepower quotient rose over time, the enemy adapted and the killing effect of our firepower declined. Korea was the first war in which an enemy was able to conduct major ground campaigns successfully while never for a moment achieving superiority in the air.

Two very difficult, related problems faced both air and ground firepower in Korea. The first, of course, was the need to achieve limited military objectives on the ground at the least cost in lives; the second was the necessity to achieve these objectives against a skilled, determined enemy who possessed unlimited human resources and political resolve. As the war dragged on and began to take the form of a World War I–style stalemate, it became increasingly difficult to maintain cohesion among Soldiers in the field. The U.S. command gradually changed its method of operation so that the primary task of engaging the enemy fell upon artillery and airpower.

By the end of the Korean War a generation of military men had come to rely on firepower alone for tactical success on the battlefield. The role of infantry in Korea increasingly became that of a "finding and fixing force." The infantry held a thin defensive perimeter and patrolled aggressively to ensure that an enemy attack was detected in time to be destroyed with air and ground firepower. All of our subsequent wars would follow the Korean template: as conflict drags on and the butcher's bill grows too expensive, our military always escalates the firepower battle. Large-scale operations have become carefully orchestrated battles of attrition, the objective of which is to slaughter thousands using hundreds of thousands of tons of bombs and shells with the least loss to the Americans.

Some aspects of a firepower-intensive battle bothered veterans in Korea. One was the apparent law of diminishing returns. Artillerymen relearned a lesson from Colonel Yahara on Okinawa and in previous firepower-intensive wars of attrition: the most important value of firepower was psychological, not physical. When the enemy dug in, few were killed, even in the densest and most intense bombardment. Instead, firepower stunned Soldiers; it created a sense of trauma and stress among them. In some cases Soldiers unused to a bombardment would actually retire to their bunkers and sleep, ignoring the fact that a ground attack was sure to follow.

The problem was that the psychological impact against the enemy eroded over time. Soldiers became inured to the pyrotechnics and blast once they realized that their bunkers secured them from harm. Thus a lesson taken back to the States after the war was that a firepower-intensive campaign had to be culminated quickly, or an enemy, particularly a taciturn Asian enemy used to hardship, would simply stand and fight no matter how intensively he had been struck by explosive power.

A second concern, again relearned from the Pacific campaign, was how difficult it was to kill the enemy with artillery. On Okinawa in particular the U.S. infantry advance would often launch confidently after intense artillery, naval gunfire, and aerial bombing; inevitably Yahara's infantry, dirty, starving, and with only rifles and a few machine guns, would appear out of their holes seemingly unaffected. Adding time and more tonnage did not seem to help. Subsequent studies done after the war by the Operational Research Office at RAND Corporation concluded scientifically what the Soldiers knew intuitively: artillery rounds and bombs were dreadfully inaccurate. Targets often were located poorly. Also, the natural dispersion of bombs and shells made it virtually impossible to hit a single point with precision.

Between Korea and Vietnam the Army deduced that the problem could be solved in two ways: first, to make the shells more lethal and, second, to make them more precise. By the end of the war in Vietnam the Army would succeed in substantially solving both problems, the first by the proliferation of bomblet (or cluster) shells and bombs and the second by the introduction of warheads guided by lasers and later the Global Positioning System (GPS). The artillery first introduced bomblet ammunition in the early sixties, with Cofram shells

("Cofram" is short for "controlled fragmentation"). When I first came into the artillery in 1966 these shells were classified as strictly as nuclear weapons, mainly because they were so deadly and easily copied if their design was ever compromised. The lethality of Cofram came from the expansion of the killing area. A conventional artillery shell is "point" detonating; it explodes at a single spot, throwing out lethal steel fragments only a few yards from the point of impact. Cofram shells popped opened in the air and scattered several dozen small, golf ball–sized grenades across a very wide area. The little grenades were encased in a steel basket that "popped" them a few feet into the air after it made contact with the ground. When the grenades burst in the air they scattered thousands of tiny, sharp steel fragments that usually did not kill but were very likely to maim Soldiers and destroy radios, weapons, and other vulnerable matériel.

The Army finally released Cofram (or "firecracker," as we called it—the sound of detonating grenades reminded us of a string of Chinese firecrackers going off) after the Tet offensive in 1968. Firecracker was an ugly surprise to the North Vietnamese. It worked superbly in the jungle, where bombs would hang up in the trees and explode at a great height, throwing fragments directly into the enemy's foxholes.

Unfortunately, the Army failed to exploit fully the precision revolution to develop and field cheap and deadly artillery rounds that could be guided precisely to the target using lasers or GPS. To be sure the Army did develop Copperhead, a large (155 mm) laser-guided shell. But Copperhead was expensive and temperamental and took too long to prepare for firing. By the time of the Gulf War if a unit in contact needed precision it turned to aerial platforms like attack helicopters or fighter jets to supply it. In time the artillery would pay a price for this neglect.

Imperfect as it may seem today, the firepower system developed during the Korean War became accepted by Western armies as the proper tactical mechanism for dealing with an intractable Asian enemy. In time, Korean War lieutenants came to command battalions in Vietnam. To them it was different terrain but the same sort of enemy. The American use of firepower in Vietnam followed a tradition of flexibility, technological innovation, and copious application long established in previous wars. Certainly, no other army in the world at that time would have been able to duplicate such a polished and complex mechanism. By war's end, all manner of ground and aerial systems, mortars to strategic bombers, could be called upon quickly and simultaneously to provide close support to combat troops. With the introduction of troop-carrying and rocket-firing attack helicopters, the U.S. Army and Marine Corps developed a new dimension in warfare and gave it credence and respectability. The computer- and sensor-laden electronic battlefields were combined with new artillery and aircraft types well suited for firing very close to troops in contact. New munitions and streamlined systems of delivery ensured that any target found and fixed by infantry forces could be dispatched with surety and precision.

Although still imperfect in many ways, U.S. forces in Vietnam came closer than any other army in any other war to creating a system that integrated into a single striking hand the destructiveness of all firepower, whether delivered by ground, sea, or air. In the right circumstances the application of this system could be enormously destructive. By its own estimates the North Vietnamese Army (NVA) lost more than a million and a half men, mostly to U.S. firepower. Our enemies learned from the NVA the lesson that the price of facing U.S. firepower in open combat is the loss of a generation of first-class Soldiers.

Despite all of these tactical and technological successes, a continuing escalation in the destructiveness of firepower never produced the decisive results achieved by lesser efforts in earlier wars. If a single lesson is to be learned from the example of Vietnam it is that a finite limit exists as to what modern firepower can achieve during the American era . . . no matter how sophisticated the ordnance or how intelligently it is applied.

Overwhelming firepower cannot compensate for bad strategy. As we subsequently learned in Iraq and Afghanistan, a war of attrition is a test of political will and national resolve. During the early years in Vietnam, policy makers decided to prosecute attrition warfare based on unrealistic expectations of the persuasiveness of U.S. firepower. When escalating doses of destructiveness failed to crack the enemy's will, the United States had little strategic alternative but to pull out of the war in unfavorable circumstances or to increase the level of destructiveness seemingly without end.

At the tactical level, firepower in Vietnam killed enemy Soldiers in hugely disproportionate numbers. But terrain, a tenacious enemy, and the very nature of a revolutionary war made the firepower system far less destructive than a similar system would have been in a conventional war against a Western enemy. The enemy rarely assembled in lucrative aggregations; he did so only in the safety of his sanctuaries or under the protective cover of the jungle. As Americans became more adept at finding the enemy, the enemy became more skilled at avoiding destructiveness by fire. The need to maintain the allegiance of the local population placed a practical limit on the degree of destruction that could be unleashed on more thickly settled and populated regions of Vietnam. In the end, exigencies imposed by political constraints, bad maps, miserable weather and terrain, unreliable allies, and interservice friction all limited to varying degrees the speed, reliability, and precision of U.S. firepower.

By the time of the U.S. withdrawal from Vietnam, an unprecedented weight of bombs and shells had failed to break the will of the enemy to fight. In fact, in 1971 the army of North Vietnam was in a stronger position than it had ever been in, with more than 350 heavy guns and 400 tanks set to invade the southern armies. Yet, no matter how adept the enemy became at countering allied firepower or how powerful its own firepower became, the stereotype still remained of the American "Goliath" pounding the helpless "David" into the ground. In the end, 6 million tons of bombs and 20 million rounds of artillery told very little about the eventual outcome of the war.

VINDICATION IN DESERT STORM

The Army used the twenty-year interregnum following Vietnam to prepare to fight a more familiar and comfortable enemy, the Soviet Union. Our template was the Israeli victory over Arab states during the Yom Kippur conflict of 1973. The Israeli Defense Forces (IDF) were a mirror image of our Army. They faced thousands of Egyptian, Syrian, Iraqi, and Jordanian armored forces equipped with first-rate Soviet matériel and doctrine. The Israeli army defeated them in a war that we considered at the time to be a template of the conflict we faced across the Inter-German border.

Firepower was the essential ingredient to the IDF's 1967 and 1973 offensives. Israeli airpower and artillery pummeled first the Egyptians in the Sinai and then the Syrians on the Golan Heights. As a major I visited the "Valley of Tears," overlooking the ruined Syrian village of Kuneitra just across the Israeli border, and counted the still-smoking Syrian tanks that marked the road to

Damascus. We knew then that a new "firepower centered" method of war based on the Israeli model would offer us some hope of defeating the Russians without reverting to nuclear war . . . and we went to work.

In the interval between Kuneitra and Schwarzkopf's "Great Wheel" maneuver in 1991 the Army became an entirely transformed institution. Thanks to the generosity of the Reagan years the "Big 5" systems—the M-1 tank, the Bradley Fighting Vehicle, the Apache attack and Blackhawk helicopters, and the Patriot missile system—gave our Army, for the first time since World War II, the technological advantage over the Soviets. The Army relearned how to train and how to fight. The all-volunteer Army restored pride in our institution, and our new AirLand Battle doctrine for the first time leveraged our dominance in the air virtually to guarantee victory.

So decades later Saddam did not stand a chance. In one hundred hours of ground combat the fourth-largest Army in the world disappeared under a storm of precision killing power. It came as no surprise to my generation that the U.S. firepower system that had been so maligned in Vietnam would experience a renaissance of sorts during Desert Storm. The artillery's most effective killer was the Army's version of cluster bombs, an improved version of the Vietnam-era firecracker shell with the ungainly title of Dual Purpose Improved Conventional Munitions, or DPICM. Research done by the Army in the eighties concluded that scattered munitions like DPICM were at least ten times more deadly than traditional single "point detonated" artillery ammunition.

The Iraqis called DPICM "steel rain." A single volley of bomblet munitions fired from a Multiple Launch Rocket System, or MLRS, would cascade thousands of these flashlight-sized bomblets across a wide pattern that would quite literally crush an Iraqi artillery unit. The troops called this combination of launcher and steel rain the "grid-square removal system." (A grid square is a map symbol representing a thousand square meters.) Needless to say, Saddam's artillery did not stand a chance.

Sadly, after the war the Army began to walk away from the use of DPICM. Part of the problem was the dud rate of the munition and the presumed collateral damage it caused. A small percentage of each bomblet volley, perhaps less than 1 percent in open ground, would fail to explode. After the Gulf War, inflated news reports, mainly from foreign journalists, declared that children were being maimed after picking up and playing with bomblets. The pressure became so great that the Army forbade the use of DPICM in Iraq and Afghanistan. The Army handled these false and inflated reports of abusive "land mine and cluster bomb" employment very poorly. By the mid-nineties personalities such as Princess Diana and some Hollywood luminaries began a crusade against "land mines" and erroneously categorized DPICM bomblet munitions as such. To be clear, mines are explosive devices that are buried in the ground and detonated by troops stepping on them; undetonated bomblet munitions lie in the open. But the antibomblet hysteria continued unabated. The mantra became even shriller when the media concluded that DPICM artillery shells and rocket warheads were also "cluster bombs." The term alone was enough to fuel enormous animus toward the U.S. military.

The Israelis employed DPICM very effectively during the Lebanon war in 2006. But, again, the press jumped on the IDF for killing innocent civilians with "cluster bombs." In 2009, under pressure from the international antiwar community and liberals in Congress, Secretary of Defense Robert Gates ordered the destruction of all stocks of DPICM shells and warheads by 2019. The process of destruction was almost complete by 2016. While the exact number is classified, suffice it to say that our stockpile of DPICM is in the tens of millions. In effect this terrible decision will rob the U.S. firepower system of its most effective means for killing enemy artillery. Make no mistake, the Russians are in love with bomblet munitions. In fact, Vladimir Putin's resurgent military deploys five different models of multiple rocket launchers, all of which can fire volleys of Russian-developed DPICM equivalents.

We gave up our "steel rain." The Russians have stolen our technology and fielded even more lethal versions. In July 2014 the Ukrainian army attempted to advance into the Donbas region of eastern Ukraine with the intent of driving a wedge between separatist maneuver forces and their supply lines. To counter this move the Russians conducted a series of fifty-five artillery "fire strikes" over a six-week period. Outside the city of Zelenopillya a combined Russian force of MLRS fired a three-minute strike using bomblet munitions that virtually wiped out two Ukrainian tank battalions.[2] Thanks to a misplaced instance of "political correctness," we have given up our most lethal firepower weapon. After 2019 the U.S. Army will no longer be capable of defeating the Russians in a head-to-head artillery duel. Mr. Putin is very pleased.

The hundred-hour-war ground phase of Desert Storm was so short that the artillery never had the opportunity to showcase its massive, industrial-strength killing power. For one thing, the ballet moved too fast; guns and rocket launchers had a tough time keeping up with the pace of the advance. A second problem was that maneuver Soldiers on the ground had an enormously rich menu of firepower to choose from and often preferred support from aircraft and helicopters to the less responsive artillery. Most seriously, the artillery had missed the precision revolution. By the early nineties the aerial services possessed an entire arsenal of laser- and television-guided precision bombs and rockets that could hit a point target like a tank with near-perfect killing effect. The artillery remained an area-fire weapon, more suited for static warfare against targets that did not move.

After the Gulf War the artillery continued to drag its feet and make very bad bets on the future. Instead of putting all its developmental dollars on precision shells and sensors, the artillery branch took as its first priority the restoration of speed and range. The sad result was the Crusader howitzer system, unveiled in the late nineties to very poor reviews. It was a huge weapon at a time when the Army sought to build a lighter and more strategically deployable force (another lesson from the Gulf War). Take too long to get to the fight and remain irrelevant. The Army cancelled Crusader before 9/11.

After having little or no impact in Bosnia and the initial campaign in Afghanistan, the artillery Army made a brief comeback during the second war against Iraq in 2003. One reason that the artillery gained renewed respect was because there was so little of it available during the brief campaign. In order to keep the number of invading forces low, Secretary Rumsfeld cut supporting artillery to the bone. With just a few guns available to support the main effort, the proportion of artillery to armor and infantry was the smallest for any force deployed in a major U.S. campaign since the Spanish-American War. Thus every tube and every round had to count, particularly given the difficult supply situation that occurred when the weather and the Fedayeen conspired to threaten a vastly overstretched line of communications. In fact, heavy helicopters from the 101st Airborne Division had to be enlisted to deliver more than three thousand rounds of artillery ammunition to the guns during the advance on Baghdad.

The artillery went into Iraq so light because Gen. Tommy Franks' plan called for speed to substitute for mass. Lighter forces would move faster, and the campaign would end more quickly, with fewer losses. Whatever might be absent in surface-delivered firepower would be offset by close air support from a sup-porting air arm recently reformed from experience in Afghanistan and greatly enhanced by the possession of greater numbers of far more deadly precision bombs than in the first Gulf War. But experience on the battlefield proved that the U.S. command had underestimated the demand for supporting fires and overestimated the ability of aerial firepower to take up the slack. Fighting in cities, particularly by light units such as the 101st and the 82nd Airborne, required a substantial amount of close-in shooting, much of it directed against Iraqis forti-fied and hidden in buildings. An enormous sandstorm stranded the Marines and the Army's 3rd Infantry Division (ID) during the fourth week in March 2003 and kept aircraft grounded. The Fedayeen sought to take advantage of the cover offered by these dust storms (or *shamals*) to attack U.S. troops. The all-weather capability of artillery became literally a lifesaver. The guns killed the enemy in very large numbers and played a significant role in keeping U.S. forces, particularly the 3rd ID, from being overrun.

Once Baghdad was taken, remnants of Saddam's army formed the mostly Sunni "Fedayeen Saddam" and later its more deadly follow-on, Al Qaeda. Soon Shia militant gangs took over the slums of Baghdad joining the fight against American "occupiers." The U.S. incursion into Afghanistan heated up as well, and soon the ground forces were fighting two long insurgencies scattered across vast swaths of inhospitable terrain. The artillery force devoted to both cam-paigns was never very large. In fact, the Army used many "fires" brigades for func-tions other than fire support, such as transportation and base security. The few gun and rocket units in theater never had the range or the numbers to cover adequately the large areas of responsibility belonging to the Army and Marine infantry units they supported.

To cover as much territory as possible, artillery units broke into small, two-gun firing platoons dispersed in forward operating bases and observation posts. Dispersed artillery units can cover more territory, but they cannot mass. The problem of mass versus area control was most problematic in Afghanistan. Bases like Wanat, Keating, and Restrepo in the Korengal Valley were so remote that they had only mortars for protection if the weather was too poor for aerial sup-port . . . and the Taliban always attacked when the weather was bad.

The killing power of artillery in Afghanistan was reduced dramatically with the prohibition against the use of "steel rain." The issue, again, was the dud rate for these shells, which in mountainous terrain could be as high as 2 percent. Also, political pressure forced the artillery to return to old-fashioned explosive shells, although upon further investigation the Army discovered that American bomblet ammunition was not killing Afghan children, as the media claimed. The vast majority of bomblets maiming children in Afghanistan came from old, discarded Russian munitions, which were far more numerous, unstable, and visually appealing to children. Point-detonating shells in mountainous terrain were virtually useless and killed very few Taliban, particularly when hidden in caves and rocky depressions. Today Soldiers often prefer to look "up" for firepower support. The weapon of choice is the ubiquitous Air Force A-10 Warthog close-support aircraft. The "Hog" is the ugliest aircraft to fly, and it is the oldest fighter aircraft in the Air Force. But Soldiers love it, because the beast can loiter for hours over troops in contact. Its 30-mm nose-mounted cannon can be fired very close to "friendlies." Next favorite is the AC-130 Spectre gunship. Spectre is a converted C-130 cargo aircraft that carries nighttime sensors and various deadly weapons, from 20-mm to 40-mm cannon to the terrifying 105-mm artillery howitzer, positioned to fire from the side of the aircraft. The Army's aerial arsenal is equally deadly. The AH-64 Apache can fly low and slow under the weather and deliver Hellfire missiles, rockets, and 30-mm cannon fire. Soldiers and Marines in isolated garrisons have gotten used to calling for support from aircraft and long-range bombers. It is no wonder that as the wars wore on the artillery increasingly lost favor among the infantry as their weapons of choice for supporting fires.

A branch of the Army that loses it utility inevitably atrophies. To regain its reputation as the King of Battle (and remain the greatest killer on the battlefield) the artillery has greatly expanded its MLRS capabilities. The huge 420-mm rocket now has a precision warhead guided with a GPS system similar to the one used by the Air Force. The range of this "precision MLRS" rocket is now twice that of the older, unguided version. This new system is undergoing something of a firepower renaissance in Afghanistan. But manpower restrictions set by the Obama administration continue to shrink the number of artillery units in Afghanistan.

Left out of the firepower equation is the unspoken concern that someday the ground services may need to mass fires again. When that day comes, the few artillery guns and rockets remaining in the force will be hard pressed to fulfill the mission. Our howitzers were designed in the sixties, and no replacements are in sight. The latest Russian and Chinese types shoot farther and have higher rates of fire. The U.S. Army has fewer artillery battalions on active service at any time since the Franklin D. Roosevelt administration. Precision still remains mostly the purview of aerial systems. Pound for pound, artillery precision is much more expensive than air-delivered precision. Due to expense it will be a long time before U.S. artillery will be able to mass precision fires.

The lesson of America's experience with firepower in the American era is obvious but often violated: a nation should never contemplate involvement in a war without a clear understanding of what firepower can and cannot do. On every occasion, the United States has overestimated the destructive killing power of its air-, sea-, and land-based firepower weapons. Inevitably this overestimation has led to optimism and expectations greater than men and machines could ever deliver. Munitions like those used in Desert Storm, intended to destroy a conventional force like Saddam's Republican Guard, had much less killing effect against an elusive, dispersed, entrenched enemy unencumbered by heavy equipment or vulnerable lines of communications. A concerted bombardment that would shock the life out of a Western or Arab conventional unit might have only a temporary effect on the fighting strength of a tough insurgent enemy inured to hardship and willing to die for a cause.

This book is dedicated to the premise that the United States can make its small units dominant, not just better. Dominance cannot be achieved simply by focusing on Soldiers in the close fight. Dominance comes only when small units have the capability to overwhelm the enemy with firepower. Infantrymen cannot carry much firepower on their backs. They need an external source, such as artillery and airpower, to overwhelm an enemy. Firepower applied with skill and audacity will kill the enemy and "break" his will to fight. In the best of circumstances, external fires crush the enemy before close combat begins. In spite of its shortcomings artillery remains the most efficient means for killing enemies at a distance in all circumstances of weather and terrain. When infantry small units move very close to each other, only artillery and infantry mortars can drop shells "danger close," within only a few meters from friendlies in contact.

The firepower system must so weaken the enemy that close-in killing by infantry becomes a coup de grace rather than a battle of attrition that lasts too long and gets Soldiers needlessly killed. We can never allow the close fight to be a fair fight. The old adage from World War II remains true in the American era: where firepower dominates, the infantry becomes a finding and fixing force, and firepower does most of the killing.

For artillery to return to the weapon of choice for killing power on a future battlefield, the branch and its matériel must be completely replaced. Sixties-era artillery and artillery munitions dating from World War II simply will not suffice on tomorrow's battlefields. The entire branch could be completely over-hauled for about the price of two squadrons of Air Force F-35 fighter planes. But in today's environment, we know, this is not going to happen. And our enemies know it as well.

[17]

AIR SUPPORT TO SOLDIERS
AND MARINES

Airpower is like poker. A second-best hand is like none at all.
—Gen. George Kenney, USAAF

Make no mistake: the successful execution of wars in the American era depends on U.S. dominance in the third dimension. Since the introduction of aircraft to war, no U.S. fighting method, from Patton's to McChrystal's, has had the least chance of succeeding without absolute, uncontested control of the skies. Our military has been seduced by past successes in the air. The last time an American Soldier had to endure the helpless horrors of an aerial bombardment was when a North Korean fighter strafed the Korean airbase at Kimpo in 1951. Only twice in the American era has our aerial dominance been challenged. On the first occasion Russians and North Koreans flying the superb MiG-15 stoutly and skillfully fought against U.S. pilots in their F-86 Saber jets. But, while dramatic and often bloody, the drama of combat over "MiG Alley" never seriously affected the ground battles in Korea.

The second occasion occurred over the skies of Vietnam in 1967 when the North Vietnamese, using sophisticated Soviet-supplied missiles and guns and fighter aircraft, embarrassed the Air Force and Navy by downing a tragically high number of aircraft. Again, while too many fliers died or were captured during subsequent battles over the skies of North Vietnam, U.S. aerial dominance was never challenged decisively in that or subsequent wars. In South Vietnam, tactical success on the ground increasingly depended on the ubiquitous presence of aircraft orbiting overhead. Few large-scale tactical engagements proceeded very far before Soldiers and Marines called for close support from Air Force, Marine, or Navy fighters or the newly introduced helicopter gunships flown by Army and Marine pilots.

The role of U.S. airpower after Vietnam changed in two significant ways. First, the ground and air dimensions of war merged. This phenomenon was first recognized officially in the late seventies with the Army's introduction of Air-Land Battle. The poor grammar was intentional. The authors of the new doctrine combined the two dimensions to indicate the obvious: no longer would there be separate air and land battles. Virtually every dimension of the land battle would have an aerial corollary, from communications to intelligence, logistics, ground maneuver, and, of course, firepower.

The campaigns in Afghanistan and Iraq and by the Israelis in Lebanon reinforced the significance and imperative of this air-ground convergence. To make the point, in 1996 I came up with the phrase air-ground "interdependence" to explain the remarkable melding of air and ground warfare that appeared after Desert Storm. Interdependence suggests a degree of intimacy far beyond just the development of joint processes and procedures intended to bring all the services together. Interdependence implies that our greatest advantage on the future battlefield, regardless of the level or type of war, will occur at the point where the aerial and ground dimensions intersect.

Winning at the "crease" will demand a level of closeness between the air and ground mediums that will allow nearly simultaneous application of fires and maneuver applied in broad patterns that strike and check the enemy everywhere he can be seen and engaged. The entire premise for interdependence rests with the ability of air and ground forces to gain unprecedented proficiency in the delivery of close-in fires.

Recent experience suggests that we have achieved success at perfecting air-ground interdependence at the strategic and operational level of war. Desert Storm proved that strategic strikes by fleets of long-range fighters, missiles, and bombers had developed to a remarkable degree. Experience in Afghanistan and during the march to Baghdad in 2003 demonstrated that the Air Force and Navy had perfected aerial operational fires to the extent that commanders on the ground no longer stopped to consider the originating source of long-distance killing fires, whether from aircraft, artillery, ships—it did not matter.

The second phenomenon of this new age of aerial warfare is the overwhelming and incontestable aerial dominance by Western militaries. Absolute dominance has led to a propensity of opposing militaries to "spot" command of what Professor Barry Posen of MIT calls the "global commons"—the air, sea, and space. To offset American precision killing power the enemy has retreated into the "contested zones," those regions of the globe that favor his style of war. The enemy has found succor and solace in distant, inhospitable regions unapproachable by conventional means. He has chosen to achieve success by fighting at the tactical level of war, where human and cultural advantages offset technological advantages. Regardless of where and at what level he seeks to fight, he will have as his principal operational objective the control of time. He will seek to win by not losing. He will use his position of advantage in remote, inhospitable, and alien places to kill enough Americans and stretch out the campaign until we tire of the effort and go home.

Our enemy's actions provide proof positive that U.S. airpower is both indispensable and uncontestable. In fact, experience in recent wars demonstrates conclusively that control of the air will provide the single greatest firepower advantage in the American era. Our Soldiers and Marines have voted for airpower by their preferences in combat. In Iraq and Afghanistan they consistently call for aerial fires: first for the AC-130 "Spectre" gunship, then Army AH-64 helicopter gunships, then fighter bombers, and, finally, artillery . . . if it is in range.

Aerial dominance in the American era, combined with the growing reluctance to risk casualties from putting "boots on the ground," has created a new approach to contemporary wars, the "light footprint" war. In effect, Western militaries have "hired out" air forces to countries in distress if support to them is important enough to engage but not important enough to engage decisively on the ground. In places like Serbia, Libya, Iraq, Afghanistan, Syria, and (in the case of drone warfare) Yemen and Pakistan aerial strikes delivered from safe altitudes and in concert with indigenous ground forces have had a salutary effect of stopping an enemy ground force and, in some cases, achieving something akin to victory. Failures of an air-only approach in Libya, Syria, and, so far, Iraq offer a cautionary tale, however. Without a reliable ground force to exploit the advantages of air strikes and to quell the chaos that too often follows aerial assault, a campaign conducted exclusively by air might cause harm in the long term.

The greatest challenge for the future will be to find better ways to kill an enemy who has learned to "hug" ground units in contact. Killing close in by air is termed "close air support" (CAS) and is the most difficult of all missions to perform, because proximity to friendly forces always adds the risk that mistakes will kill our own Soldiers. But in spite of difficulty and risk, when a Soldier's life is at stake and an enemy is "hugging" him in close combat he expects the aircraft orbiting above to kill the enemy no matter how close the fight.

Enemies have also learned to open fire and then disappear in the period between the request for support and the arrival of aircraft overhead. The enemy has also countered precision bombs by using the media to raise the stakes for occasional failures. Efforts to lessen response times have been met by an enemy who has developed his own creative means to enable him to move frequently and fight in ever more dispersed formations. In limited wars fought by the United States since the end of World War II, approximately 96 percent of all combat deaths occur within the "last mile" from the line of contact. In order to reach enemies huddling within the last mile the Army and Marine Corps must develop new ways of planning, delivering, and controlling close-in fires.

SOURCES OF FRICTION

Close air support is hard, as noted, because it offers both the most certain means for killing enemy combat forces and the greatest likelihood for harming friendly troops. Historically, both the air and ground services have been tentative in using CAS unless absolutely sure of the need. The conventional wisdom used to be that it was better for ground forces to use artillery, mortars, or attack aviation first and reserve CAS for targets farther away from troops in contact. Air forces likewise favored the freedom inherent when striking more distant targets, where collateral damage to friendly troops was least likely. In fact, CAS has always suffered from several sources of "friction" that collectively have prevented it from being fully effective as the primary source of killing power in support of ground operations.

Without question, GPS- and laser-guided killing power has effectively reduced if not eliminated "target location error" (TLE), the distance between the target location identified by the Soldier on the ground and the spot where the bomb lands. TLE has traditionally been the greatest source of imprecision in the delivery of close-in fires. In Vietnam TLE averaged about 250 meters. Today, thanks to handheld observation devices with embedded lasers and GPS, Soldiers can locate targets with accuracy of a meter or less. Precision weapons now land within a few feet of the identified target location. Unfortunately, as we have seen recently in Iraq and Gaza, very precise weapons serve to heighten the trauma and embarrassment when weapons hit the wrong target precisely. Mistakes occur infrequently, but when they do the global media are first on the spot to declare that since U.S. weapons are so precise, any discretionary "error" surely had to be intentional. Nothing is worse than being precisely wrong. The enemy recognizes the impact of discretionary errors on morale. As we have seen with the Israelis in Lebanon and elsewhere, the enemy will continue to find diabolical and creative ways to enhance the probability that aerial fires will strike innocent civilians and friendly ground forces. A single discretionary error can have a devastating effect on the success of a campaign.

A great deal of moral courage and trust is needed to restart a close-support mission after a severe incident of fratricide. Past experience suggests that such errors often compel commanders to slow mission times, increase minimum safe distances, and restrict the use of certain weapons and platforms. These additional sources of friction favor the enemy. Marine and Army close-combat units discovered in Fallujah in 2004 that even with the aid of superb tactical intelligence and precision locating devices they were never able effectively to deliver bombs very close. Fear of collateral damage and confusion over exactly where the enemy was located compelled those in close contact to pull back at least four hundred meters. A rule of thumb still useful today is that the minimum safe distance a ground force should be from a bomb is about "a meter a pound." Thus today's heavy bombs preferred by the Air Force might push back the point of contact between friendlies and the enemy a thousand meters or more. The sight of withdrawing ground troops often was the signal for the enemy to withdraw, leaving the aircraft to bomb empty buildings. To be as safe as possible the delivering fighter plane would carry the smallest bomb available, usually a five hundred pounder. But the rule-of-thumb five-hundred-meter separation might as well be five hundred miles when the urban fight is joined at point-blank range.

An emerging and very troubling aspect of modern aerial warfare is the proclivity of the enemy to resist attack by even the heaviest bombs. Before the beginning of Operation Protective Edge, the 2014 Israeli attack into Gaza, Hamas militants constructed heavily reinforced defenses along parallel housing blocks on the outskirts of Gaza City. During the opening phase of the seven-week campaign the Israeli Golani Brigade suffered heavy casualties when attacking these well prepared defenses. The Israelis had badly underestimated the amount of destructive close air support needed to crush the Hamas defenses. The Israeli air force tried to reduce collateral damage among civilians by dropping five-hundred-pound bombs. Soon the bomb sizes increased to one thousand and then two thousand pounds, just enough to collapse the concrete bunkers and thick building walls that constituted the Hamas defenses. The lesson the Israelis learned was that heavy urban defenses dictate that infantry forces must either move back or hunker down and risk casualties when heavy bombs are delivered very close. They relearned the painful rule of thumb taught by the Marines in Fallujah, that the contact distance in the urban fight is often fifty meters or less and at that distance a two-thousand-pounder can be just as deadly to the attacker as the defender. So increasingly we are witnessing ground units taking extreme risk in ignoring "minimum safe distances" to kill a close-in enemy who is heavily protected and willing to die.

Timeliness is the greatest source of friction in supporting the close fight with airpower . . . and the enemy knows it. ISIS in particular takes effective advantage of lengthening mission times. Rules of engagement, poor intelligence, and the ability of the enemy to hide have increased mission times over Iraq and Syria to an hour or more. Because of what Soldiers term the "latency" or "dwell time" of these missions, the enemy has plenty of opportunity to disappear before an orbiting aircraft is cleared to deliver bombs. As a consequence more than 75 percent of air missions against ISIS return to base without dropping. All too often the time that it takes to deliver close air support is so long that even those missions cleared for drop end up killing only buildings. As ISIS has adapted and learned to operate under the U.S. aerial campaign, its losses have fallen dramatically. No longer do its forces travel in convoys. Like their Hezbollah brethren they move in twos and threes in civilian cars and pickups. They hide critical items well inside buildings or bury them in the desert. They no longer brandish very large and distinctive captured U.S. equipment in the village square. Most ISIS offensive operations are conducted the old-fashioned way: with suicide bombers followed by mortar fire and dismounted infantry attacks.

In the campaign against ISIS, just like previous campaigns against Fallujah, Ramadi, and elsewhere, the Army and Marines discovered what generations before them already knew: missions are slow principally due to human, not technological, factors. With today's constrictive rules of engagement every bomb or shell has a commander's name on it. Mistakes can be both fatal and career ending. The embedded journalist is waiting behind the next wall to report the incident to the world . . . often with a video playback.

Layering aggravates the problem of latency. On average, each level of decision making takes at least eight minutes, a figure that has not changed substantially in half a century. The standard for latency in the future will depend, as always, on actions by the enemy. Most challenging will be the engagement of moving targets, such as terrorist vehicles and foot-borne enemy on the move. The standard for aircraft on station to engage moving targets should be two minutes. Stationary targets, particularly those with uncertain intentions, may wait longer for engagement, but under no circumstances should the time from identification to attack be less than ten minutes. Clearly, missions after an hour or more do very little harm in proportion to their expense.

In Afghanistan, thanks in large measure to drones and long-endurance fighters and bombers, the air services are getting better at maintaining a constant aerial presence over troops in contact. But problems still remain. Response times measured in only a few minutes can be achieved only if supporting aerial platforms are constantly overhead. High-performance aircraft are not very efficient when circling as they wait for something to happen. Even a flight time to target measured in minutes might be too slow when supporting today's fleeting and brutal engagements.

Of course, we have learned that aerial observation does not have to be done by manned aircraft. Any vehicle overhead (even if unarmed and unmanned) changes the enemy's behavior. When he sees a drone he immediately goes to ground and disperses. He turns off his electronic communications. Reinforcements and supplies fail to arrive, out of fear of being spotted. When he withdraws deep into urban structures he gives up the advantage of direct observation.

The variable most likely to reduce all sources of friction is trust. Trust between Soldier, his commander (or the approving authority), and the pilot overhead must be earned. It is purchased gradually and can be forfeited instantly if a bomb accidentally kills friendlies. Technology can do little to establish trust. Trust comes slowly, from long-term association and proven performance in combat. Trust cannot be established between strangers.

REDUCING FRICTION

As we develop the means to deliver fires closer to friendly troops, the enemy finds ways to move even closer. As our response times quicken, the enemy learns to retreat even more quickly. As our weapons get more precise and destructive, the enemy becomes more proficient at hiding, dispersing, going to ground. As fratricide and collateral damage decreases, the enemy finds a way to exploit the media to heighten the psychological impact of each event. Thus we are in a footrace with an enemy who knows the weaknesses of our firepower systems and works constantly and cleverly to diminish their effectiveness.

Close-air-support mission responses are slowed because of too many layers in the decision-making chain. The only way mission times can be improved is to eliminate layers. The question is how to eliminate layers while ensuring that fires are delivered at the right time and place. Army and Marine infantry, those closest to the enemy, should be solely responsible for controlling the delivery of aerial fires. Only a maneuver Soldier can actually sense the threat. Only he has the inalienable responsibility for protecting his men and accomplishing the mission. Artillery and Air Force observers may have access to the latest sensors and superb connectivity to higher fire-support agencies, but no one except a close-combat Soldier possesses the fingertip sense of the battlefield necessary to determine the risks and the means to attack the target immediately to his front. Taking intermediaries out of the firing chain is no great technological challenge. Web-based sensors on board overhead drones linked to GPS and downloaded to a Soldier's cell phone would remove any ambiguity about the exact nature of the target. A Soldier's cell phone would provide a simple and reliable means for communicating directly with airplanes overhead. Special Forces small units today frequently act as their own observers for CAS. There is no reason all infantrymen cannot as well.

CAS is an incredibly intimate and personal mission. Thus, successful close air support depends on building trust between those who call for the mission and those who drop the bombs. Mistakes made by pilots dropping weapons in the wrong place and by Soldiers mistakenly shooting at friendly aircraft only exacerbate the problem. The trust curve can be increased bloodlessly by habitually associating air units most likely to support troops with troops they are most likely to support.

The Marines make their air wings part of each Marine division, and every smaller Marine expeditionary unit habitually takes along its share of pilots and planes. Marine pilots like to brag that they are infantrymen first. Sadly, such associations do not exist between Army and Air Force units. They should. A habitual relationship should be enduring and should never be a pickup exercise. Every Air Force fighter squadron commander should be held responsible for training Army maneuver observers in techniques and procedures for calling in and managing close air support. Higher-level commanders should be evaluated on their ability to make optimum use of aerial fires. Some squadron officers and enlisted airmen should literally live with their associated ground units. Maneuver tactical commanders must know each fighter pilot personally and understand the strengths and weaknesses of each.

In the past, effectiveness in CAS platforms was defined by the axiom "lower and slower is better than higher and faster." Often in the era of limited wars the air services were obliged to swap the new for the old when older weapons proved to be better suited for closer support of troops in contact. During the early days of the Korean War the Air Force brought back World War II–era propeller-driven aircraft to replace jets after discovering that fast movers were incapable of spotting a dispersed enemy and bombing with precision.

This lesson was repeated in Vietnam. The Air Force and Navy again brought propeller-driven observation and attack aircraft out of mothballs to meet the same demand. Today venerable firepower platforms such as the AC-130 gunship and the iconic A-10 Warthog close-support jet seem to reappear time and again as essential firepower providers, even though the Air Force declares both to be too vulnerable for modern war. Since the earliest days in Vietnam the ageless B-52, designed during the forties as a strategic bomber, has been continuously drafted into the role of a conventional bomber. Some argue that today the availability of shared video images between pilots and Soldiers promises to make "low and slow" an anachronism. If both Soldier and pilot could see the same image of the target, and if the pilot trusts in the veracity of the commander in contact, perhaps the mission could be accomplished with precision bombs flying at high speed and altitude. One lesson seems to be accepted by all: that a real-time view of the target shared by the unit in contact, the pilot, and the critical decision makers is perhaps the most important single technological requirement to improve timeliness and effectiveness and lower the risks of CAS.

In today's environment the process is the problem. Captain Swenson can certainly vouch for the fact that friction comes from those in the decision-making chain who are uncertain, poorly trained, and inclined to allow procedures to interfere with decisive action. Every decision maker who orders a bomb to be dropped must have the skill, instinct, and authority to make very critical judgments, often with insufficient information and when the target is unseen or indistinct. He must be able to differentiate friend from foe and enemy from the innocents. He must be immune to attempts by the enemy to deceive. None of these changes will happen until the air and ground components accept the truism that close air support has become far too important to be left substantively unchanged in the face of a strikingly different and more challenging conflict environment. Today the enemy is the catalyst for change. He understands how lethal we are from the air. He's done all he can to lessen our advantage there. We must begin now to restore our ability to kill him with efficiency from the air if we are to defeat him and lower the human cost of close combat.

[18]

WIN FOREVER . . .
IN COMBAT

Know the other and know yourself. Fight one hundred battles
without danger.

—Sun Tzu, *The Art of War*

Pete Carroll, coach of the perennially successful Seattle Seahawks football
team, is a friend. We met in 2009 during the first international small-unit
symposium that I put together for Joint Forces Command (JFCOM), then
commanded by the legendary Gen. Jim Mattis, the most venerated war fighter
in the Marine Corps at the time.

To our surprise, Carroll did not come to be venerated. He came to learn
and to help. Over three days he would walk into a work group and explain how
he developed small teams, in his case of eleven men each for offense, defense,
and special teams. We asked him to sum up his experiences at the end of the
symposium, and his observations were simple and direct. He recounts his time
with us in his book *Win Forever:* "I am grateful to [General Scales] for allowing
me to participate in the conference and for helping me understand just how
universal the basic principles of leadership, competition, and self-knowledge
really are."[1]

My most memorable encounter with the coach came after a day's work
when he sat with my business partner, Jack Pryor, General Mattis, and Professor
Marty Seligman from the University of Pennsylvania. As Carroll talked, we were

struck by the remarkable similarities between a football team and an infantry small unit: two "elevens," one trying to win and finish uninjured, the other trying to win and stay alive. Marty Seligman remarked that teams of nine to eleven were the same for the squad and most outdoor contact athletic teams. Eleven was the number of most primitive, aboriginal hunting groups in the Kalahari Desert and Australia. Perhaps eleven is in our DNA. Eleven was ideal because a smaller group would not have the heft to run down and kill large mammals, whereas any larger and the group would be too ungainly for extended expeditions.

Carroll talked about the effort he put into selecting and conditioning his coaches and players. A few months later, when we were his guests at the University of Southern California, he showed us his remarkable Trojan fitness centers, with row after row of machines. He introduced us to his incredibly professional fitness staff. We talked about the extensive and imaginative drills and player exercises he employed in daily practices in an effort, as he says, to "win forever."

On both occasions, he asked if the Army and Marine Corps were as thorough and lavish when putting together their "elevens." Sadly, of course, the answer was no. However, his questions during the conference had intrigued General Mattis and his team. Afterward, we talked extensively about the need to do for our teams what Coach Carroll did for his. How would it be done? What would be the cost? Where would such conditioning and training best be conducted?

At the time the ground services fielded about 6,000 small units, Army and Marine squads of infantry, sappers, tank crews, Special Forces, Rangers, Deltas, SEALs, and the occasional CIA direct action teams—6,000 teams from a nation of 330 million. Surely, the nation could afford to lavish the same care and attention on those who go out every day to face death as the NCAA spends on student athletes. So, we put together a wish list for how the 6,000 might be turned into armed Division I varsity athletes.

To tell the story, let us begin, as always, with some history. During World War II and Korea, the "exchange ratio" for American air forces was extremely favorable. The ratio between enemy and friendly killed in air-to-air combat over Europe versus the German Luftwaffe was nine to one, against the Japanese about thirteen to one. The advantage in Korea against North Korean and Russian flyers was, again, about thirteen to one. For a time in Vietnam, however, the ratio dropped embarrassingly. In 1967, it approached parity.

The response within the Air Force and Navy was immediate and dramatic. Both services began to restore the traditional dominant ratios by creating advanced tactical fighter schools, made famous by Tom Cruise: Top Gun for the Navy and Red Flag for the Air Force. The air services quickly developed new tactics for air-to-air combat. The shock and embarrassment of this tough era also led the aerial services to develop a new series of tactical fighter aircraft, such as the F-16 and F-15 for the Air Force and the F-18 for the Navy. Since Vietnam, these aircraft in the hands of U.S. and Israeli pilots have achieved incredible exchange ratios, well over two hundred to one. Today, thanks to the airpower pioneers of the seventies, the United States cannot be challenged in the air.

What about on the ground? Let us do some more arithmetic. During the battle for Fallujah in 2004, at least ninety Marines and Soldiers perished in brutal street-to-street and house-to-house fighting. The arithmetic loss rate in this urban fight was virtually the same as those in Korea and Vietnam, about six to one in open street fights, approaching parity once the fight moved into buildings. So at JFCOM, Jim Mattis and I asked why the ground forces should suffer such discouraging ratios. We concluded that it was not about Soldier and Marine quality. The performance of close-combat Soldiers and Marines was high. When compared to the enemy, there was no contest. Look at any news report or photograph of tactical engagements in Afghanistan and you will notice enemy combatants running about, shooting wildly. U.S. Soldiers and Marines move in tightly formed groups and, even in the tensest moments, carry their rifles with fingers outside the trigger wells. These images prove the value of rigorous training, and no one respects and appreciates first-rate training more than close-combat Soldiers, who consistently rate the importance of good training higher than pay and benefits. They know that first-rate preparation for war is the best life insurance. In Vietnam, two-thirds of all small-unit combat deaths occurred during the first two months in the field, in part because the training system had mass-produced Soldiers too quickly to prepare them properly for the complex, difficult task of close-in killing. So we asked what a difference it would make if we could adapt some of Pete Carroll's methods to create a ground version of "Top Gun."

We needed a "win forever" strategy—an attributable, measurable, service-wide system for selecting, training, and verifying the fighting ability of small units and their leaders. Such a system would begin with selection and testing of all infantry volunteers. Much as in the National Football League, this testing would include measures of physical prowess and neuro-cognitive levels, along with assessment of adaptability, character, and commitment. This baseline of information would guide training of Soldiers and Marines before combat begins. We concluded that, as in the air services, no small unit should be sent into a shooting situation until both leaders and followers had experienced bloodless battle on a virtual practice field.

So the challenge for the future was clear in 2009: we needed to *create superb small teams during a protracted period of peace that we knew was coming.* This was a tough sell in 2009. At the time, infantry leaders had as many as five or six tours in the combat zone. Some special operating forces had as many as twelve. But we knew budget cuts and radical reductions in training and operations budgets were coming and would threaten to dull the sharp edge honed after nearly a decade of war. We foresaw the emergence of a "garrison" Army and Marine Corps that would be locked into bases with little chance of overseas deployment. Given normal career attrition, we feared that units would increasingly be made up of new Soldiers who did not have close-combat experience . . . and had no chance to inoculate themselves for combat before again going to war inadequately prepared.

Unfortunately, the enemy rarely takes downtime. The enemy's tempo along the "Arc of Instability" continues to increase while fighting skills atrophy at home. If the past is prologue, our ground forces will inevitably be required to deploy directly into a combat zone with little or no notice. First priority must be to keep combat proficiency high, so units will not have to go to war without extensive training-up or last-minute personnel reshuffling. Individual small-unit proficiency must be constant, not subject to the same pendulum swings that diminished fighting proficiency in past wars. Tomorrow's training regimes will increasingly become more episodic. Just before deployments, units are at their peak. Soldier assignments, both internally and externally, are more stable, and turbulence is at a minimum. Distractions are few, and leaders concentrate on those tasks to be accomplished in battle. Most deployments are preceded by a rotation through a combat training center, where leaders get the opportunity to practice skills in rigorous simulated combat. All too often, however, even in combat, these skills deteriorate quickly.

For a solution to this vexing problem, we discovered a mirror image of Carroll's win-forever philosophy in our elite special operation units. In 2009 these men were engaged in direct action "night raids" and established a remarkable record for killing many Al Qaeda and Taliban with very small losses. To be sure, as in all aspects of human behavior, bad things happen: a lucky shot by a rocket-propelled-grenade gunner downs a Chinook helicopter, and dozens of SEALs or Rangers die. Yet the "exchange ratios" achieved among these Tier I forces were remarkable. Based on my discussions with special operators in the field and at Fort Bragg, North Carolina, I estimated that direct-action teams, Special Operations Forces, Delta, the Rangers, and the SEALs, routinely achieve an exchange ratio of about forty to one. Of course, we could not expect such extraordinary ratios among Army and Marine general-purpose forces. Perhaps a more achievable ratio might be twenty to one. Adding those enemy killed at a distance by drones, close air support, artillery, and mortars, we concluded with reasonable confidence that a ratio of at least sixty to seventy to one is possible—depending, of course, on the mission, the nature of the enemy, and conditions of terrain and weather. With ratios like these the president's decision making would not be driven just by the arithmetic. He would have more time and strategic maneuver room to win before the American people grew tired of the exercise.

Pete Carroll and the special operations community share similarities we could build on. First, there was the imperative to have a realistic, repeatable system for hammering the realities of war (or football) into the primal reflexes of the brain. Think of two-a-days on steroids. We thought of building a small-unit Top Gun– or Red Flag–style exercise into team training. Maybe we could exploit the gaming industry to find an immersive simulation that put Soldiers virtually into harm's way without ever firing a shot. Carroll had told us that the key to winning was repetition—constant, unending, and boring repetition. Ideally, repetition in practice would not be rote football drills; instead, each repetition would be unique, making every player think about what was about to happen, not just going through the motions.

So we envisioned a "virtual gym" where the senses, brain, and body would be highly developed and fully integrated, sort of an NFL training facility in every combat brigade. Experienced military and civilian coaches and facilitators would run these gyms. The centerpiece of the gym would be an instrumented open space, like Top Gun's but indoors. Soldiers and Marines would don gaming headsets and walk through a virtual battlescape. No two repetitions would be the same. As the trainees crept through this virtual space, images and targets would appear. Some would be innocents caught in the crossfire. Others would be bad guys, perhaps some wearing disguises. Others would charge the squad wrapped in suicide belts. Some engagements would be in virtual villages and cities. Others would occur in open spaces, where enemy snipers would engage from long distances. Soldier and Marine small units would have to react reflexively and make decisions intuitively. All of these engagements would be caught on tape to be repeated, like game films, after each exercise.

These virtual "combat immersions" could be immediately paused and restarted, time after time, under a variety of circumstances. Repetition has two important effects on the quality of the training experience. First, the small unit develops what behavioral scientists term "collective muscle memory," a condition that fuses together the collective action of nine Soldiers into a cohesive and effective whole. Second, unexpected and seemingly random sets of circumstances demand that the small-unit leader make immediate "in extremis" decisions that reveal whether he possesses the intuitive "right stuff" to lead young Soldiers in combat.

Perhaps virtual immersions could be connected to Soldiers in the combat zone over the net. Such virtual "right-seat rides" would allow a Soldier at Fort Lewis or a Marine at sea to watch an action in real time, transmitted through a fighting Soldier's helmet cam. After the battle was over, both Soldiers could discuss and replay the episode. Monitors and "coaches" would transcribe the tape into another scenario for the virtual trainer.

Think of how proficient our small units would be if they could go through a thousand rotations per year, all of them at Top Gun standard. Variable scenarios would allow small-unit repetitions to be done many times per day; each with different missions, enemy situations, terrains, and at different levels of tactical tempo and complexity. The simulation facility would embrace all the goodness of the larger training centers. World-class and diabolically skilled "opposing forces," or OPFORs, would play the enemy. The OPFOR would always play to win; each repetition would be a free-play exercise in which either side could prevail. All repetitions would be recorded, and after each exercise the evaluated team would undergo an after-action review, during which every player would share his successes and failures with his team. As in football, every Soldier in the gym would hear "footsteps" from competitors eager to take his job. Acceptance into tomorrow's small units would have to be earned, and the teams would be required to compete every day. As they age, Soldiers lose their edge. Like professional football players, they slow and become less aggressive and eventually unfit for operating in life-and-death situations. The virtual gym would be an instrument for accountability. Repeated failure would disqualify leaders and teammates for deployment. No one should have to die because training and performance assessments did not hold a Soldier or his leaders accountable.

Coach Carroll puts as much or more emphasis on selecting and training his coaches as he does on his players. He told us that he does not coach players, he coaches his coaches. From a ground-service perspective the takeaway is universal: a team is only as good as its junior leaders. Small-unit leaders must be taught at a much earlier age to lead indirectly, to think quickly, and to "see" a battlefield that is dispersed, complex, hidden, and ambiguous. The isolation inherent in urban fighting puts even greater demands on small units and requires a degree of cohesion never before seen in the U.S. military. Today, learning and brain science can help identify those who can make tough decisions intuitively. Intuitive decision making is a learned skill; it is learned through a system that is experience based, rigorous, accountable, and repetitive. Decision-making simulations today can replicate conditions of uncertainty, fear, and ambiguity. If used properly, these immersions can help identify the natural leaders, perhaps even before taking the oath of enlistment or commissioning.

Good commanders know how to lead in combat. Great commanders possess an intuitive sense of how to transition quickly from kinetic warfare to a subtler kind of cultural warfare, distinguished by the need to win the narrative and well as the kinetic battle. Rare are the leaders who can shift between these two disparate universes and lead and fight competently in both. The key to achieving excellence in both combat domains is what combat leaders call "combat inurement"—that is, the intuitive ability of leaders, Soldiers, and small units to fight together with an unprecedented level of proficiency.

Pete Carroll's fitness centers have dozens of workout machines that his players use to increase muscle strength, endurance, and flexibility. An Army virtual gym could easily do the same thing. Soldiers could also increase visual and perceptual acuity and the ability to see, sense, and react to unseen enemies using "surround" screens that present infinitely varied situations. Virtual firing ranges would allow Soldiers to improve their shooting and sniping skills. Virtual Soldier gyms could be made portable; a unit flying (or floating) to a distant, unfamiliar objective could download the latest intelligence and geography of the area and practice the operation many times before doing the real thing.

One lesson I have learned from combat and from observing close small units in action for more than a decade is that there is no magic formula for finding the Vikings within the officer and NCO corps. No personnel selection system will reveal who can sense the battlefield and make decisions "in extremis" using innate intuitive skills. There is no examination for courage or coolness under fire. A lieutenant graduating from West Point or the Reserve Officers Training Corps may want passionately to wear the crossed rifles. His father and grandfather may have served with distinction in combat. Maybe he is tall, blond, played football, and married the general's daughter. But none of the traditional indicators tells anything about his potential for leading a platoon in combat. In fact, a review of past performance using today's subjective selection criteria would have left Sergeant Giunta and Captain Swenson off the list. Sadly, at present the Army and Marine Corps must put young officers in front of forty men and risk their lives in a live-fire crapshoot to find out if he has the right stuff.

The right answer, of course, is to put every young man who wants to lead in the close fight through a virtual gym. To be fair, the infantry aspirant should undergo a lengthy string of immersions that objectively test his leadership and command skills. Only then can a West Point tactical officer or a Marine instructor tell a young man that he has made the cut. Squad-leader selection for NCOs must be even more stringent. As part of his qualification for every stripe earned, a young enlisted infantryman should prove his ability to make intuitive decisions in the heat of battle. He should be given more time to correct his mistakes in the virtual gym, but he should never be certified to lead a squad in combat until he has proven himself in a simulation.

Today, the National Football League is making great progress in developing decision-making simulations for quarterbacks. Quarterbacks are trained to observe and orient, visualize, focus, and execute to a standard of seven seconds or less.[2] This standard is exactly the same for a small-unit leader exposed to first contact with the enemy. Unfortunately, nothing has happened to create a similar virtual immersion for combat leaders. This must change. As a first priority, the Department of Defense must create a national-level small-combat-unit "simulations and gaming" effort managed by the ground services but funded by a separate (and fenced) line within the Defense budget. To ensure that such an effort would survive internecine budgetary battles, legislation should be enacted that would set aside a percentage of all Defense simulations funding (say 20 percent) for small units and small-unit leader simulations.

The nation spends at least two million dollars to select and train a Navy carrier pilot. Pilots, civilian and military, must spend time in multimillion-dollar simulators several times per year in order to maintain flying proficiency. Just one Navy F-18 pilot has died at the hands of the enemy since 1972. Today, small-unit leaders are still dying. Yet the cost of preparing them for small-unit leadership is very small. The video-gaming industry has been creating realistic close-combat simulations for decades. Professional sports teams use them routinely. Thus the critical question: Do pilots deserve better training than infantryman? Even if every close-combat Soldier and Marine were given the exact same treatment as a Tier I Special Forces team, the total cost would be significantly less than what the nation spends to train fighter pilots.

So let us pick a number . . . say a million dollars, dedicated to training every regular Army and Marine squad using cutting-edge technologies. And then let us put it into law. Forget the humanity for a moment and just think of the long-term cost saving. Such a commitment to world-class simulations would save money over time by reducing the number of Soldiers and Marines who wind up in VA hospitals.

Yet here we are in 2016, fourteen years into war, and a Soldier or Marine can play his Xbox and fight a virtual enemy for entertainment in the barracks, but his service cannot spend the money to give him a simulation that will save his life in combat.

[19]

STRATEGIC GENIUS

Every special calling in life, if it is to be followed with success, requires peculiar qualifications of understanding and soul. Where these are of a high order, and manifest themselves by extraordinary achievements, the mind to which they belong is termed genius.

—Carl von Clausewitz, Book 111

In recent years, the media has taken particular aim at generals, both in their professional and personal lives. Revelations of extravagant lifestyles fueled by excessive spending on the "care and feeding" of generals at a time of crushing budget deficits have angered many inside and outside the Beltway. Perhaps unfairly, revelations of personal failures and embarrassments have reignited and accelerated the debate about the quality of American generalship.

Western democracies characteristically hold military leaders accountable if wars last too long or cost too much in treasure and human life. The public tends to hold their fire at the beginning of wars, either through uncertainty about the progress of the enterprise or out of respect for those fighting it. Criticisms tend to accelerate in times like these, when unpopular wars wind down into messy or indeterminate conclusions. Unlike past wars in the American era, the public and politicians tend not to criticize the tactical fighting abilities of young privates, sergeants, or lieutenants. They tend to reserve their fire for perceived strategic errors, made by more senior leaders, who are depicted in wartime literature and the media as unable to adapt to the inevitable fog that accompanies all human conflict. The public does not always differentiate between decisions made by generals and those by their civilian masters.

So as we exit from our second war in this new century, many in authority sense that something's missing in American strategic generalship. This perceived weakness at the strategic level is all the more remarkable when considering how well Army leaders have done at maneuvering large formations at lower (tactical and operational) levels in past wars. U.S. ground forces demonstrated in the 1991 "Great Wheel" and the 2003 "March to Baghdad" that they were brilliant practitioners of conventional operations. This skill was acquired just after Vietnam in the late seventies by a generation of Vietnam-era officers who put a unique American spin on German armored blitzkrieg warfare. The Army called this AirLand Battle and perfected it during the matériel, training, and doctrine revolution that changed the Army's focus from tactical victories to winning at the operational level. Still, today U.S. ground forces are unbeatable in large-scale conventional mechanized maneuver in open terrain, such as northern Europe and the heartland of the Middle East.

However, wars in Iraq and Afghanistan have shown that the services have come up short at the strategic level, the level at which national security and political objectives are translated into war-winning plans and policies. The military was too slow to understand and adapt to an enemy who changed the game from open warfare to insurgency. Likewise, the military was clumsy in its efforts to conduct what Tom Ricks, author of *The Generals,* termed "civil-military discourse." As a result, much of the leadership and decision making in Iraq and Afghanistan has gone through tumultuous annual shifts both in leadership and policy.

Before becoming too critical of generals, it is important to put their service in the context of the last decade of conflict. Generals are Soldiers . . . and people. They are personally vulnerable, often uncertain, likely to be very tired from the physical demands of their jobs, and more often than not rightfully distrustful of those around them who are too ambitious or jealous to offer unvarnished counsel. The truth is that the overwhelming majority of serving generals do in fact live "above the common level of life": patriotic, churchgoing, and family oriented; most are workaholics, at the top of their games at managing one of the world's most complex organizations, and doing very dangerous things that have great consequences. Virtually all are accomplished linear thinkers, who have proven themselves able to make the global trains of war run on time. Most generals have given virtually a lifetime's effort to their country. Those in combat jobs have been overseas since Bosnia, involved in the stressful task of winning impossible wars and dealing with the loss of those under their command. Few corporate chief executive officers could possibly understand or endure this level of emotional stress and number of hours on the job.

Today's generals deal with a conflict environment that is enormously complex and constantly changing. These are not dumb people. Yet since 2001 in Iraq and Afghanistan, they have been confronted with a set of strategic variables that are unique in the history of American wars. They have had to deal with an unprecedented level of ambiguity and uncertainty. Most were educated and acculturated to fight a European-style war on the North German plain; then they were unexpectedly faced with alien conditions of weather, distance, terrain, enemy, and culture. Add to this the pressure of a media that immediately flashes to the world any missteps, either personal or professional. Then add to the challenges that unique personal trauma imposed on them by our longest and most emotionally debilitating wars. From Bosnia to Afghanistan, many of our generals have been at this for almost two decades.

THE REQUIREMENTS OF STRATEGIC GENIUS

Strategic genius is hard to define. Great strategists of the past were not all military men; not all were appreciated in their time, nor did they all achieve great rank and stature. Four categories of generals embrace the collective sum of strategic circumstances and attributes that define strategic genius in war.

COMBAT GENIUS

These are leaders like George Patton and Stanley McChrystal, who fight beyond the plan; they innovate as they fight and stay well ahead of the enemy in imaginative application of combat power. Their demonstrated genius affects the future course of warfare . . . and they become immortal. Exceptional combat excellence, of course, comes with exemplary immersion in the art of war, both in practice and vicariously through the study of military history.

POLITICAL GENIUS

Generals like Colin Powell and David Petraeus are able to swim in the political ocean and survive the sharks. They know how to wield and meld the elements of military power with allies, coalition partners, and politicians. They are masters at "civil-military discourse." They possess the skill to influence wartime policy while remaining subservient to their civilian masters. Their key trait is the ability to offer meaningful and prophetic advice to civilian leaders while remaining respectful and true to their professional values. Political skill comes from an exposure to war, to be sure. These leaders also develop within the military bureaucracy, by studying the political arts and by serving within civilian institutions that habitually rub shoulders with the military services.

INSTITUTIONAL GENIUS

Gen. Peter Chiarelli, former Army vice chief of staff, was a leader who was brilliant in his ability to manage a very large institution and represent its equities in tune with the needs of the nation. Others, like Gen. Creighton Abrams, former Army chief of staff and commander of U.S. forces in Vietnam, were able to showcase their services in a new and creative manner. The legacy of these men is measured by a uniform regard among Soldiers, politicians, and administrations for their selflessness and ability to restructure and shape budgets and legislation to meet the future needs of the service. These Soldiers learn strategic brilliance though a complex career path that includes combat service melded with deep immersion into the internal staff mechanisms that make the Army run. They understand war, certainly, but they are also master manipulators of the bureaucracy that constitutes most of the day-to-day workings of the Army.

ANTICIPATORY GENIUS

These generals possess the unique ability to think in time, to imagine conceptually where the nature and character of war is headed. Anticipatory genius is capable of piercing the fog of war and seeing into the future. Anticipatory thinkers are more intuitive than logical or linear. That is one reason why their ranks, compared to those of other kinds of generals, are so thin. However, those possessing anticipatory genius must also be gifted enough to shape the institution to meet the future a generation ahead. They must be able to meld vision with the practical art of inducing achievable change. These "seers" are not well known, nor are they appreciated during their time of service. Their knack for future-gazing seems to be inherited rather than learned. They study war but view it through a different lens. Anticipatory genius is the most rare and precious of all four attributes and the one least likely to be developed through any predictable pattern. The only single features that seem common to all anticipators are a questioning (often acerbic) mind, lack of patience for those who cannot see beyond today . . . and retirement at an early age.

So what influences the system that nurtures strategic genius? How are generals selected? And what can the institution do to make sure those who lead our Soldiers at the strategic level will lead with a brilliant and refined intellect? As in all large institutions, it begins with culture . . . and culture too often suppresses the ascent of brilliant strategic leaders. Only two categories concern us here: the combat and anticipatory geniuses. The military does revere a few political generals who, like Colin Powell, are able to cross the civil-political divide and prosper in both domains. Likewise, the institutional genius is respected for his or her ability to keep the bureaucracy turning. But the ultimate expectation from the American people is that the military is to win wars. There is an old saying that "tactics wins battles, but good strategy wins wars." Wars are won by *anticipatory geniuses,* the seers, who craft the proper force and doctrine to win the next war, and by *combat geniuses,* the doers, who employ that instrument to achieve victory at a cost acceptable to the American people.

SEERS AND DOERS

The problem with combat generals is that too often in our history the Army has prepared and selected them to fight one war and then suddenly immersed them in a war of a different kind. American armies have paid a high price for this preparatory gap. Great Civil War heroes like U.S. Grant, William T. Sherman, Winfield Scott Hancock, Phil Sheridan, and (of course) George Custer performed badly when faced with a counterguerrilla war against Native Americans. Then, just as the U.S. Army learned how to fight frontier wars, it failed to make the shift back to big wars in 1917. Likewise, the British Army during its heyday in the nineteenth century promoted and rewarded those "colonial" generals who proved adept at defeating tribal enemies. These same generals were responsible for the deaths and maiming of millions in World War I, when they failed to understand that the Germans were a very different and deadly enemy indeed.

The lesson learned is that the gods of war are a perfidious lot. They do not give away where, how, when, or for how long a future war will be fought. Thus anticipating shifts in the nature and character of war is impossible, given that the wavelength of the sine curve of change is often measured in generations. We simply cannot know if a general prepared for one war will be confronted with an entirely different war. The only solution, of course, is to create a very broad (and deep) bench, wide enough to hold every strategic talent, each capable of going to the mound when his or her particular pitching skill is needed at the moment.

Some generals are particularly revered within the intimate confines of the general-officer club today because of their gifts as seers and doers. They are almost exclusively combat-arms officers. Generals like Peter Chiarelli, Martin Dempsey, and such fellow travelers from other services as Gen. James Mattis of the Marines share a common provenance. They all began the serious study of war very early in their careers: Mattis through intensive self-study; Petraeus, Chiarelli, and Dempsey through academic sabbaticals at name graduate schools followed by tours as instructors at West Point.

War makes the Army different from a bureaucracy. The pitiless Darwinian hand of war cleanses the bureaucrats and elevates those previously hidden in the shadows of the bureaucracy who come alive in the crucible of human conflict. Such leaders thrive in the uncertainty and fog of war. They adapt and anticipate actions of the enemy. Failure cannot be hidden for long, particularly in the light of the U.S. media. Much is suddenly expected from those who must lead and make strategic decisions that affect the lives of their Soldiers and often the fate of the nation. Often the time available to shift from business and administration to combat is very short, and since Soldiers' lives are at stake, the opportunity to learn from failure is very limited.

WHAT TO DO

The U.S. military must develop the means for finding just a few who possess the strategic right stuff to be dominant at the strategic level of war. Today's structures, policies, and institutions simply fail to find those individuals most gifted to lead at that level. Identifying them will require reform of the way the Army selects, promotes, assigns, rewards, and educates officers, from precommissioning to selection for general.

The most significant problem with the system today is that the Army's method for officer advancement selects out those due for stardom at a point in their careers when their potential strategic genius has yet to be observed or tested. In effect, the Army promotes young captains early who have proven their bravery on the battlefield. A tactician gets the job done. He is the officer whom senior leaders admire for his abilities to get the formation to the parade on time and in the proper uniform. He leads a unit he can see immediately before him, a platoon or a company of perhaps no more than a hundred men. A gifted tactician fills holes in the battle line when it is threatened and makes immediate decisions based less on information from above than on "gut feel."

The Army's system of paper evaluation finds tactically proficient young captains and promotes them early, or "below the zone." While not all selected below the zone make general, it is safe to say that most selected for general were at one time in their lives selected below the zone, mostly very young. This would be a fine system if tactical genius and strategic genius were related, but experience has shown that great tactical skill does not equal great strategic skill.

In fact, tactical and strategic genius are unrelated. Officers with potential for strategic leadership are morally as well as physically brave. They may not be able to make the convoys run on time, but they have a special talent for seeing the future, for conjuring a battlefield that has yet to appear. These are young men and women who are intellectually gifted. They can think critically. They are more interested in studying warfare than practicing it. Tactically talented officers can move hundreds. Strategically talented officers can maneuver hundreds of thousands, if not millions. Tactically talented officers know how to fight enemies they know. Strategically talented officers are prepared to fight enemies as yet unforeseen. The tactically talented read the manuals and put existing doctrine into practice. Strategically talented officers continually question doctrine and eventually seek to change it. Tacticians see what is; strategists conjure what might be.

SELECT THE BEST AND BRIGHTEST VERY YOUNG

To solve this conundrum, the Army must consider how it manages officers. First, the Army must begin by deepening the bench for early selection to major in order to increase the odds of netting the most promising strategists in the midst of their tactically competent brethren. Second, the promotion selection board must have some objective insight into an officer's intellectual merit. This intellectual component could take many forms. Best would be an intellectual résumé that highlights the officer's academic standing, performance in graduate school, and skill as an instructor, supplemented by candid comments by commanders and mentors concerning the officer's capacity for strategic leadership.

LEARN EARLY, LEARN FOR LIFE

I believe that strategic excellence can be detected among the very young. Creativity, cognitive acuity, imagination, and the ability to "see" and anticipate the future can be discovered though observation and, most importantly, examination. Strategic talent as demonstrated by moral courage, vision, cognitive ability, and cultural awareness appear early in an officer's career. Most behavioral scientists conclude that inquisitive learning begins at about twenty and substantively ends at around forty.

Civilian graduate study is the surest means for elevating tactically competent junior officers into strategically brilliant generals, but a degree alone is not sufficient. It is more important that those who complete graduate studies be rewarded for the experience. Officers are ambitious by nature. They will do those things that they think will get them promoted. By the same token, today's young officers are natural learners. They learn differently from my generation, in that they learn principally for a purpose, usually for career advancement. They tend to learn in increments—just the right information, just in time. Much of what they learn comes from nontraditional, virtual means, eschewing traditional brick-and-mortar institutions. They are more comfortable with learning online, often as members of informal communities of bloggers and social media.

Many of the most successful commanders in Iraq and Afghanistan actively pursued learning opportunities very early in their careers, often at great professional risk. Of course, the public is well aware of David Petraeus' PhD and dissertation at Princeton. However, as we have seen, many others, such as Peter Chiarelli and Martin Dempsey, followed the Petraeus model by gaining an advanced degree from a name university, followed by an instructorship at West Point. As also mentioned above, an intellectual propensity for success at the strategic level appears early in an officer's career, in the late twenties and early thirties. Most gain their strategic footing at a top-tier graduate school. As a young major on his way to teach at West Point, Andrew Krepinevich wrote a dissertation, *The Army and Vietnam,* later published commercially, that synthesized perfectly the strategic failures in Vietnam. In a similar vein, then-captain H. R. McMaster's dissertation, *Dereliction of Duty,* revealed the Joint Chiefs' complicity in supporting the war in Vietnam. David Petraeus' dissertation on the impact of the Vietnam War was followed by Capt. John Nagl's *Learning to Eat Soup with a Knife,* a case study of past counterinsurgencies. All of these works were done by very junior officers, all writing with the passion and imagination of youth and unfettered by the political reticence of more senior officers. These works proved to be highly influential, not only to inform future generations but to sharpen and deepen the capacity of their authors for original thinking and rigorous analysis.

All four authors have gone on to positions of great responsibility in the community of strategists. The point is that these men, along with a generation of others, clearly demonstrate the proven value of the Petraeus model: early attendance at a challenging graduate program, followed by time to complete a dissertation on a relevant strategic subject. Yet the Army command culture still continues to discourage bright young scholars from pursuing higher education early in their careers. This phenomenon has been a part of the Army's personnel theology since the program for advanced civil schooling was created after Vietnam. Too often, officers who earn a terminal degree, such as a doctorate, are sent into early "active retirement" at a service- or joint-school instructorship. This must change, and change can only occur if it is forced on the institution.

STRATEGIC EXCELLENCE IN SERVICE SCHOOLS

Service schools are the crown jewels of Army learning. A different system exists for each level of warfare: tacticians, usually captains, are finished at Army branch schools; majors learn operational art at service staff colleges; and colonels are taught strategy at the war colleges. Staff and war colleges are competitive, with fewer than half the Army's majors and slightly more than half of colonels selected to attend. Formal preparation for a strategist begins at the staff-school level. Today, staff schools teach a wide variety of students: Army, of course, but also foreign officers, civilians from other federal agencies, and officers from all the other services. Accordingly, however, while the curriculum is thorough, it teaches to the lowest common denominator and thus lacks the focus and rigor for challenging the most gifted and motivated.

Since the eighties, the Army and other services have understood that strategic genius can only be discovered and cultivated by stressing the best and brightest in an "honors" program—for the Army, the School of Advanced Military Studies (SAMS). SAMS graduates make up a disproportionate number of successful strategists. Many have been promoted to the highest ranks in the service. The concept of a military "honors" course came to maturity when Gen. Norman Schwartzkopf selected a small group of young SAMS graduates, the "Jedi Knights," to do his strategic war planning for Desert Storm.

The Gulf War taught the Army leadership that intense study of war cannot be a gentlemen's course. Those who do the intellectual heavy lifting must be found, rewarded, and promoted to general. The Army must find strategic and anticipatory genius by an intellectually ruthless strategic "honors program" at the war colleges, as well as the staff colleges. A strategic SAMS course should be reserved only for those who pass a very rigorous screening and formal entrance examination. Matriculation would be conditioned on the basis of proven intellectual ability and educational achievement. The course should last at least a year; all segments of this strategic SAMS should be rigorously graded, with termination a consequence for those who fail to make the grade. Reward for completion should be selection for higher command and staff positions and a fast track to general. Oversight should be exercised by the Army Chief or Vice Chief of Staff. Instruction to the brigadier general's board should include a strict quota for the "strategic SAMS" graduates with the intent that they will fill particularly sensitive strategic general-officer billets.

SELECTION TO COLONEL

Good strategic generals come from a very large and varied assortment of very good colonels. The bench can best be broadened by preparing enough colonels from all strategic backgrounds, so there is enough talent and promise to fit the times and circumstances of the moment. A deep strategic bench would include members of every experiential skill: from big maneuver warfare to counterinsurgency and nation building. It would offer colonels for consideration to general who are well educated and experienced as thinkers and teachers. These strategic colonels can fill the vital general-officer positions, not only in combatant commands but also in the national security apparatus, and in joint and international billets as well. The goal of creating strategic exceptionalism should be the principal task of service chiefs and secretaries. The point at which these leaders can have the most immediate and lasting impact on the process for finding strategic generals is the "board."

THE BRIGADIER GENERAL BOARD

Once a year at Fort Knox, Kentucky, a team of about eighteen generals consecrate the "inner temple, the holy of holies": the brigadier general board. In a period when the press and pundits rail against the bloated number of generals, it is instructive to note how small the product of the board actually is: only about thirty-one for the active Army. Most of these selectees will eventually serve in positions that demand talent in strategic decision making. The debate among board members as they choose from perhaps two thousand colonels is often heated, and the voting very close. It is a timeless truism that board members tend to select men and women in their own images. On occasion, the four-stars have the upper hand in the voting. Secretary Robert Gates knew this in 2007 when he changed the membership of the board from big-war to counterinsurgency generals (headed by David Petraeus) to ensure that those who performed well in Iraq and Afghanistan would make the cut.

If it did its work properly, a board would be able to choose in each selectee both a quality officer and one who is particularly gifted in a needed strategic skill. For example, the brigadier general board might be required to select three strategic colonels for a two-star opening at the National Security Council two years hence. The Army will continue to select generals who are both good bureaucrats and skilled operational artists. It is important to note that such a fully functional "strategic general" effort would yield a relatively small cadre of very talented men and women, perhaps no more than a third of the Army's three hundred active-duty generals.

THE LONG-TERM INTENT

The career pattern that leads to general officer must reward intellectual over operational skill. No officer should be presented before a general-officer board who has not served at least two years as an instructor in the Army's professional military education system. After selection for advanced promotion to major, the most promising must be sent to advanced civil schooling in subjects related to the military and strategic arts. Matriculation in military schools must be contingent on rigorous examinations. Though it seems trite to say, no officer should be promoted who cannot read, write, speak, and think at the strategic level. Thus all military colleges must institute graded curricula. Senior educators must have the authority to sideline professionally any officer who cannot meet the intellectual standards of an advanced strategic position.

Some might conclude that such a program is elitist. It is not. All large organizations, the Army included, want the most capable to reach the top. This program merely seeks to guarantee that only those gifted with strategic genius become strategic decision makers and commanders. Likewise, the accountability embedded in such a system will provide an objective and fair barrier that will keep from responsibility those who do not have the necessary depth of intellect. Harsh? Perhaps. But war is harsh. And as we have seen throughout our history, mediocre generals get Soldiers needlessly killed and put the nation at risk.

[20]

THE DRAFT

[Conscription] rests on the assumption that your kids belong to the state.
—President Ronald Reagan

Before 9/11 the draft was a five-letter word that no thinking politician would utter in public. But after years of war, our ground forces almost collapsed from overcommitment. The shock of seeing Soldiers suffer from the consequences of too many deployments is causing politicians of all stripes, some retired generals, and bureaucrats in the Pentagon to rethink the issue. The draft would fill the ranks with cheap and plentiful men and women. No wonder the idea is gaining ground.

Advocates for national service do make some compelling arguments. They point to the intrinsic value of service. "A reinstated draft, or compulsory military service," writes Joseph Epstein in *The Atlantic*, "would redistribute the burden of the responsibility for fighting wars, and engage the nation in military conflicts in a more immediate and democratic way." Old Cold Warriors like Epstein believe that every young American owes his or her country something as part of a debt of citizenship. Proponents are always careful to point out that service does not necessarily mean service in combat. They argue that the young can plant trees for the Forest Service, serve the elderly in retirement homes, help clean up cities and rivers, or mentor and be "big brothers and sisters" to the disadvantaged.[1]

Older veterans like Epstein venerate their own time in service, because the experience exposed them to their fellow countrymen. Many of them still believe that the barracks is a place for therapeutic social leveling. Rich and poor, black and white all mingle in the barracks, and profess that before leaving (for Harvard, in Epstein's case) they gain a better appreciation of their countrymen. They argue that a drafted military, comprising a more socially, ethnically, and economically diverse cohort is better (and more fair). Of course, Epstein served his two years writing for an Army post newspaper. I often get a different perspective from Vietnam-era infantrymen, who sweated and rotted in the jungle for months waiting to die from in a Viet Cong ambush . . . and today still suffer flashbacks from their near-death experiences.

Many, mostly liberal, academics look to a drafted army as a hedge against a professional officer corps intent on suborning the Constitution and civilian control of the military. They often argue that an army mostly manned by citizen-Soldiers will be more questioning of authority and might temper U.S. overseas ambitions. The argument goes that voter-parents with sons potentially in harm's way will always resist the needless spilling of their darling children's blood. Critics are quick to compare the national ambivalence toward war in the Middle East to the revulsion of Americans toward Vietnam. Massive protests served to end that unpopular war—the consequence, they argue, of an engaged society with skin literally in the game.

Draft supporters often mention countries that maintain the draft, like Switzerland and Israel. But while the Swiss still draft, virtually all other European nations have eliminated conscription. The Swiss retain the draft because they have not gone to war since the Renaissance; for them, national service becomes a means for achieving social cohesion rather than defense of the country. The Israelis draft because they are a hated minority of eight million, surrounded by hundreds of millions of Arabs hostile to their existence.

In this era of severe fiscal constraint comes the argument that a drafted army is cheaper than a professional one. I find it interesting that draft proponents seem to bring up the costs of Soldiers when no one is shooting but that when the bullets start to fly, so does the cost argument. When the price of a Soldier is dear, military pay goes up, benefits accrue, and the quality of Soldier life inevitably improves. When wars die down, like today, the electorate suddenly becomes outraged at excessive salaries and shameful military spending. It is a cycle that never ends . . . and, by the way, the argument for the economy of a drafted military ignores the fact that amateurs die in hugely disproportionate numbers when compared to professionals. The lifetime cost to the VA for a paraplegic who went to war unprepared is tens of millions of dollars. No proponent for the draft ever mentions this unpleasant fact.

Let us be very clear: the draft is not really about national service. It is not about planting trees or emptying bedpans . . . it is about the Army. Other services rarely draft—the Air Force, Navy, and Coast Guard never, and the Marines only in extreme situations. To be even more specific, the draft is about Army infantrymen: the Army never has a problem recruiting linguists, intelligence specialists, medics, or computer operators in wartime. No, the draft is about the unwilling, poor, and unlucky who lose the lottery and are dragooned into a specific part of the service that most Americans view as demeaning, uncomfortable, and dangerous.

The numbers are telling: 70 percent of all Americans who died at the hand of the enemy in World War II were infantrymen. From World War II to the present, that percentage has actually gone up, to 80 percent. In other words, four out of five of all those killed at the hand of the enemy from Korea to Afghanistan come from a population that constitutes less than 4 percent of the uniformed force within the Department of Defense. Some old vets might look nostalgically on their service, particularly if it was in peacetime. Yet I can assure you that most infantry veterans would rather have been doing something else when facing a brutal death in extremely close combat. Proponents of the draft simply have no clue about the corrosive dynamics of impressing young men into life-threatening service against their will.

One very disturbing aspect of arguments for national service is that they ignore the impact of the draft on the fighting abilities of the Army. So, the real question is: Does the draft make a better Army? I think the answer to that is overwhelmingly no. Do more drafted Soldiers die compared to professionals? Again, I certainly know this to be true from my own personal experience. I have served in both a drafted and a professional army. There is no comparison. A professional army beats a drafted army, hands down. Professionals make much better Soldiers for many reasons. Choosing to serve begins the process of making a Soldier a member of a calling, a band of brothers that demands far more from a young man or woman than putting in time waiting to be discharged. Warfare has become so complex and demanding that just two years of short service is not enough to make a competent Soldier. The "Willie and Joe" generation carried a rifle for Uncle Sam in World War II. These poor souls could be manufactured quickly, but they paid a high cost in blood. Today's Soldiers are required to do more than fight. They must also learn to interact with alien cultures, to be builders, advisers, and trainers. Gen. Charles Krulak, a former Marine Corps commandant, put the issue of the complexity of today's wars in context when he contended that the modern close-combat Marine needs to prepare to fight a "three-block war": one block a high-intensity battle, another block a counter-insurgency battle, and the third block humanitarian aid. Infantry work today is done at the graduate-school level, and it is no place for high-school dropouts.

In past wars, Soldiers relied on leaders to make key life-and-death decisions. Today, young Soldiers standing guard at checkpoints in Afghanistan often must make split-second, life-altering decisions . . . alone. Wrong decisions have strategic consequences, as we have seen so often in Iraq and Afghanistan. Making Soldiers good at crisis decision making takes time and requires Soldiers who have the "right stuff." Soldiers like these cannot be mass-produced in a few weeks of basic training. Good Soldiers, like good wine, take time to mature.

During America's conscription era from 1940 to 1973, you can bet that young men vulnerable to the draft knew the odds of dying in the infantry, and the good ones usually found a way to avoid the front lines. Fear of dying in infantry combat inevitably perverted the selective service system. The upper class and well connected did not want Johnny to die, so they went to extraordinary lengths to keep him out of the infantry. The system became even more perverted when grossly unpopular wars like Vietnam made avoidance of the draft suddenly socially acceptable among much of the population.

The perversion of draft laws was tragic for those of us who had to lead these men in combat. As soon as the bullets start to fly, the selective service system falls apart. The consequences of having a draft today would be even more tragic. On the contemporary battlefield, there is no room for poorly trained, poorly motivated infantrymen. Less intelligent Soldiers get killed in hugely disproportionate numbers. Drafted armies are by their nature self-killing machines, meat grinders for young, postadolescent kids, virtually all of whom are poor. The most difficult task in war is to fight close to the enemy. It takes extraordinary strength, endurance, skill, and an intuitive sense of surroundings. Yet in my father's war, thanks to a corrupt draft, infantry came from the lowest mental categories and were universally smaller and weaker than Soldiers drafted for noncombat specialties. Thus it should surprise no one that better-trained and acculturated German Soldiers had a field day killing Americans in the hedge-rows of Normandy. The same can be said for my Vietnam generation, where the ranks of infantry units were too often filled with young men who hated the fact that they were there.

Drafted Soldiers serve for as little as six months to two years before discharge. As we learned in World War II, a drafted army of amateurs can be made professional over time, but the price of learning is measured in blood. It takes years to build a cohesive band of brothers within close-combat units. A draft would rush unprepared, undertrained, and poorly bonded Soldiers into battle, only to get them killed. If you think that post-traumatic stress disorder is a problem for a volunteer force, just watch the consequences of putting unwilling, poor-quality, psychologically unprepared drafted Soldiers under fire.

The draft becomes even more of a loser's choice when juxtaposed with American wartime values. On the one hand, proponents of national service speak about the values of service to the personal betterment of the individual. On the other hand, nothing could be more antithetical to personal betterment than being dead. And make no mistake, a drafted army needlessly kills Soldiers.

National service sounds like a utopian concept for social leveling, and it might be, if it were applied fairly. Those who call for a renewal of the draft proclaim that the social and racial inequities of the Vietnam-era draft would not happen again. The realities of how wars are fought make such pronouncements nonsense. There is no way that a draft could fairly discriminate between those who are likely to die and those who are not. Infantry units in a drafted army would comprise overwhelmingly draftees, most of them poor, disadvantaged, and collectively incapable of dealing with the complexities of modern war.

Reading between the lines of the pro-draft movement is an unspoken contention, that good Soldiers cannot be recruited during wartime. Can we fill the ranks given the reluctance of America's youth to join in wartime? Yes, we can, if we are willing to accept a peacetime rather than wartime system of recruiting. First, we must change the fifties-era remuneration system and pay Soldiers for risk as well as skill. Private security firms in Iraq have no problem finding good-quality volunteers, because they are willing to pay handsomely for the risks they take. In today's military, a computer programmer in the Pentagon makes a great deal more than an infantryman humping a hundred-pound rucksack in 120-degree Afghan heat. No wonder infantrymen are hard to recruit and keep. Lately, the Pentagon has tried to solve the problem by offering substantial recruiting bonuses. Bonuses are bribes. Increased pay over the course of a career is an investment. Those who continually go into harm's way should also be allowed to retire earlier. Selling back three years for each year in a close-combat unit would be about right. In such a scheme, an infantry Soldier would be able to return to civilian life before his psyche or his body is broken. These men should be excluded from the tender mercies of the VA. They should be allowed permanent access to the terrific military medical system for a lifetime.

We should recruit foreigners. For millennia, great powers have allowed indigenous Soldiers in their ranks. To this day, the British Army retains Ghurka regiments from Nepal, and the French army still has its Foreign Legion—both highly respected and competent fighting formations. During the Cold War, we recruited Special Forces Soldiers from Eastern Europe and later from Cuba, because their intimate knowledge of prospective theaters of war could not be replicated from the general population. We could leverage the power of citizenship as an inducement for filling the ranks with young men who are intimately familiar with places like Africa and the Middle East.

Most importantly, we must increase the number of close-combat Soldiers in infantry units before war begins. Recruiting more fighters so as to retain those whom we need most would give those most likely to die time to recover between deployments. A denser population of infantrymen would allow the bravest to reconnect with their loved ones before returning to combat. More time at home would be a long-term investment that would prevent experienced Soldiers from voting with their feet.

Were we to be so foolish as to return to the draft, we would bring back an army of amateurs. The army that we saw performing so magnificently in Iraq and Afghanistan at the tactical level would be a thing of the past. Surely, a nation of three hundred million should be able to recruit and retain the very few long-service professionals it must have to fight its wars.

[21]

Earning the Right

I do not believe in using women in combat because women are too fierce.
—Margaret Meade

Two events in my life describe my time on this planet. During the summer
of 1992, I conducted a parachute jump with my oldest daughter, newly
commissioned Lt. Maria Scales, at Fort Benning, Georgia. She's a hoot: self-
motivated, driven by success to a degree I still cannot comprehend, and tough.
It was her fifth and last parachute jump. I had pulled strings and gotten permission from the commander of the Infantry School at Fort Benning to join her.
She was a tiny thing, no more than maybe one hundred pounds. I was, to be
honest, a bit heavier. She stood in the door of the shaking and rolling C-130
aircraft as we lifted off the airstrip. Very quickly, the aircraft swerved to the
right to line up with Pryor Drop Zone just across the Chattahoochee River in
Alabama.

I was her dad, of course, and an experienced paratrooper. I decided to take
a brief moment while bouncing around the aircraft to offer a few bits of advice
on the finer points of parachuting. From many years with the 82nd Airborne
Division, I was used to an hour or more of approach flying during which the
Air Force pilots devised any number of torturous means for making our flight
as uncomfortable and terrifying as possible. I leaned over to her as she stood in
the open door, started to shout . . . and suddenly she was gone . . . gone into

the slipstream, disappeared into the ether, my little girl. I did not have much time to reflect on her disappearance before I was gone as well. I had failed to understand the geometry of airborne school. The distance from take off to first jump was about fifty seconds. It was a nineteen-"PAK" landing zone, meaning the aircraft was over the drop zone only long enough to disgorge about half its jumpers. No time for fatherly wisdom. The jumpmaster pushed me out. I had a terrible body position as I hit the airstream, "all asses and elbows," to use the common term. I was twisted up to my ears in parachute risers and stunned by the utter violence of it all. And there was Maria, merrily drifting far above.

Again, I looked up to offer a few words of wisdom on how to land . . . and immediately slammed into the earth . . . hard, like a sack of potatoes, legs apart, elbows exposed, spine stiff, clearly unprepared for the compression. All I can remember once on the ground was collecting my chute in enormous pain. My beautiful daughter said to me, "Hey Dad, we're all going over to the Black Angus to drink. Want to come along?" No, not this time. I had a very important meeting with the general officer commanding and had to leave immediately. Wrong, of course. All I was able to do was draw a bath and soak for an hour. I never jumped again.

Fast-forward six years to April 23, 1998. My youngest daughter, Monica, Notre Dame Reserve Officer Training Corps (ROTC), made it through Airborne School without my wisdom. Soon she was a lieutenant in Bosnia, surrounded by very angry Serbs who wanted to attack her convoy. She was escorting a cardinal and a group of Croatian Catholics who had been displaced by Serb Soldiers from the town of Derventa. They were returning to Derventa to celebrate mass in their heavily damaged church. A large group of Serbs armed with automatic rifles, Molotov cocktails, and rocks started attacking the cardinal and several pilgrims as they tried to enter the church. Monica's group—part of a United Nations contingent—drew their weapons and started pushing through the crowd. The crowd grew violent and turned on Monica's Soldiers. Not able by the rules of engagement to open fire, she ordered a retreat and barely made it to a cluster of Norwegian armored vehicles before being overwhelmed. All this remained unknown to my wife and me until her division commander and dear friend, Gen. Larry Ellis, wrote Diana (not me) a letter telling her how close her daughter had come to being killed. So I have skin in the game when it comes to the subject of women in the military: two paratroopers, two commanders of their respective ROTC battalions, great Soldiers. I could not be more proud. Their sense of honor, patriotism, valor, and dedication to duty, all this they get from their mother.

Needless to say, in December 2015, my family watched closely as Secretary of Defense Ash Carter opened the gate to allow women into "direct ground combat"—specifically, units below brigade level. Much of the media hype was misplaced at the time, writing and speaking about "women being allowed in combat." Actually, the issue is not about women in combat. They are already in combat and have been since the 1991 Gulf War. It is really about women in the infantry. A few experiments dictated by circumstances (and a laudable effort by the ground services to experiment) have put some carefully selected women in the Army's elite Ranger School and a few in the equally demanding Marine Infantry Officer's Course in Quantico, Virginia. So far, three incredibly fit and dedicated female officers, all graduates of West Point, have earned the Ranger tab. Well done.

I asked my two experts their opinions on all this. As usual, they led me down an unexpected path of logic. They told me, "It's not about which levels of command to assign women or which jobs they can perform in war. The real issue is one of acceptance," they said. "Like it or not, the culture of the military is defined by the ethos of the warrior. Forget the fact that even in Iraq and Afghanistan, fewer than one in ten actually engaged the enemy in close combat. It's all about perception. The more we are excluded from a presence on the battlefield, the more we are protected from any probability of participating in the acts of a warrior, the less chance we will ever have to be embraced by the warrior caste."

Placed into the context of history, their argument makes sense. Prior to the Civil War the regular Army considered the Irish to be great revolutionaries but poor material for Soldiering. However, that opinion was reversed after Antietam and Gettysburg, when units like the Excelsior Brigade and the Irish Brigade fought and died valiantly. Irishmen earned with their blood the right to be accepted as fellow warriors and for nearly a century were disproportionately represented in the front ranks of the Army and Marine Corps.

Politicians are fond of recognizing Harry Truman's 1948 executive order as the instrument that integrated the services, but in fact Truman did not integrate the services. The North Koreans did. The Army that landed at Pusan in 1950 was still segregated, thanks to resistance by Dixiecrats in Truman's party. Most

Army posts, then as now, were located in Dixiecrat states, and in 1948 there was no chance southern Democrats would allow black Soldiers to frequent white-only establishments or mingle with white boys in the same units.

I remember like it was yesterday when all this changed. It was 1954, and I was in the fourth grade at Barden School at Fort Belvoir, Virginia, and for the first time in my short life I went into the classroom surrounded by black kids. One picture in our family album shows Miss Palbicki's class, with ten of the twenty-five kids in the picture African American. I remember telling Mom. I thought this wonderfully southern, aristocratic woman would have a heart attack. My dad intervened and (for the first time in my memory) shouted at Mom, "So what, Clyde [my mother was named Clyde, how southern was that?]? It's right that black kids are in Bobby's class. Their dads paid for the right for their children to go to school with my son. They shed their blood in Korea. Their kids can go to Barden." This was not about the Supreme Court's *Brown v. Board of Education* decision or Harry Truman's signed order to integrate the services. My dad had served in the 2nd Infantry Division's 2nd Engineer Battalion in Korea. By the time Dad arrived in Korea, thousands of white Soldiers in the division were dead, wounded, or captured. In order to fill foxholes and hold the line, the Army sent solders from all-black rear-area units to fight and die in previously all-white infantry units. The subtleties of segregation were forgotten when empty foxholes in Korea had to be filled. Black Soldiers died with great gallantry and earned with their blood the right to serve as equals. When I commanded a battery in Vietnam, there was no question that black Soldiers had the right to serve. Today, it is no different.

Fast-forward to 2013: the public hardly noticed that gays have been accepted into the military's ranks with virtually no fanfare. This had to be the most significant nonevent in recent history. "Don't ask, don't tell" disappeared with hardly a whimper. Why? Because the professional officer corps had been serving with homosexual Soldiers for all of their careers. Until he died, my dad talked fondly about gay warrants and noncommissioned officers who had held his unit together during the dark days in Korea. During my thirty-five years of service, I worked for gay generals and commanded gay officers, enlisted men, and women—no big deal. We were glad the charade was over.

With women it is different. Just a few years ago, the officer in charge of preventing sexual harassment in the Air Force was himself charged with sexual harassment against women in his office. How, I asked, can a culture noted for advancing social change be so regressive when it came to gender equality? We are almost forty years into gender integration, and it seems as if we are going backward. So, again, I asked my two veteran daughters what they thought. Their answer was sobering. As with African Americans and gays, it was not about regulations, laws, or executive orders; it was about culture. For whatever reason, the rank and file in the services still have yet to accept women into their social brotherhood. Women have fought and died in Iraq and Afghanistan. But we have yet to witness a full acceptance of them or their contributions.

Women serving in Afghanistan and elsewhere in harm's way are well aware of these precedents. They have earned the right to become full members of the warrior caste. During fourteen years of war, women have fought in very close proximity to infantrymen and have been exposed to violent death to a degree unprecedented in American wars. Thousands of women have died or been severely maimed. Fourteen years of war have taught the lesson that it is impossible to protect women from harm, and we must accept the fact that the unique circumstances in Iraq and Afghanistan also make that difficult. To sustain the impulse to do so would perpetuate the cultural barrier that unfortunately still exists between male and female Soldiers. Every general officer I have spoken to in the field agrees that women Soldiers should continue to serve as they do now, in conditions that will put them in harm's way.

Even now that they are accepted by Defense Department decree to be infantrymen, for the most part they are not pressing to join the close-combat branches. So the debate today is no longer about women in combat. However, if history is a window on the future, then neither feminist pressures nor presidential fiat can guarantee the acceptance of women in the warrior band. Membership is a privilege. In the past, the dues were paid in blood. Please do not misunderstand. I am not in favor of sending young women out to die. I wish that none of our young Soldiers had to suffer. But this is war. It just so happens that the unique circumstances of this war give women the unparalleled opportunity to earn the right to be accepted as full members of the warrior band. In our recent wars women have been willing, like their predecessors, to earn the right to full membership. We should honor their service, mourn those who die, and encourage our women Soldiers to continue to demonstrate valor and courage under fire. And we must never go back. Let them fight and earn their red badges of courage.

To be sure, part of this is about sex. The chest-bumping manly culture rejects the presence of females in their ranks. Sad to say, but Soldiers still view their domain as a male preserve. I remember asking my oldest daughter about what she worried about most in her first command. She said she feared falling out of a run. When men fell out, it was due to a hard night of carousing. When women fell out, it was due to their physical shortcomings. After a few years of service they shrugged off occasional unwanted advances. They laughed about boorish colleagues who, fueled by alcohol, made fools of themselves in the presence of female officers. They look back at commanders who neglected to include them in golf outings or nights at the bar. They always sought to be more pure than Caesar's wife, in the hopes that their professionalism would overcome the innate prejudice of their peers. After four years of dedicated service, my daughters resigned their commissions.

Protestations by the president and secretary of defense against this boy's-club atmosphere can only do so much. If the culture of the rank and file rejects the presence of females as their professional intimates, nothing will change. The presence of African Americans is now transparent. Gays have been part of the military culture as far as I can remember. Women are different. It breaks my heart that this is so, but I do not know what anyone can do to make it better.

We must wait to see if the new policy allowing women in the infantry will succeed. The outcome is not guaranteed. Women are now allowed to participate in the horrible privilege of intimate killing. Killing close is done in small units, normally squads and teams. In these engagements, Soldiers fight and often die not for country or mission but for each other. We borrow a phrase from Shakespeare's *Henry V* and term this phenomenon the "band of brothers" effect. This is the essential glue in military culture that causes a young man to sacrifice his life willingly so that his buddies might survive. Contemporary history suggests that U.S. infantry units fight equally well when made up of Soldiers of different ethnicities, cultures, intelligence levels, and social backgrounds. The evidence is also solid that gays make just as good infantrymen as do straight men.

I have been studying the band-of-brothers effect for almost forty years and have written extensively on the subject. We know that time together allows effective pairings—or "battle buddies," to use the common Army term. We know that four solid buddy pairings led by a sergeant compose a nine-man, battle-ready squad. The Marine squad is slightly larger. We know from watching Ranger and Special Forces training that buddy groups often form spontaneously. Yet the human formula that ensures successful buddy pairings is still a mystery, and that is the key stumbling block in the debate. Veteran SEALs, Special Forces, Rangers, tankers, and line infantrymen will swear that the deliberate, premeditated, and brutal act of intimate killing is a male-only occupation. No one can prove it with data from empirical tests, because no such data exist from the United States. They just know intuitively from battlefield experience that it is true. I am not convinced.

To be sure, women Soldiers may be fit, they may be skilled, and they may be able to "hang." Many have proved with their lives that they are willing to make the ultimate sacrifice. However, many of our senior ground-force leaders, as well as generations of former close-combat veterans from all of our previous wars, are virtually united on one point: that the precious and indefinable band of brothers so essential to winning in close combat would be irreparably compromised in mixed-gender infantry squads. Again, I am not so sure. The military has only about six thousand squads . . . and the number is getting smaller by the day. This thin red line is already fragile from overuse in Iraq and Afghanistan. Let us get the data, study the band-of-brothers effect to make absolutely sure women will fit in before we take the plunge. We must not let political expediency hurry this effort. We have to make sure that women allowed into the infantry are able to meet all the standards of fitness and endurance. In fact, in the infancy of the new policy, women grunts will probably have to exceed the standard, because just one female dropping out due to fatigue or injury in the heat of the close fight will prejudice the entire effort to change the culture.

Until the data proves that women can fit into male-dominated buddy groups, there are numerous things the Army can do to make the situation for women Soldiers better. As my daughters will tell you, the military has never been a family-friendly organization. The retention statistics are horrendous. Many more female than male cadets and officers leave the ranks prematurely. So at a time in service when young female officers and Soldiers really need female mentors, too few women are present. The reasons women leave are complex. But the most common denominator is the lack of a family-friendly ethos in the ranks. Amazingly few two-soldier families prosper. Those females who stay have to make heart-wrenching compromises about family and personal relationships, choices that their male colleagues rarely face. Those few females who are well adjusted and content often do things like teach at West Point or in ROTC or serve on higher-level staffs in Washington.

The Army and Marines are not like corporate America. In fact, these services are far more demanding on females than the more sedentary and physically less demanding air and sea services. Hours are long. Separations commonly last years, because the ground services have many fewer opportunities for shared assignments. More often than not, either the male or the female member of a serving husband-and-wife team has to give up competitively selective and professionally rewarding assignments. Disproportionately, the loser is the wife. The arrival of children too often means the mother resigns her commission.

Yet there are many things that the Army and Marine Corps could do better. One common thread among women who leave the service is a sense of isolation from other females. I certainly know that was true for my daughters. Perhaps the ground services could exploit social media to do better at connecting women who share the same jobs. I believe that women who serve in isolated units should be given periodic "time outs"—a few weeks off to spend with other women. Think of a social sabbatical, sort of a single-female version of "R and R" that their male colleagues enjoyed in previous wars.

Both married and single women consistently say that their careers became too hard after the birth of their children. The situation often becomes career ending when an overseas deployment looms. Today, the services have excellent day-care facilities, certainly as good or in some cases better than their civilian counterparts. Most women Soldiers cannot afford home care, and an argument can be made that mothers and their children thrive better when care is in the home. The Army should consider a home-care program, one that capitalizes on the large number of young married women who populate many of our larger military installations.

Female long-service professionals tell me that the hardest moments for such women occur when reaching the midcareer point, when the biological clock starts to tick loudly and they have had no time to start families. The Army should consider two-to-four-year absences for these women to get their personal lives back in balance. Such a program would allow a long-service midgrade officer or NCO to revert to the reserves. They would perhaps lose a year's seniority for two years of regular service. While away, they would be required to stay professionally current, perhaps completing Staff College or intermediate NCO professional schooling by distance learning, something the Army now accepts as normal career credit for all officers and NCOs.

Some would argue that these allowances are unfair to male Soldiers. Perhaps so. However, one thing is clear: after forty years, women are not well accepted in today's Army. That is terribly unfortunate, because women make great Soldiers, and our Army needs them. So I believe the Army must make extraordinary accommodations to keep them. I fear that Secretary Carter's decision to allow women into the infantry was made for political expediency and not to improve the fighting power of our Army. I still believe that all the data about a woman's physical suitability for close combat has yet to be collected or fully assessed. Nothing could be worse for our young women than to have an administration force the ground services to take in women close-combat Soldiers and then watch them fail.

CONCLUSION

In Times of War and not before
God and soldier we adore
But in times of peace and all things righted
God is forgotten and the soldier slighted.
—Rudyard Kipling

The strategic circumstances in today's wars reflect the fact that the gods of war have a sense of irony. For the most part, the ships have sailed back to port, and the bombers and fighters are secure at home bases. The steel phalanx that rolled over Iraq has been evacuated. The few remaining Soldiers in Afghanistan are performing "grunt" tasks no different from those of the British Army in Palestine in the 1930s and Northern Ireland in the 1970s—or, for that matter, the Roman army in first-century Judea. In all wars in the American era, infantrymen have borne most of the burden. Yet, Army and Marine grunts make up less than 4 percent of the U.S. military—a force only slightly larger than the New York City Police Department.

The tasks these Soldiers perform are timeless to be sure—and dangerous. By day, Afghan streets bustle with commerce much as they did when Soldiers of the British Raj patrolled them. But at night across the country, these same streets turn into free-fire zones where the thugs, criminals, and Islamic fanatics come

out to kill. Those who have seen war firsthand and close up know the debilita-
tion that comes with facing the constant fear of violent death. Unlike firemen
and cops on the beat, a Soldier goes out on patrol every night expecting to kill.

During fourteen years of war in Iraq and Afghanistan, a Soldier's routine
has remained pretty much the same. In the afternoon, young Soldiers undergo
the necessary routine of briefings, inspections, and rehearsals. At dusk they don
heavy body armor, helmets, weapons, night-vision devices, radios, and all the
other impedimenta that make up a Soldier's burden. At dark they move out
into a miserably hot, humid, and dusty night to do the job. Only a Soldier can
describe the gut-churning fear that accompanies the moment when the "search
and clear" team kicks in a door to confront whatever is inside. Within the confines of a tiny room, the Soldier looks through the two dimensional, grainy-green
image of his goggles to determine if his welcome will come from a Taliban terrorist or a child huddling with its mother in terror. Dripping with sweat, gripped
with anxiety and fear, the Soldier has only an instant to determine whether to
shift his finger into the trigger well or reassure the occupants inside. Today, this
scene is repeated daily in Afghanistan, as well as other places too secret to recount
here. These young Soldiers "walk point" for a thousand dollars a month and the
promise of a trip home to a nation that, they hope, understands and appreciates
the true meaning of sacrifice.

These young men do not usually talk about war. They think about their
buddies. They talk about families, wives, and girlfriends and relate to each other
through very personal confessions. For the most part, they are volunteers from
middle- and lower-class America. They come from every corner of our country
to meet in harsh and forbidding places. Soldiers suffer, fight, and occasionally
die *for each other.* It is as simple as that. Patriotism and a paycheck may get a
Soldier into the military, but fear of letting his buddies down gets a Soldier to do
something that might just as well get him killed. What makes a person successful
in America today is a far cry from what makes a Soldier successful. Big bucks
gained in law or real estate and big deals closed on the stock market are making some of their peers rich, but those comforted souls have no buddies. There
is no one whom they are willing to die for or who is willing to die for them.
William Manchester served as a Marine in the Pacific during World War II and
put the sentiment precisely right: "Any man in combat who lacks comrades
who will die for him, or for whom he is willing to die is not a man at all. He is
truly damned."

The Anglo-Saxon heritage of buddy loyalty is long and has been frightfully won. Almost six hundred years ago the English king Henry V waited on a cold and muddy battlefield to face a French army many times the size of his own. Shakespeare captured the pathos of that moment in his play *Henry V*. To be sure, Shakespeare was not there, but he must have been there in spirit, because he understood the emotions that gripped and the bonds that brought together both king and Soldier. Henry did not talk about a failed national strategy. He did not try to justify faulty intelligence or ill-formed command decisions that had put his Soldiers at such a terrible disadvantage. Instead, he talked about what made English Soldiers fight and what in all probability would allow them to prevail the next day against terrible odds. Remember, this is a monarch talking to his men:

> This story shall the good man teach his son; And Crispin Crispian shall ne'er go by, From this day to the ending of the world, But we in it shall be remembered—We few, we happy few, we band of brothers; For he to-day that sheds his blood with me Shall be my brother; be he ne'er so vile, This day shall gentle his condition; And gentlemen in England now-a-bed Shall think themselves accurs'd they were not here, And hold their manhoods cheap whiles any speaks That fought with us upon Saint Crispin's day.[1]

Our young Soldiers and Marines fighting in far places inherit the spirit of St. Crispin's Day. They alone know and understand the strength of comfort that those whom they protect, those in America now abed, will never know. They live lives of self-awareness and personal satisfaction that those who watched them from afar in this country, who hold their manhood cheap, can only envy.

I care deeply that America honors but does not well understand the service these young men perform today. It bothers me that war is a television image, one that 99 percent of the American people, those who have not served, would rather ignore. I wrote this book because I am afraid that this serial ignorance and institutional neglect will inevitably lead to the collapse of U.S. ground forces again. In fact, it is happening now. The administration is fond of telling America that we have "the best military in the history of the world." We do have the best air and sea forces. They are dominant and undefeatable.

On the ground, it is a different story. Most of your Army is poorly trained and has no hope of receiving training above the squad level for another five years. The Soldier's best friend, his rifle, was unreliable and weak fifty years ago. Our Soldiers carry the same rifle today, and their grandchildren will carry it for decades. While the Air Force and Navy are in the midst of a rebuilding renaissance, the Army has essentially ceased the purchase of new weapons. Gen. Mark Milley, the Army's chief of staff, has admitted that the Army has not the money to field a new suite of tanks, infantry carriers, helicopters, and artillery for at least a decade. My grandchildren will fight with Reagan-era weapons.

If present budget trends continue, the Army will "break" for the fifth time in my lifetime. It will happen in about three years. An Army breaks about six months before the Army knows it is broken, but the signs will be there. First, noncommissioned officers will vote with their feet and leave the service. Fewer young Soldiers will sign up. The best and the brightest young officers will transition into civilian life after serving for four or five frustrating years in an Army they see falling apart.

Sometime in the near future, an incident will occur that tells America that it has a broken army on its hands. It could be another Desert One, the hostage-rescue operation that failed so tragically. It could be a spike in indiscipline, chaos emerging after the backbone of the Army, its NCOs, is gone. Or it could be a silent, creeping atrophy that sends the Army into another tragic dark age.

History tells us that armies break quickly and need at least a generation to rebuild. It takes at least fifteen years to educate and acculturate a good platoon sergeant or battalion commander. It takes at least as long for today's turgid weapons-buying bureaucracy to build a new helicopter or tank. In the meantime, our enemies adapt and learn and get better. They will continue to spread their Islamism across the Middle East and Levant to the far reaches of Saharan and equatorial Africa . . . and eventually and inevitably to our homeland.

Inside the Beltway the perennial promise from all administrations is that they will not put "boots on the ground," but they will. The day will come when the nation needs its army, and the U.S. Army, as always, will respond with boots on the ground—just like in 1950, when President Truman sent Task Force Smith to Korea. When called to battle, Task Force Smith was performing constabulary duties in Japan. Its Soldiers were eager but soft and untrained. Its equipment was worn and out of date. The task force had only six rounds of antitank ammunition to face a North Korean division equipped with the newest-model Soviet tanks. The North Korean army quickly overran these poor, wretched Soldiers. Many died. Many others were wounded. Many survivors were in such bad physical shape that they could no longer run away and became prisoners of war.

Most of these poor young men were infantry. And it is the infantry who are America's "canary in the coal mine." When the infantry loses its edge, America loses its ability to win its wars. And, very sadly, that day is just around the corner.

NOTES

CHAPTER 2. THE CINDERELLA SERVICE

1. Lindsey Neas, "Undercutting Our Armed Forces," *Washington Post,* April 23, 2015.

CHAPTER 3. THE AMERICAN ERA OF WAR

1. This narrative is taken from Hiromichi Yahara, *The Battle for Okinawa*, translated by Roger Pineau and Masatoshi Uehara (Hoboken, N.J.: John Wiley and Sons, 1995).
2. Brig. Gen. R. Clements, USAF (Ret.), Letter: Subject: The Invasion of Japan, September 16, 2006.

CHAPTER 4. ADAPTIVE ENEMIES

1. Carl von Clausewitz, *On War,* edited and translated by Michael Howard and Peter Paret (Princeton, N.J.: Princeton University Press, 1976), 77.
2. This thesis originally appeared in Robert H. Scales Jr., "Adapting Enemies: Dealing with the Strategic Threat after 2010," *Strategic Review* 27, no. 1 (Winter 1999): 5–14. Portions of the above articles are reproduced here with permission.
3. Mao Tse-tung, *Selected Works of Mao Tse-tung*, vols. 1 and 3 (Beijing: Foreign Language Press, 1967); William H. Whitson, *The Chinese High Command: A History of Communist Military Politics, 1927–1971* (New York: Praeger, 1973).

4. Frederick Fu Liu, *A Military History of Modern China: 1924–1949* (Princeton N.J.: Princeton University Press, 1956).

5. Robert H. Scales Jr., *Certain Victory: The U.S. Army in the Gulf War* (Washington, D.C.: Office of the Chief of Staff, U.S. Army, 1993).

Chapter 5. Forecasting War

1. Philip Tetlock, *Superforecasting: The Art and Science of Prediction* (New York: Crown, 2015), 232–37.

2. Thoughts in this and subsequent paragraphs I share with my colleague and gifted friend Douglas Ollivant. Most are contained in our op-ed "Terrorist Armies Fight Smarter and Deadlier than Ever," *Washington Post,* August 1, 2014.

Chapter 6. The New Age of Infantry

1. Frank G. Hoffman, "Hybrid vs. Compound War, the Janus Choice: Defining Today's Multifaceted Conflict," *Armed Forces Journal* (October 2009): 15 [emphasis original].

Chapter 8. War in Two Epochs

1. Obviously my juxtaposition of Patton and McChrystal is in large part a metaphorical "trick" to make the point about how warfare has changed in the American era. In fact, credit for the McChrystal method belongs to a generation of special warriors, many of whom are personal friends of mine, such as Lt. Gen. John Mulholland, who was first into Afghanistan after 9/11; Gen. Charles Cleveland, who commanded Special Forces in Central Command; Gen. Mike Flynn, who was the first to break though the intelligence barriers that kept Soldiers in the dark for too long; Adm. William McRaven, for his codification of the theory of special operations in this new era; and Gen. Tony Thomas, a longtime friend.

2. Most of the ideas depicted here and in subsequent paragraphs I jotted down during a personal interview with General McChrystal at his Alexandria, Virginia, office in May 2015. Subsequently, many were repeated in McChrystal's book, *Team of Teams: New Rules of Engagement for a Complex World* (New York: Portfolio/Penguin, 2015).

Chapter 9. Feeding the Narrative

1. Much of the detail and all of the ideas in this chapter are taken from my monograph *The Past and Present as Prologue: Future Warfare through the Lens of Contemporary Conflicts* (Washington, D.C.: Center for a New American Security, 2009).

2. Mark Mazzetti and Michael R. Gordon, "ISIS Is Winning the Social Media War, U.S. Concludes," *New York Times,* June 12, 2015.

Chapter 11. Intent and Intuition

1. I owe a special thanks and recognition to Lt. Gen. Don Holder (Ret.) for many of these ideas concerning the special requirements for developing operational-level commanders.
2. Col. Tom Kolditz, interview, West Point, June 9, 2006.

Chapter 15. Mother Ships and Battleship Bureaucrats

1. One example of this traditionalist approach is a very influential House Armed Services Committee briefing by a retired colonel, Douglas McGregor, "Transformation and the Illusion of Change."
2. S. L. A. Marshall, *The Soldier's Load and the Mobility of the Nation* (Quantico, Va.: Marine Corps Association, 1980).

Chapter 16. Firepower

1. Col. G. F. R. Henderson, *Stonewall Jackson and the American Civil War* (London: Longman Green, 1978), 611.
2. Phillip Karber, "Lessons Learned from the Russo-Ukrainian War" (Draft, Johns Hopkins Applied Physics Laboratory, July 6, 2015).

Chapter 18. Win Forever . . . in Combat

1. Pete Carroll. *Win Forever: Live, Work, and Play Like a Champion* (New York: Portfolio, 2011), 282.
2. According to Pete Carroll, seven seconds is the accepted maximum allowable reaction time and the decision-making standard for most contemporary quarterback assessments.

Chapter 20. The Draft

1. Joseph Epstein, "How I Learned to Love the Draft," *Atlantic* (January–February 2015): 86.

Conclusion

1. Shakespeare, *Henry V,* 4.3.56–67.

INDEX

Names beginning with Al, al, and al- are alphabetized under the main element of the name. For example, Al Qaeda is alphabetized under Q.

ABOUT THE AUTHOR

MAJ. GEN. BOB SCALES, USA (RET.), is one of America's most respected authorities on land power. He commanded two units in Vietnam, receiving the Silver Star for action during the Battle of Hamburger Hill. He commanded units in Korea and the United States and completed his service as commandant of the Army War College. He is the author of seven previous books on future warfare and military history. He graduated from West Point in 1966 and earned a PhD in history from Duke University.